A GIRL
AT
TWENTY

Books by Mrs Robert Henrey

THE LITTLE MADELEINE (*her girlhood*)
AN EXILE IN SOHO (*her adolescence*)
JULIA (*as a London shopgirl at the age of 17*)
A GIRL AT TWENTY (*she works in Coventry Street*)
MADELEINE GROWN UP (*her love story and marriage*)
MADELEINE YOUNG WIFE (*war and peace on her farm in Normandy*)
LONDON UNDER FIRE 1940–45 (*with her baby in London*)
HER APRIL DAYS (*the death of her mother*)

WEDNESDAY AT FOUR (*a Buckingham Palace garden party and a journey to Moscow*)
WINTER WILD (*clouds on the horizon*)
SHE WHO PAYS (*the French student revolution of 1968*)
LONDON (*with water-colours by Phyllis Ginger*)
PALOMA (*the story of a friend*)
BLOOMSBURY FAIR (*three London families*)
THE VIRGIN OF ALDERMANBURY (*the rebuilding of the City*)
SPRING IN A SOHO STREET (*some Soho characters*)
MILOU'S DAUGHTER (*she goes in search of her father's Midi*)
A MONTH IN PARIS (*she revisits the city of her birth*)
A JOURNEY TO VIENNA (*her small son becomes briefly a film star*)
MATILDA AND THE CHICKENS (*the farm in Normandy just after the war*)
MISTRESS OF MYSELF (*a summer by the sea*)

A GIRL
AT
TWENTY

*Six months in the life of
the young Madeleine*

Mrs Robert Henrey

J. M. DENT & SONS LTD

LONDON

Made in Great Britain
at the
Aldine Press · Letchworth · Herts
for
J. M. DENT & SONS LTD
Aldine House · Albemarle Street · London

This book is set in 11 on 13 point Garamond 156

ISBN: 0 460 04193 2

FROM THE AUTHORESS TO THE READER

The whole of the action of this book takes place in 1926, during which year I became twenty. This was the period between my time as a shopgirl at the Galeries Lafayette in Regent Street and my going as a manicurist to the Savoy Hotel in the Strand.

Several of the characters such as Daisy and the Tall Louise who appear in *Madeleine Grown Up* have their beginnings here.

It was in order to qualify for my employment at the Savoy that I spent these preliminary months in a picturesque but long since disappeared barber's shop in Coventry Street, a stone's throw from Piccadilly Circus which was then the heart of a great and throbbing Empire.

The book is written with the same scrupulous attention to accuracy as *The Little Madeleine* and *Madeleine Grown Up*.

In delay there lies no plenty;
Then come kiss me, sweet and twenty,
Youth's a stuff will not endure.

Shakespeare
Twelfth Night

I

I N THOSE DAYS, on the south side of Coventry Street, half
way between Piccadilly Circus and Leicester Square, was a
very small, old-fashioned shop, a tobacconist's judging from
the contents in the window, but also a barber's shop from
the hanging sign—the manager of this latter a Belgian who, out
of pride at having become a Londoner, had anglicized his difficult
Flemish name.

Imagine the scene from the inside one afternoon in 1926 with
its sleepy, calm air and agreeable fresh smell of Virginia tobacco
and Havana cigars in cedarwood boxes. Outside the usual traffic,
some of it still horse-drawn, especially City vans and brewers'
drays, and all the people hurrying along the pavement. London
had a calm dignity, an awareness of importance, the war over not
so long ago, the Empire still embracing, sterling soaring above
the fallen currencies of Europe. Oh, how I loved it all! How
ecstatically I viewed the passing scene with all the girlish wisdom
of my not quite twenty years and my job (waiting for a better
one) as manicurist and errand girl in the barber's shop in the
basement.

A man walked into the shop, seemingly a little embarrassed,
but anxious to pass the time of day—to talk. He looked us over
in turn—Wendy, seated behind the counter, her head, shoulders,
bust and waist alone visible, but all this well worth scrutinizing,
certainly pretty, the rather prim English miss with light auburn
hair, rosy cheeks, dimples and small twinkling blue eyes—and
me, golden headed in my white working coat tightly belted.

'Good day!' he said to Wendy, while giving me a long, side-
ways examination. My white coat appeared to intrigue him, or
perhaps it was something else, the fact that I was new. He asked
Wendy for some cigars and several ounces of pipe tobacco, and

Wendy, very professional, asked him all the questions necessary in such circumstances. Clearly he had all the time in the world and so had we. It was as if we had been conducting business in a small Spanish town during siesta.

'I think, sir, that you should try some of this, and some of that,' said Wendy, dealing out small, square packages of pipe tobacco as if they were cards in a pack, laying them out on the long counter. She had risen from her seat and stood with a hip slightly touching the highly polished cherry-wood frame, the glass and mirrors scratched and tarnished, the shop fittings being old, probably Victorian.

'I'm staying at my club,' said the man, addressing Wendy. His conversation continued to be levelled at her, though his eyes kept on stealing glances at me. 'The Engineers' Club, at the corner of the street,' he said. 'In fact, almost next door. You know it?'

'Yes, indeed,' said Wendy. 'Everybody knows it.' She smiled at him. 'You must find it very gay. Piccadilly Circus on one side of you and Leicester Square on the other. You could hardly be nearer the very centre of the universe, could you now?'

He chose his cigars and pipe tobacco, and Wendy carefully added up the cost. The man took something out of his waistcoat pocket and threw it lightly on the glass counter where it spun in a gleam of hot light. I gave a little cry of astonishment because it was a gold sovereign, and this was the first time I had seen a man take a gold sovereign nonchalantly from his waistcoat pocket and toss it on a shop counter. Wendy showed no surprise at all, but she said to him:

'So you are from South Africa?' I am not sure why she surmised this but he answered:

'Yes, from Cape Town.' Whereupon he picked up his purchases and walked out of the shop.

From the far end of the room there suddenly appeared, as if from the wings of a stage set, a little man with a pasty, yellow complexion and a curiously pointed beard of many colours. His domain of infinitesimal proportions, cut off by a door from that part which served as a tobacconist's, was the ladies' hairdresser's, just large enough, at a squeeze, to contain two customers and Frenchy, the Parisian coiffeur, whose frivolous occupation of

8

tending and colouring ladies' hair was expected never to interfere with the male seriousness of a customer choosing cigars and tobacco. His door, therefore, as a rule remained tightly closed, but from time to time, when he was certain that the shop was empty, except for us, Frenchy would emerge from his dungeon in order to take deep breaths of Coventry Street air scented with tobacco in the leaf and cedarwood boxes containing the most expensive cigars. At such moments he liked to exchange a few words with Wendy. If his customers had been generous he might buy a packet of Gold Flake, but if not he would content himself with Woodbines.

Wendy had not yet picked up the South African's gold sovereign that still radiated a sort of pleasant warmth on the glass-topped counter. Frenchy looked at it and said reflectively:

'To think we all took those lovely gold coins for granted before the war!' He took the piece up and considered it fondly:

'Well, girls—money! That's what makes the world go round!'

'Oh!' I exclaimed. 'You, a Frenchman, saying such a thing! Love! Isn't it love that makes the world go round?'

From behind the half-open door of the ladies' hairdressing salon rose a high voice rendered curiously metallic from the fact that its owner was under the heavy helmet of an antiquated drier:

'The girl is right, Frenchy. Love is every bit as powerful a force as money. Take me, for example. The fact of being in or out of love has positively directed the entire course of my existence, given me both the bumps and the inestimable joys.'

'It's Mme Daisy,' said Frenchy in an aside to Wendy. 'I have left her under the drier.'

'So I hear,' said Wendy. 'Her voice comes out like muffled drums.'

'If it were not that just now I feel myself to be utterly abandoned,' pursued Daisy. 'I have never felt so low, so miserable. But what do I care? The next man I meet may prove the winning number—the man I shall cling to for the rest of my days.'

Wendy gave a great sigh: 'My choice is made,' she said. 'I am stuck with the number I drew no matter how he turns out in the end. I found it hard enough to land a man at all and was it my fault that he turned out to be an Able Seaman on the Peninsular and Oriental Steam Navigation Company—come today, gone tomorrow? I try to follow his whereabouts in the Shipping Intelligence. He sends postcards also from time to time showing a line of camels in the desert or a coloured view of Bombay. "Beautiful weather. I'm thinking of you. Love, Dick." What am I supposed to think of that? Still, I have learnt to ask no questions. You know what people say: "Ask no questions and you'll be told no lies."'

Her blue eyes and pink cheeks had an air of innocence, but there was doubtless more behind her pretty features than she cared to show. What do Able Seamen do when they are given shore leave in a foreign port? 'Maybe mine's different,' she said philosophically.

'Oh, Wendy,' I hazarded, 'if you had your time over again would you still choose him?'

Wendy looked puzzled. 'One never really has a choice,' she said.

'Correct!' came Daisy's musical comment from the room next door. 'But, of course, there are different ways of saying yes. Personally I am inclined to cry out in the affirmative even before they have time to pop the question.' Her rich throaty laugh broke across the sound of traffic in the street. 'I tend to be of a trusting nature,' she continued, unperturbed. 'I give men the benefit of the doubt. Oh, make no mistake, I soon discover my error! Men are all the same. The terrifying part of it is that I have put two future men into the world. Yes, I have two small sons, mere schoolboys for the moment, but anybody can see that they are the spit image of their father—and yet there they are, spoilt by their grandmother and by me, thought the world of by their school chums. Oh, Frenchy, I have the most appalling confession to make. I haven't a cent to pay for my shampoo and tint. Say that you forgive me, Frenchy. I'll settle what I owe you when I come again. I've been promised a job in a chorus—a touring company opening in the Provinces next week. The theatre is in my blood, Frenchy. You do appreciate that, don't you?'

She emerged from under the drier and now stood framed in the half-open door, one arm raised, her delicate hand holding the fringe of the curtain. I thought her intriguing and definitely exotic with her prodigiously dark eyes, the white almost oriental. She spoke English and French indifferently without the trace of an accent.

'I thought you had been abroad?' said Frenchy.

'Exactly,' she answered. 'To Brussels from which city I have returned without a shilling to my name and yet I was offered a simply fabulous job in one of the best hotels. The wage was small and maybe that ought to have made me suspicious, but I was tempted by the prospect of working in a foreign city. Besides, the job offered me suited my qualifications. I sounded just right for it—reception girl, telephonist, manicurist, fluent English. I couldn't fail. So I set off on the Ostend mail packet in high hopes, wearing a new ensemble and extremely proud of myself. In the train from Ostend to Brussels I had qualms. It's never much fun for a girl to be by herself on a journey. Expensive hotels have a romantic side, but the staff entrance is less so and the bedroom allotted me was cold and unfriendly.

'The next morning I was introduced to the girl I was to work with in the hairdressing salon. She eyed me with obvious suspicion. Blonde, sexy and out to kill, she clearly had no disposition to waste time over me. I spent most of that morning taking calls at the end of a phone, too busy to notice what was going on. The other girl would disappear and then come back half an hour later looking pleased with herself. It did not take me long to solve this mystery. As soon as it was my turn to replace her, facts spoke for themselves. In addition to the hotel guests who used the salon, men came in through a swing door that communicated with the busy Brasserie. These gentlemen appeared to think it necessary every time they passed me to put a hand under my skirt and pinch my bottom. I might not have minded so much if it had gone no further than that. It happens to most of us, if only during the rush hour in the Underground. But in this case I realized that it was all part of the job. The other girl and I were engaged to satisfy the personal needs of a busy, European clientèle. For which reason the management thought fit to pay us merely a token wage. Hence my companion's frequent absences, her look of personal triumph on her return. Well, if she liked it, that was her business.

Personally I felt tricked. I was mad enough to ask the manager if he knew what was going on.

' "Mademoiselle," he said, "with those lovely eyes of yours and that pretty face, what are you complaining about? Why don't you wait till nobody looks at you. I'm not responsible for making life what it is."

' "I want to go back to London," I said. "Will you pay my fare?" '

' "Earn it," he answered. "I've no time for fools!" '

I wonder if we were more naïve in those days or if it was more difficult for a woman to earn a living. There were so few openings for us then. I remember thinking it extraordinary that this woman of thirty—she might have been even less—should without rhyme or reason, being a total stranger, think fit to have embarked on this slice of her life. I did not for a moment suppose that this trip to Brussels had been her first adventure abroad. Indeed from the moment I set eyes on her I had sensed that there was something curious and mysterious about her, and in the circumstances, if my suspicions were correct, it was all the more surprising that she should have reacted in the manner that she did to what had been asked of her in the Brussels hotel. Momentarily what worried me was the thought that Mr Y, my employer down in the barber's basement, might at any moment come up to inquire what I was doing. I would have hated to have been sent out by him on some trivial errand at this stage in Daisy's piquant confessions.

Assuredly Wendy had all the life of London passing by her window. The tobacconist's shop she managed was owned by one of those city companies whose branches constellated the West End and they in turn leased our barber's basement as well as Frenchy's dismal Ladies' Salon to Mr Y, who had quite discarded his native Flemish tongue to speak English with an almost affected cockney accent.

A steep stair, the steps lined on each side by a narrow width of brass that shone in the semi-darkness like gold, led from the shop down into the basement. People went up and down it noisily, one hand on the banister, passing under a lighted globe across which was written in bold letters: *Barber*. Primarily all this was a man's world. Men swung into the tobacconist's shop, bought their cigarettes and pipe tobacco, decided to have their hair cut and descended into the barber's shop, sure of themselves and the world around them. Thus it was that Frenchy felt at times somewhat ashamed of his futile, feminine commerce, his curling-tongs and hair dyes, his two customers' chairs and loquacious female customers—and, as I have already said, when men were about, closed his door.

Wendy used to say that her customers came in for a packet of twenty Players, went half way across the world and then came back for a box of matches. What she meant was that no man can come to London without finding himself at one moment or the other in the heart of it. So back went her customers to South Africa, to Canada, to India, to the Fiji Islands. Then months later she would see them again:

'Hallo, miss, what's new since I was last here? Are there any good shows in Town?'

She sat at the heart of the British Empire as a penguin might lazily flap its wings on the ceiling of the world. She gathered the most extraordinary information, and her opinion, as she delicately put a box of Swan Vestas on the counter, was sought on the best restaurants for taking a girl out to supper or if Charlot's new revue was worth going to.

Mr Y was always very polite to her. She had the power by gentle persuasion to send a customer running down the stairs to have his hair cut. Though she talked about her door being ever open onto the effervescence of Coventry Street there was, in fact, no door at all—just an opening in the shop front that could be shuttered at night or when the shop was closed. Thus a man needed to expend no physical strength to enter her domain—not even the pushing of a door handle. Wendy was at one with the world outside and the world with her.

Mr Y's subterranean territory, which was also mine, stretched not merely under Wendy's shop and the Ladies' Salon but terminated like the eye of a prehistoric monster under the sidewalk of Coventry Street, so that the feet of passers-by could be dimly seen through the thick squares of frosted glass if one craned one's neck upwards. The cellar barber's shop was gaily lit when we had a customer, but if there was none Mr Y put out all the lights except one—a naked, feeble thing in a corner round which the barbers crouched to study racing form. Betting on horses was their passion, putting a shilling on the winner of the three-thirty their dream. It struck me that they had very little real life outside of this, and I began to wonder if in many ways, with so little to worry about, the German barber and the Hungarian barber and their like were not a great deal more fortunate in their naïve simplicity than women full of complexes like Daisy, Wendy and me.

Not that I was unfamiliar with the language of bookies and punters. Stacey Street, off Cambridge Circus, where I lived with my widowed mother Matilda, was a cul-de-sac at the end of which a bookie with his two bowler-hatted acolytes had their pitch. They would arrive in mid morning with their Gladstone bags and stand hunched together while the first punters moved stealthily towards them close to the fetid walls of early Victorian houses which should long ago have been pulled down. But this was the London which, with all its imperfections, one quickly learnt to love; and horse-racing was still an integral part of it, no less than its street brawls and public houses, its costers, its open-topped red omnibuses and horse-drawn brewery drays. Both barbers, the German and the Hungarian, sought to acquire Mr Y's studied cockney accent, though with less than partial success, which in no way affected their deep conviction that to be a citizen of London was the happiest state to which a man could aspire. Our Hungarian had a way all of his own of exclaiming between his teeth, when he perceived hurrying down the steep stair a customer known to be mean with his tips: 'That blighter again!' He was looked upon as the undisputed specialist of the Turf. There was not a famous jockey of the time whose past performances he could not recite without so much as a glance at the book. The names of Carslake and Donoghue dropped from his lips like the dew from heaven. He was always certain of making today or tomorrow the fortune that had slipped through his fingers hitherto. 'Two bob each way and one to win!' I see him still, squeezed between his German colleague and Mr Y under the abominable naked electric bulb at the far corner of the dungeon, peering short-sightedly through a magnifying glass at the small print on the back page of the *Evening News* racing edition, muttering the reasons for his choice. 'That man Donoghue is bound to win.'

Mr Y was by adoption more cockney than any man born within the sound of Bow Bells. He had come to London as a refugee during the winter of 1914 and had so utterly renounced the land of his birth that I never discovered whether he was originally from Antwerp, Bruges or Ghent. But if in a sense he was a renegade, he retained from the land of his fathers an incredible capacity for hard work and a determination to cut every penny into four. Nothing escaped his notice. What he could not see in front or behind him he ferreted out. In spite of this, according to the Hungarian, there was one thing he could never spot—a winning horse! His occasional shillings invariably backed a loser.

That afternoon, after leaving Wendy, Frenchy and Daisy, I discovered Mr Y in his alchemist's 'kitchen' under the pavement of Coventry Street mixing his secret tonic, or hair oil, that he told his customers had the magic property of preventing men from going bald. The empty bottles, ready to receive this concoction, stood on a long shelf beside him. They were, in his own words, of a serious, manly shape—the sort that a man could hold firmly in his hand without fear of breaking or upsetting. Impressively labelled they would sell at a guinea apiece.

One of my occupations was to iron the towels that showed no visible sign of having been used before. I kept a flat-iron on a small gas burner where the black kettle was always ready to make tea. The towels that we did not dare damp and iron after use were washed at home by Mrs Y, but the others, those that were merely crumpled or lightly smeared with lather from the razor, could be made to look tolerably new and crisp again with a hot iron. It may not have been hygienic, but it saved money. The secret was to slip the reconditioned towels between the others so that the customer did not notice.

This piece of dishonesty found an echo in what Gabrielle, a strange acquaintance of my mother's, was paid to do in certain houses in Paddington. Gabrielle, like the Tall Louise, our neighbour in Stacey Street, was a Belgian. But whereas the Tall Louise was a woman of nearly fifty, Gabrielle was still in her twenties and decidedly piquante. It would be difficult to paint a picture of that part of London in which my mother and I lived at that time without describing how so many of the streets all round Piccadilly Circus looked when the street lamps were lit. The London street lamp cast a soft glow over the houses, many of them Georgian with their shuttered offices or shops on the ground floor. In Shaftesbury Avenue, in Coventry Street, in Regent Street and Piccadilly cars and taxicabs, many carrying men and women in impeccable evening dress, hurried towards the fashionable restaurants and brightly lit theatres. Only in Soho did the Italian food shops, the Belgian pastrycooks, the French newspaper shops remain open till late, but then Soho was a republic of its own, a blaze of light and sound, of cheap foreign restaurants, of clubs and street barrows. The darker streets on both sides of Piccadilly Circus—Wardour Street and Gerrard Street, between Shaftesbury Avenue and Coventry Street, with Bond Street, Conduit Street and Cork Street to the north of Piccadilly, and Jermyn Street to the south of it, were—just as soon as the shops were closed and the offices empty—dark, mysterious, lit only by that soft street lighting, full of shadows, very still, virtually empty of traffic, historically romantic and the haunt of elegantly dressed French girls whose foreign *souteneurs*—Italian or French —sipped their black coffee in reverie or idle discussion in the café-bars of Soho.

One could live in this world without being tainted in any way by it. My mother, who made the most exquisite dresses for many of these young women, though alive to all that went on around her, was herself modest to the point of prudery. It was her theory that one was born with a nature that was seldom affected by one's environment. Girls of wealthy families, jealously protected in youth, can be naturally vicious; others reared with vice all round them can be models of purity. This is not to say that my mother did not enjoy the picturesqueness of this strange cosmopolitan world in which we continued to live until I had left the barber's shop in Coventry Street, gone to work at the Savoy in the Strand and married. She was never really afraid that I would be led astray by the strangeness of my surroundings or by the women who came in or out during her dressmaking sessions. She probably

16

thought that a knowledge of how other people live is a girl's best education.

At this period I first met many of the characters that were later to people my formative years. The Tall Louise, who served a truly beautiful French girl in Conduit Street, occupied, when she was not with her mistress, the back room on the same floor as ours in Stacey Street. The ladies themselves seldom left their flats except to work at night or to come to my mother to try on a dress. They recounted their affairs of the heart and the quarrels with their rivals. They stole each other's hair styles, each other's dressmakers or maids.

The Tall Louise, like all the rather specialized foreign 'maids' who looked after the French girls who walked those dark, deserted streets of the West End, remained on duty in her mistress's apartment during the girl's busiest working hours, which extended from the hour the shops and offices closed to far into the night. Because no girl would have felt safe all alone in a flat, the maids slept in and served them breakfast in the morning. Thus the Tall Louise seldom used her room at the back of ours except at weekends, when her young employer, whom she invariably referred to as 'Mine', went out with her *souteneur* or visited her family. Thus it was an understood thing that the Tall Louise's young friend and compatriot, Gabrielle, who lived at Brixton but worked in Paddington, could go and rest there whenever she felt so inclined. But though Gabrielle frequently took advantage of her friend's kindness, she became bored whenever she was alone, and would therefore knock and softly whisper at my mother's door to ask if, instead of remaining alone in the Tall Louise's room, she could come and lie down on my couch which was placed just under our one window which looked out on to Stacey Street. My mother, who rejoiced in Gabrielle's quite extraordinary Flemish way of talking, was only too happy to accede to her request.

Both the Tall Louise and Gabrielle sprang from much the same social stratum. In a land where so many men worked extremely hard in the coal mines or in the various branches of metallurgy, a great many women worked equally hard as waitresses, bar attendants, chambermaids in small hotels or in brothels. Their rough, picturesque language never quite left them and, accustomed to long hours and hard work in the vice-ridden, colourful streets of crowded cities where women played an ever-present role, nothing surprised them.

But Gabrielle at twenty-six, or perhaps twenty-seven, had never ceased against all the odds to remain the pure, white lily. She was pretty enough to have turned the head of a very good-looking young man of impoverished but aristocratic family who was still looking for some employment worthy of his superior qualities and refined nature. He had a mother who lived with them at Brixton, and because of her admiration for her son vetoed every attempt he made to earn a living. Nothing, in her opinion, was ever good enough for him.

Gabrielle, whose married name was Mme de ———, on the theory that money had no odour, and because she desperately needed it, not only to supply the needs of her husband and his mother, but also for their little girl of seven whom they had put as a boarder in an expensive convent, had found herself this job in Paddington. The brothels of Paddington were numerous, but seldom talked about in polite society. Few of the thousands of passengers who daily thronged the railway station, gateway to the Cornish Riviera and the rich dairy farms of Devonshire, were aware of these discreet establishments behind solid and inspiring Victorian façades. Gabrielle, who worked in the linen-room, was one of a number of women who took eight-hour shifts. White linen sheets that were merely creased were sprayed with water and ironed so that they could be used a second or third time; the rest were boiled in giant coppers and re-starched.

That is why in Mr Y's basement barber's shop under Coventry Street, while ironing customers' towels, my thoughts had turned so appositely to Gabrielle. I wondered if, at that very moment, she might be resting on my couch under the window vaguely entertaining my mother with her strange tales. Gabrielle could, of course, with her elegance and pretty face and her comparative youth, have done like the Tall Louise's 'Mine' and made herself £80 or £100 a week, but even to speculate on such an eventuality would have been entirely to misunderstand her character. Her morals, as they touched upon her own body, were as rigid as those of the most faithful and affectionate young wife. Conversely she might have worked as a 'maid' to one of the young French girls, but the nocturnal hours would have conflicted with her scrupulous desire to be back home with her husband and her mother-in-law at a reasonable hour in the evening. In Paddington she could take the day shift. The wage and the tips, that were often princely, were sufficient to keep her family in quiet dignity.

'But why have you put your little girl in a convent?' my mother asked her.

'Because nobody better than I,' said Gabrielle, 'is more bitterly aware of the dangers that surround a young girl.'

One day my mother hazarded the question: 'Does your family know?'

'About me?'

'Yes.'

Gabrielle eyed my mother suspiciously, knowing her to be endowed with no small amount of feminine perspicacity. 'My mother-in-law thinks that I work at a Belgian pastrycook's in Baker Street. There are so many of them that she could never find out. My husband pretends to believe what my mother-in-law thinks and, as for my daughter, she does not need to believe anything. She is far too young and happy with the Sisters in her convent.'

My mother smiled. She never judged women who were faced with the hard problems of life. She had struggled and worked too hard herself. For the poor her understanding was infinite. Besides, as she always repeated, the important thing was to be aware of everything so as to be in a stronger position to pass relatively unhurt through a world in which women were more often than not the victims. And of course she liked to listen. Her days at home were often lonely and dull. Women were wise in their conversation and it was invariably spiced with a depth of feeling that was absent when men were present. Even when I happened to be at home neither the Tall Louise, nor her young and elegant employer 'Mine', if she came to try on a dress, nor Gabrielle herself, ever treated me otherwise than as an intelligent, fully awake being. Truth occasionally shocks but it does no harm. Only innuendoes corrupt.

'I have yet to meet anybody,' Gabrielle once told us, 'who as a child was so miserably poor. My father was always drunk and my mother worn out by too many pregnancies. I seldom remember her without a protuberance like a Zeppelin. As for me, I was born with a deformed leg that turned inwards, so that I learnt to sit in a wooden crate and to propel myself by my elbows with such speed and adroitness that people in the street stopped to look at me as I tore forward with the noise of thunder in my chariot. I was determined to do everything that other street children did and I managed to join in most of their games. One day a man who had been watching me for some time as I manœuvred in my soap box, convinced that I was inventing my infirmity to beg money from passers-by, which was utterly untrue, followed me home. There he saw my brothers help me out and pull me up the stairs. He must have been struck by pity because he asked my mother what was the matter with me and why I could not walk. She said that it was because when I did try to do so my good foot tripped up on my bad one so that I fell on my face. "But you don't need to feel sorry for her," she added. "She is the gayest of all my children and spends her entire time playing in the street."

'He turned out to be the most famous surgeon in Brussels and he decided to cure me. I spent several months in hospital, and after several operations walked as well as any other child with nothing to suggest my early infirmity except that one leg is slightly slimmer than the other, but I doubt if anybody would notice it.'

Gabrielle ran from reminiscence to reminiscence with scarcely enough time to take breath. It was as if she felt the need to pour the incredible incidents she had witnessed out of a sack, and all these were spiced by her Flemish accent and the pure Flemish words intermingled with French, words that surprised us, sometimes even blurred the sense or in our ignorance made us laugh. Her long stay as a child in hospital left her with the conviction that there were others far less happy or contented than she was. 'The infirmities that don't show are the lethal ones,' she would explain. 'I was fortunate that my bad leg was visible and could raise sufficient pity in a man to want to cure me.'

Back in the streets with other girls of her age, she learnt with them what men in lonely roads or waste land show to girls—a silver franc balanced on their sex to tempt their greed, thighs pinched in crowded trams, enticing smiles from hennaed, Walloon procuresses. Always she came back to her predominating thought, that she must protect her own girl by the very obverse of all that had formed her own experience, the cloistered calm of a nuns' garden in some quiet spot far from the commotion and tumult of town. Once when we were all three together she laughed enigmatically and said:

'My husband on this score is of the same opinion as I am. He claims that a girl of seventeen, a member of his family, while returning from Mass one Sunday morning at Brompton Oratory, was kidnapped in Brompton Road and has never been heard of since.'

'Oh!' exclaimed my mother. 'Do you really believe that?'

Gabrielle shrugged her shoulders. 'Nobody ever believes anything till it happens,' she said.

Now my towels were ironed and stacked away in a neat pile. The German hairdresser, seeing me fold the ironing-board, signalled that it was time for me to make tea, but I suddenly felt the need of fresh air and said to Mr Y who was still bending over his mixture:

'It's time for me to make tea, Mr Y, but there is none left in the canister.'

'Don't you use it up rather quickly?' he asked suspiciously. 'I seem to remember sending you out to buy some less than ten days ago.'

'Yes, Mr Y, but as you forbid me to buy more than a quarter of a pound at a time it is difficult to make it last even ten days. I keep on having to ask your permission to buy more.'

'Very well,' he agreed, 'but watch the pennies, young lady.' He lifted up his long white coat and, putting a hand in a trouser pocket, produced a shilling. He never took money from the black box which served as a till. The black box was for putting money into, not for taking it out until the end of the day when he did his accounts.

Whenever he sent me out to buy tea I went to an emporium, long since demolished, called the Haymarket Stores. This short journey to the top of Coventry Street and round the hubbub of Piccadilly Circus allowed me to spend some moments looking at

21

the photographs of the actors and actresses appearing in C. B. Cochran's 1926 Revue. Then into Haymarket where a jeweller's shop of a delightfully old-fashioned kind sold elegant Victorian rings with sapphires, rubies or diamonds, or a combination of all three, and invited passers-by to come in and sell their 'old' gold as if gold were any less valuable because of its age. On the opposite side of the road stood the Haymarket Stores which was momentarily a great favourite of mine. I liked it for its modest size and its homely atmosphere. The German barber had asked me to buy him a cheese sandwich because he had forgotten to lunch, and my mother had told me before I left home to see if I could not find her a nice piece of gammon. What I saw did indeed appear tempting. The assistant who looked at me with eyes full of tenderness gave me a splendid piece for two shillings, saying as he wrapped it up:

'Remember to tell your mother to cook it with a Spanish onion. That's how *my* mother cooks it at home.' As he handed me the parcel he added: 'I do wish I could be sitting next to you, miss, when your mother brings the dish to the table.' Then as a whisper in my ear: 'I could hold your hands under the tablecloth!' The soft words brought a blush to my cheeks, but there was a murmur from other customers waiting to be served.

On my return to the barber's shop, Mr Y was waiting frantically at the foot of the stairs. I had a customer. A gentleman dressed lugubriously in black without the trace of a smile on his features. Every new customer put terror in my heart. I feared most when cutting a cuticle to nip a piece of flesh and set the blood running without being able to stop it. The only thing I could do was to become suddenly very gay—gay enough for two, but mostly for myself to give me courage. While I was putting soap and water in a bowl, I began telling him where I had been and why I was late. I told him about the old gold, the barber's cheese sandwich and the piece of gammon I had bought for Mother. I told him how fortunate I was to have obtained it for two shillings and how the assistant had expressed a wish to come home and eat it with us. Not a muscle moved on my customer's face. I must have bored him terribly. Had he been thinking of his business problems while I had gone rattling on? It was no good stopping now. I described what Mother and I intended to eat at lunch on Sunday.

His hands were long and narrow and rather well shaped, but three fingers of each hand were curved inwards and it was impossible for me to hold one of his hands in the way I should normally have done. I suddenly understood why he had come for a manicure. He could not possibly cut his nails himself. My thoughts flew to Gabrielle and the story of her poor leg turned inwards, seated in her wooden box, paddling with her elbows to flee from a crowd of urchins.

My customer remained silent until the end. Then, having silently paid the bill, he handed me a silver half-crown piece. 'Oh!' I exclaimed, surprised and overjoyed. 'That's sixpence more than my gammon cost!'

At last he smiled. He was not angry with me after all. All his face was touched by sunshine—the sunshine of a smile. 'I'll come again next week—the same day, the same time,' he said. 'Try not to keep me waiting.'

'Oh no, sir. Oh no, sir. She shall not keep you waiting!' exclaimed Mr Y, who had overheard him. 'She shall be on time, sir. She shall be waiting for you. I shall write it down in my appointments book—and believe me, sir, I never forget a rendezvous.'

Mr Y's effusions were part of his character, part of his immense satisfaction of having become a Londoner by adoption. All Londoners were his brothers under the skin. He felt the need to smother them in politeness. I was quite pleased myself, not only because of the half-crown but also because this was my first appointment to be marked by Mr Y in his appointments book. It is wonderful to feel oneself needed.

The barber's shop had relapsed into stillness and Mr Y made a sign to approach. One light had been left on and the German barber had retired into a dark corner to eat his cheese sandwich. What was Mr Y going to say to me? I felt nervous.

'I am going to teach you how to give a face massage,' he said. 'I am the person to whom you are going to give your first facial.'

He swung a barber's chair round and prepared to heave his great girth into it. My ears were attuned to the sound of passers-by walking on the thick glass studs above our heads. The high heels of young girls struck the studs with the sound of sharp hammer blows, the men's footsteps seemed to fall slowly, aggressively. I began to feel quite sick and I could feel my heart pounding. My nervousness was extreme. Mr Y had armed himself with a jar of cold cream and a bottle of a special lotion he made in his alchemist's kitchen. Meticulously he told me what I must do, but the sight of his enormous face tilted at an angle against the metal head-rest of the barber's chair gave him the appearance of an ogre in a fairy story and I thought him even uglier than usual in this absurd position. Not only uglier but more terrifying. However, it was vital that I should not panic. I needed this job in order to get a better one, but I fancy I had never before been so frighteningly conscious of the difference in size between the slim girl I was and the bulk of a fat, middle-aged man. There seemed to be something symbolic in this sudden awareness of a young girl's lack of physical force in face of the opposite sex. He could have squeezed the life out of me with his thumb. Gingerly I picked up the hot towel that I was supposed to throw over his features like some poor girl lost in Africa trying to net a lion, but I must now be careful not to burn him or to stifle him. I watched the steam rising from the hot towel, waited till I judged the heat to be just right and then dropped it on him, allowing the enormous nose to peep out. This was something he had lengthily insisted upon:

'Make sure that the customer can breathe, miss. You must dispose the hot towel snake-wise round the nostrils.'

This I did and he was thus virtually annihilated by a mountain of steaming towel. Not to see his features peering up at me gave me reassurance. He was there and yet not there. His eyes could no longer follow my nervous movements. Inert under his hot covering he was at my mercy. I laughed at the thought of it and put out my tongue at him. It was wonderful to reflect that he could not see me.

The German barber, who by now had finished eating his cheese sandwich, was standing in the shadow of the alcove and to my horror I realized that he had been watching me. A large, happy Teutonic smile revealed the worst. I put a finger to my lips to dissuade him from speaking. I was almost sure that I had heard him whisper: 'Ach, Fräulein, how dare you?' Please, I wanted to say to him, please keep the secret! He nodded his good kind head. He was far too nice a man to do me any harm.

A gurgling sound began to be heard under the hot towel, and fearing that I might have unwittingly stifled Mr Y I quickly removed it. The sight that met me was rather frightening for the young girl that I was. The great tired face was pitted with pores that had opened out under the heat of the towel and there were blackheads on the ungainly nose. I set about massaging cold cream into the flabby flesh, the chin rough with a stubble of un-shaved beard. I stood on tiptoe to compensate for the shortness of my arms. Under gentle massage my patient appeared to relax, and to my relief I found the work less repugnant than I had feared. After a while I applied a second hot towel and then a cold one. I now recalled Mr Y's instructions to apply his own magic lotion, that which he sold to his customers at a guinea a bottle. I therefore poured a few drops into the palm of my hand and started first on one cheek, then on the other. I worked frantically, determined to succeed in the task I had undertaken. I felt that my honour was at stake. By the time I had finished I was in a state of utter weariness, my dress clinging to me as if I had passed through a tropical forest.

Mr Y, raising himself heavily from the barber's chair, said: 'You have done very well, miss. I am pleased with you. A young woman who can learn so quickly to conclude a successful facial is an asset to her firm.' He added thoughtfully:

'You may charge your customers five shillings.'

'Why five shillings?' I asked. 'The barbers charge half a crown.'

'A facial by a young girl is worth twice as much,' said Mr Y.

The streets had their evening appearance. Sometimes I went home through Leicester Square, past the Empire Theatre where Fred and Adele Astaire were bewitching London in *Lady be Good*, whose tunes were sung and whistled all over Town, and past Daly's and the London Hippodrome with long queues of people waiting patiently for seats in the pit and gallery. At other times I turned up Wardour Street, that first short stretch of it, not more than a hundred yards in length, in which so much colour, so much dust, so much romance and vice were crammed. I liked the restaurants with evocative names—the Boulogne with its picture of a fisherwoman in her native *coif*. I liked the small bookshops with their Victorian bindings and prints of old London. I liked the windows of Willy Clarkson's shop, full of theatrical wigs and photographs of famous actresses past and present. These wigs of every period reposed on wax models of sweet or sinister appearance as at Madame Tussaud's, and here and there framed letters of the famous such as Sarah Bernhardt proclaimed effusive admiration for the rather frightening bearded man who could occasionally be glimpsed behind the lace curtains of the double doors and whose presence was a feature of every London theatrical first night. I seldom dared do more than give these wonders a passing glance. Prostitution lay heavily along the street. Unfortunates who had none of the elegance of my mother's wealthy and youthful customers, who never left the purlieus of Bond Street or Conduit Street, stood here almost as motionless as the models in Willy Clarkson's windows. They were old, gaudy and henna'd, and watched with a sort of wistful longing the innocent young couples who would step out of a taxi on the romantic business of dining *à la carte* with a bottle of Chianti oblivious of anything around them but their first young love. Now here was Shaftesbury Avenue with other theatres just springing into life, its dress shops, its fire station ever on the alert, and my own landmark—the Palace Theatre with *No, No Nanette*. From here I could already see the street in which we lived, the very window also at which my mother would doubtless already be standing, waiting for her daughter to arrive.

Saturday was seldom busy at the barber's shop. Two young men came in to have their hair trimmed. They were 'babies', almost as young as I was, and because of that I looked at them with something like contempt. I thought that men were interesting only after a certain age. Too young I judged them immature. These two youths must have sensed the little impression they made, for having seated themselves in adjoining chairs they talked impressively to each other about their new motor-cycles and the girls they intended to drive down to Brighton for the week-end in their sidecars. Mr Y paid them scant attention. They had no need of a facial, obviously did not own a guinea to buy a bottle of his after-shave lotion, were not in danger of going bald, at least for a number of years, and would have laughed at the idea of having a manicure. Finally, young men were not generous with their tips.

As soon as they were gone, Wendy came down to make herself a cup of tea. She would bring her kettle down and put it on the gas ring in Mr Y's alchemist's kitchen. 'It's in the lease,' she explained mysteriously. 'I have a right to do it.' This also gave her the opportunity to run unperceived into the downstairs 'Ladies', this commodity being absent from her upstairs domain. She would give me a conspiratorial wink and come back a moment later with an air of triumph. Sometimes when her kettle had boiled we made tea and I accompanied her upstairs. She lived with an aunt who was an excellent cook, and while she dusted the pipes and tobacco jars in the window of her shop she would tell me what new gastronomic masterpiece her aunt had produced for her last night's supper.

Wendy had a passion for dusting her wares. Because there was no door the wind and dust blew in from Coventry Street and particles of London smut settled on her glass counter. Frenchy had a customer under the drier and, because he had tinted her hair, his own short pointed beard was smeared with the mixture so that it had become stiff and of the strangest colour. I asked him why he felt impelled to finish off the henna on his beard.

'I just can't stand the idea of wasting it,' he said. Then confidentially: 'Shall I tell you who she is?'

'Please,' I answered.

Frenchy answered proudly: 'My customer is cashier at a famous ladies' hairdresser's in Mayfair. I expect you have heard of it. She was telling me just now that the Duchess of York was there only yesterday to have her hair done. What more need I tell you! You may think it strange that somebody who works in so superior an establishment should choose to come to me in my obscure hide-out, but she does not want anybody to know that her hair is turning grey at the roots and so every Saturday when her own high-class firm is closed she pays me this discreet visit!'

'Yes,' I mused. 'I think I have heard of it. Some of my mother's customers go there. Is it not in Curzon Street?'

Frenchy nodded. 'Would you like to go and talk to her?' he asked as if offering me an audience with a lady of high rank. 'Go in, I pray you. She is very kind and an extremely good-looking woman.'

I stepped rather nervously over the threshold of his domain, but very much on the alert in case Mr Y should discover my absence and call up the stairs for me. Frenchy must already have discussed me with his customer because she said without the slightest preamble: 'My poor girl, it's dreadful for you to be working in a barber's shop. You'll never get a worth-while reference. Shall I try to get you a job at my place?'

The idea of working in a ladies' hairdresser's did not particularly tempt me. I was impressed by the name of this firm which served royalty, but I was suspicious of my own qualifications. Most men are indulgent when their fingers are inadvertently nipped by a young girl nervously doing their hands, but I did not relish the sarcasm of society women who would have nothing but contempt for me. However, I was wise enough to keep such reflections to myself and merely thanked Frenchy's customer for her kind intention.

Down in the barber's shop all the lights except the one in the alcove had been turned off and the barbers were still discussing what horses to back for the three-thirty race. It was too dark to sew. The Hungarian had asked me to turn the cuffs of his white shirts. I could tack them in the alcove and Mother would finish them off on her sewing-machine when I went home for lunch. He was grateful in a good-natured, picaresque way.

'Have you no woman to look after you?' I asked him. He tapped the little book of racing form he always consulted.

'No,' he answered. 'I'm too busy studying other people's horses to have a mare of my own!'

The German barber was shocked. 'Ach!' he exclaimed. 'You must not speak about women in that way. My wife, she is an angel.'

While Frenchy's customer was examining the result of her hair tint,

Wendy was putting dust sheets over the wares in her shop. We walked together from time to time as far as Leicester Square tube station, where she would bid me farewell before disappearing down the stairs, her serious little features giving her the air of a prim school marm. She was very proud of her hair and wore it in a chignon, which was rare by then, most women having cut theirs short to be in the fashion; and as our hats were designed to go with the 'little boy' look, Wendy's chignon had trouble in lodging itself in her cloche. She lived somewhere beyond Putney in a part of London I had not yet had time to explore.

When at last she was ready, Frenchy's customer decided to join us. She was a little woman whom one might have described as plump but appetizing, her skin ivory coloured, her eyes not large but jet black and full of fire and life. She must have caught me staring at her because she exclaimed: 'Don't tell me. I remind you of somebody, don't I? Everybody tells me so. They say I'm the image of the actress Yvonne Arnaud. Even our most important customers remark upon it. Some women might mind this continual comparison, the look of disappointment when people discover that I am merely the cashier at a ladies' hairdresser's, but it makes me feel proud to be thought as beautiful as a famous actress and it gives me status with the rest of the staff. They are impressed.' She laughed happily and showed a set of beautiful white teeth. At Leicester Square tube station we deposited Wendy and, when I looked inquiringly at my companion, she said:

'No, I never take the tube. I live in Bloomsbury and shall catch a bus at the corner of Shaftesbury Avenue. Where do you live?'

'I live less than a hundred yards away in Stacey Street.'

She did not take me up on this, but, turning sharply on her heels, led the way along Charing Cross Road, conscious of her seniority, some ten years older than I was but ten years younger than Matilda, that's how I worked it out – Matilda being my mother. She continued to do all the talking, as might have been expected in a woman full of worldly wisdom, sure of herself and of her place in the universe and, since she was smaller than I was, I caught myself looking down, as we walked so briskly along, at her hat. I can see it now as clearly as on that far-away Saturday, a small red felt, full of gay coquetry. Her hair rejuvenated by

Frenchy had a becoming warmth which toned beautifully with the red hat which anybody could see was an expensive one of excellent quality. On the whole this woman whom I had never set eyes on before rather intimidated me, but as soon as I was able to break into her monologue I said:

'Your hat is delightful and what a rich felt!'

'Oh, do you think so?' she exclaimed. 'I bought it from a titled woman, very young and pretty, for whom it was specially made by the most famous modiste in Mayfair; but while she was un-wrapping it from waves of tissue paper in the shop in order to show it to us she received a phone call from her fiancé to say that he could not go out with her that night. Her disappointment was so bitter that she took an instant dislike to this little masterpiece and declared that she would never wear it. She asked me if I would like it, and as it happened to be pay day I bought it from her for £2—a lot of money for me but only a fraction of what it was worth, and as it was so obviously an exclusive model from a famous modiste I felt I could rival the wealthiest and best dressed of our customers.'

By this time we were almost in sight of the Palace Theatre where *No, No Nanette* with George Grossmith and Binnie Hale had been running sensationally for over a year. She started to tell me about her colleagues, the girls she worked with, all jealous of one another, scratching one another's eyes out at the least provo-cation. 'I don't trust anybody,' exclaimed my companion, draw-ing herself up to her full height so that I determined then and there never to accept her invitation to work in such an establish-ment.

How was I to break the news that it was here that I lived and that it was time to part company? I stopped. So did she.

'By the way,' she said, 'my name is Marion. Actually it's Maria, but Marion sounds more aristocratic, don't you think?' We had begun to walk again, and before I knew what had happened we were in my street and there was Mother looking out of the window between a red geranium and an empty bottle of milk.

My mother had her anxious look. She must have been waiting for me. I waved to her and Marion did the same as if she had always known her, laughing gaily as she did so, and when I put the key in the door and let myself in, Marion followed me. Matilda did not seem too surprised to see us enter the room together. She saw in every woman a potential client who might need to have adjusted to her size some dress too optimistically bought in one of those dress shops in Shaftesbury Avenue (or elsewhere) only to discover on her return home that it was too large, too small, too long, too tight under the arms. That is where my mother, so clever with her needle, would come in! Marion removed her red felt hat, placed it at a rakish angle over the cold-water jug and went over to sit on my couch under the window.

I tried to tell my mother in a few words something about Marion. She knew all about her firm, of course, one of her best customers having an apartment immediately opposite this famous establishment; and rather to my surprise and somewhat to my resentment my mother and Marion got on very well together.

'Oh!' exclaimed Marion, making herself comfortable on the edge of my couch. 'What a relief not to be bothered by a lot of men!' Personally I was far from agreeing with her, and the thought of a long, dismal Sunday with only my mother and her women friends to talk to was depressing in the extreme. I almost looked forward to starting work again on Monday morning. Coventry Street seemed by comparison with this positively exciting. I wondered if Wendy would be as bored with her aunt in Putney as I was at the prospect of an interminable evening. Meanwhile Marion was making an increasingly good impression on my mother and even gave signs of showing off. She was going to tell them at her place what a valuable asset a young French girl trained in Paris as a manicurist, so young and pretty and adroit, would be to the firm. Not only this. She would drop a word or two in the ears of her aristocratic customers that she knew personally of a remarkable home dressmaker. 'Women are all the same,' she confided in my mother (as if Matilda did not know about women!). 'None can resist jotting down the address of a new hairdresser, a new dressmaker or a new fortune-teller.'

It was not easy to impress Matilda. I never met anybody so insensitive to flattery. So few recognized at its true value her amazing skill with the needle. What profit had she ever derived from her inherent good taste, her subtlety, her infinite capacity for

31

hard work? Polite promises like those that Marion had just thrown out generally produced on Matilda's lovely features a cloud of sarcastic disbelief. I looked up at her to see if she were on the point of giving vent to annoyance. Marion's chatter tired me and I kept on regretting that I had been unable to part company from her in Cambridge Circus. Matilda to my surprise showed unaccountable patience and was obviously turning something over in her mind—not just the money that a few wealthy customers might bring to her if she could tempt them into this obscure room, no, not the money alone but something more important— a widening of her interests. How lonely she must have been during my absence! She said rather slowly, as if thinking aloud:

'Yes, it would indeed be nice if you could send me some of your important ladies. When a new customer takes off her dress so that I can take her measurements I am invariably surprised to find how widely we women differ in our good and bad points. The variations in the feminine body, from the dressmaker's point of view, are without number. Believe it or not, on such occasions I become a mental thief. I steal from one customer her delicate waist, from another her ivory shoulders, from yet another her long, elegant legs and slim ankles. It is my revenge for being compelled to admire the qualities I envy in them, and it gives me a sort of inward pleasure to leave them with what is ugly or ungainly about their persons. Dispossessed of their good points they become in my eyes mere hulks! I can thus laugh at their sarcasms, at the way they look down their noses at the squalor of my room, at the modest way I myself am dressed.'

Marion was delighted by my mother's outburst.

'Oh!' she exclaimed. 'That's exactly what I do to the haughty society women who sail past my cash desk. I tell myself that in spite of their fortune or their title most of them wouldn't even get followed by a man in the street whereas I, Madame Gal, I am frequently accosted by some importunate stranger as I come home from work!'

This thought obviously gave Marion momentary satisfaction. She got up from my couch and, taking her little red felt from the cold-water jug, started to adjust it carefully on her head. As there was no lighting on our stair I accompanied her to the front door.

It was a beautiful warm night. I thought I would walk with her as far as Cambridge Circus, whose lights glittered at the end of the street, but before we had quite reached it Marion said to me: 'Don't bother to come any farther. Just as soon as the policeman holds up the traffic I'll jump on a passing bus. I liked meeting your mother. She's fun.'

When I got home again, Matilda said: 'I liked meeting your friend Marion. She is very intelligent.'

I said nothing. With each of them finding the other so much to her liking, I felt superfluous and rather empty headed. I removed the cover from the couch, turned down the sheets of my bed and, having undressed and put on a nightdress, slipped deliciously between the cool linen. Nanny, our cat, who had hidden in a corner while Marion was there, came to curl up beside me. She disliked strangers and, though her empire was small, guarded it jealously. During the day time, when my mother was sewing or cutting out a dress, Nanny slept on a corner of the table, opening from time to time her golden eyes to see what she was doing. At the sound of footsteps on the stairs she would dive under my couch, but she never failed to recognize my quick step in the street, the sound of my key in the front door lock, the way I would burst into the room. Our reunions, those of Mother, Nanny and myself, were tumultuous.

2

SUNDAY MORNING, and the lovely awareness that I could stay in bed as long as I chose. There was nowhere else I would have preferred to be at that moment. My heart was filled with content. Nanny had gone out into the yard. I could hear the Tall Louise moving the sparse furniture in her room. She had not yet dared to knock at our door, but the smell of my mother's newly made coffee would doubtless soon prove an irresistible temptation. My blonde hair had lost during the long night's sleep the carefully thought-out waves I had produced with the curling-tongs. The permanent wave was as yet an expensive dream, and I heard Marion tell Frenchy that customers at her place spent many guineas and several hours of discomfort to achieve a result not always entirely satisfactory. Cheap perms left women with tight curls like the fur of a Persian lamb, and the first rainy day took out the curls and left the hair hanging down in damp wisps. I envied Nanny whose fur was so lovely in its natural state and who could stay at home when it rained. The Tall Louise called Nanny 'la fille de joie' on the theory that she had never had anything to do but to make herself beautiful for the tom cats of the parish of St Giles.

Every Monday morning at the barber's shop we turned the place upside-down to make sure that there was not a speck of dust or an inch of unpolished brass. A new week was about to start and already the great theatrical managers, many of whom were our customers, were preparing their autumn shows. André Charlot, whose revues were amongst the most spectacular in Town, was often our first customer, immediately going over to the German barber's chair in which he allowed himself to sink heavily. He was taciturn but scrupulously polite. None of us would have dared to ask him news of the 1926 Charlot show which he was rehearsing with Jessie Matthews and Anton Dolin, but we knew that it was due to open at the Prince of Wales Theatre, which was practically next door to us, in October. In my eyes he possessed, like Charles B. Cochran whose 1926 Revue had opened a few months before at the London Pavilion, the key to a girl's theatrical paradise, and I told myself that any young girl fortunate enough to attract his notice and find herself being given the smallest role in one of his 'revues' was bound to become eventually a star and see her name in lights in Piccadilly Circus or Leicester Square. June was the young actress we all admired. When Mr Y inspected his barber's shop every Monday morning he talked about the brilliance of the autumn season and the necessity of making every-thing in the establishment worthy of it, rather as if he also were preparing a theatrical event, despite the fact that he, unlike the great impresarios, was an unknown grain of sand in this little world in the heart of the Empire. He issued his instructions in a quiet voice that was not without authority. The Hungarian was told to empty a high-up showcase of its dummy bottles of Mr Y's lotion and hair oil, dust them carefully and put them all back again. We were all assigned our different tasks, and as we were continually interrupted by the arrival of a customer we stayed in during the lunch hour in return for which Mr Y would provide tea and sandwiches. It was I who bought the sandwiches. I was given a list and dispatched to a shop in the neighbourhood. The entire operation took on a holiday air. We burnished the scissors and dusted the shelves, we washed the brushes and combs, we rubbed and polished and changed all the furniture round, we cleaned the mirrors and shook the curtains. It was all very gay and I never heard anybody quarrel or utter a hard word.

But the German barber always did the most work, just as he was the first to arrive in the morning. We would find him waiting in Coventry Street in front of the half-open iron shutter of the tobacconist shop inside which the char, kneeling on her damp pad, would be scrubbing the linoleum floor or vigorously clean-ing the brass with metal polish. What was her age? I never could determine whether she was young or old. I doubt if I often saw her except in a kneeling posture, so that her large black hat hid her tired features, or again leaning over whatever she happened to be burnishing. The tone of her good mornings differed in accordance to our rank. Mr Y was addressed as 'sir', Wendy as 'miss'; the foreign barbers, Frenchy and I received scant salutation. She liked Wendy, and Wendy provided her with cigarettes and tobacco for herself and her old man at a cut price. What I learnt about her was by way of Wendy. She lived in a tenement near Moorfields Hospital and one of her sons had been killed in the war. Her 'old man' had worked in a munitions factory, but since the end of the war he had never kept down a job for more than a few weeks. 'Them was the good days!' she told Wendy. Yes, even though they had lost a son 'them war days were the best'. They were younger and wages had been high. Everything had gone to pieces after the Armistice. As her next job was not until ten o'clock she would occasionally prolong her work a few minutes after the appointed hour. She charred for one of the 'ladies' who did Leicester Square, and because for obvious reasons she was on her high heels until the small hours, she did not care to be awakened by her char until ten o'clock had struck.

The German barber's propensity for work, and the fact that he arrived so early every morning, interrupted my description of the free lunch Mr Y provided on certain Mondays prior to the autumn season. Wendy had asked me to buy her a ham and cheese sandwich at the same time. Her aunt had forgotten to prepare her a packed lunch and, because it was such a fine morning, she had set out for work earlier than usual. On stepping out of the tube station the sun had positively shone down upon the glory that is London at the beginning of a new day. 'I felt glad to be alive,' said Wendy, 'and because it was early I just walked round a little while.'

I also had enjoyed my expedition to buy the sandwiches at the Haymarket Stores. The Kit-Kat Club was being given the same sort of joyful renovation as Mr Y's barber's shop. Everywhere one saw men on top of ladders with pots of white paint. Bands of ex-service men paraded up one side of the street and down the other. They played 'Tea for Two' and 'Lady be Good', their medals shining on their frayed, shabby suits. These men blowing into their trumpets or beating their drums were far too young and soldierly to be maimed and unemployed. How long was it since they had been heroes in the front line? Eight years? Nine, perhaps? 'Them was the good days!' as Wendy's char had told her.

My own fear was to be ill. Even a common cold was catastrophic. Mr Y's customers fled at the sight of red eyes or a running nose. Our German barber invented all sorts of excuses to hide his frequent colds in the head. He would tell his customers that if he sneezed it was because he had inhaled some of the shampoo with which he had washed their hair. Mr Y was unsympathetic. What he feared most was that one of his barbers should arrive smelling of embrocation that in the heat of the downstairs barber's shop should render the atmosphere pestiferous. I was at the age when cold followed upon cold. My dress was never warm enough, my coat too thin against an east wind. So, like the German barber, I lied. It was face powder from my powder puff that had got into my nose.

The German barber, when there were no customers and the lights had been turned down, would come and sit beside me in my alcove. He had a leather dispatch case from which he would bring out four sandwiches and two slices of home-made cake which his wife had packed lovingly for him. Sometimes he would share this meal with me, and it gave him an opportunity to tell me how fortunate he was to have married such a pearl of a woman. Our barber was a Prussian and wore his moustaches like the Kaiser had done when he was German War Lord. His grey hair was cropped in the German way so that there was no mistaking his origins. He had come to England in 1910 to escape, curiously enough, the military regime which he feared and disliked, for though he resembled the Kaiser physically and had admired him as a good German he would not have hurt a fly. 'Ach!' he would sigh, 'I shall never forget that beautiful August morning when two London policemen came to tell me rather shamefacedly that I would have to follow them. "But I love England!" I cried. "It is my home. I have not once been back to Germany since I left it." "Yes," said the two policemen. "We believe you, but the mob would tear you to pieces if we did not remove you to a safe place. Have you not seen what they have done to every shop with a German name! And don't you worry, sir, the war will be over in three months."'

What pained him was that in a few more months he would have obtained his naturalization papers. In fact the British treated him rather well. He was allowed to work as a gardener, mowing the lawns, tending the flowers and growing vegetables and, several months before the Armistice, they released him. I asked him if he had seen the Zeppelins. 'Yes,' he answered, and when he looked up at them, silver cigars in the nocturnal sky picked out by the sweeping arms of a dozen searchlights, he felt both frightened and proud. How clever his compatriots were to have invented so beautiful a thing.

'Now,' he said, tapping the vest pocket in which he kept his wallet, 'I have the British passport I dreamt so much about. I am a British citizen. I love everything about this country, the way they live, their police, their parks, the liberty we all enjoy. With my wife I speak German, and in order that we should not forget the country from which we spring she cooks me delicious German food and German cakes like those you are now eating. I doubt if any man is happier than I am, and I have only one fear in the world, that I might suddenly fall ill and lose my job.'

The other barber and most of his customers called him George. There were English words he simply could not pronounce. When he made the bill out for a haircut he would call out: 'On shilling!' His tongue was incapable of enunciating the word one. We used to bait him about it, but he simply smiled rather sweetly and threw up his plump hands in despair. Having written out the bill, he would take the clothes brush and brush down his customer with a look of adoration on his kindly features. There was no servility in this, merely, I repeat, adoration. In his mind there was something sacred in any man who needed what little he had to offer, and his heart went out in gratitude.

His wife was called Gertrude. In some ways, he admitted, she was more German than he was, although she had been glad, when the German currency collapsed after the war and went to several hundred thousand marks to the pound, to have an English bank account so that she could send money to her relatives in Germany who were not only beaten but ruined. With one single pound they could live for several days, almost a week. Then also Gertrude clung to the idea that German cooking was superior to English and that the German *Hausfrau* did a better job with the weekly wash than her British counterpart, but all this, said George, was woman's stuff and did not really concern him. Everybody knew that a woman's task was cooking and the house.

'Also children?' I queried, remembering the three 'k's which were the pride of the German housewife.

'Yes, indeed,' said George. It had been a matter of great regret to both of them that Gertrude had been barren, but on the other hand they felt almost grateful not to have had children on that terrible August morning in 1914 when two policemen came to take him away. Now that the war was over, and that clearly there would never be another one, they sometimes started regretting again their married solitude, but there is a time for everything in life and now it was time to think of other things.

'Of what things?' I asked.

'If I were not so awkward with women,' said George, 'I would like to take a course in ladies' hairdressing. I sometimes dream of having a small establishment in Croydon where we live. It would give me a new interest in life and save me this long train journey every day to and from Town. But I am so terribly gauche with women!'

'You could ask Frenchy to give you lessons,' I suggested. 'I have a wig at home. I'll bring it, and if you don't want to bother Frenchy I could give you a few lessons myself. I'm rather good at it!' I added importantly. 'It's a question of having a supple wrist—like playing the violin!'

I had become quite enthusiastic, and with my mouth full of Gertrude's home-made German cake I felt as anxious to project myself into a world of men, as my poor George seemed to be, to exchange our barber's shop for the frivolous gossip of a ladies' hairdressing salon.

The days come back to me with surprising clarity. I was almost twenty, not quite a girl, not altogether a young woman. I had the experience of two countries behind me, my girlhood in Paris, my adolescence in a London convent, my first job as a secretary to a City of London silk merchant in Aldermanbury Street, my year at the age of seventeen as a shop-girl at the Galeries Lafayette in Regent Street, that month in which I learnt manicure and hair-dressing in Paris—and now this experimental job in Coventry Street while waiting for an opportunity to find myself miraculously catapulted into heady, exciting days amongst film stars, writers, newspaper owners and millionaires at the Savoy in the Strand.

I remember a certain Thursday, for instance, a magnificent hot, sunny morning when the London streets glistened and everything seemed charged with electricity. I flew rather than walked along the streets, and I felt as light as a feather in my short frock and high-heeled shoes. This was the month in the year when every-body talked about holidays by the sea—everybody except George, the Hungarian, my mother and I. Mr Y had spent a week at Ostend, but Mr Y was different. He was the boss. George had been left in charge, and in order to proclaim the dignity which had been conferred upon him took over the first barber's chair in the salon—the one Mr Y reserved for himself when he was there. It was next to the cash box and the bottom of the stairs. A temporary barber had been engaged to help out. He was a Bohemian from the then recently created republic of Czecho-slovakia, and though he doubtless knew little about the Treaty of St Germain-en-Laye, he was, to George's delight, a nice judge of horseflesh. As he was merely a stand-in he had no particular need to make himself agreeable, and we knew very little about him except that he lodged in Kennington and walked all the way to and from work every day because he loved streets. He replaced barbers on holiday or on sick leave, and when somebody wanted to engage him all the profession knew that he could be found every evening in a certain café in Windmill Street behind Picca-dilly Circus where out-of-work musicians went to exchange gossip and try to get wind of a suitable job. There was a notice-board not only for musicians but also for our Czech. He would find a note from a firm anxious to engage him, and the next morning he would go off on foot with a white coat rolled up in a covering under his arm. His white working coat, a comb and a pair of scissors were his only baggage, his only known belong-ings, more than sufficient to allow him to carry on his trade and thus, from one day to the morrow, from one job to the next, he would criss-cross London.

Mr Y had never exactly impressed me with his authority, but when he was away the entire atmosphere in the barber's shop changed. George was far too modest to make himself feared. He had been chosen by Mr Y for his immense integrity. In addition to this Mr Y had known him for years. On Thursday, which was early closing day, we all went home—except George who stayed down in the basement to go through the accounts. He even put out all the lights save the one above the table in the alcove. He gave up his half-day with pride and pleasure.

The Czech smoked those horrible black Italian cigars which have a straw down the middle and give out a choking, acrid odour. Mr Y never allowed his employees to smoke during working hours, but George just did not have the heart to object. I did not dare tell him that the Czech's cigars made me feel violently sick. When the cat's away, the barbers play.

I was myself in no great hurry to go off for my half-day. Matilda was busy. Mme Sandret, from whom we bought our coffee at her famous shop in Old Compton Street, Soho, had put her in touch with a client who lived in Pembroke Square. My mother was to help this woman and her young daughter to go through their wardrobe before sailing for Bombay. The husband had been appointed to some important governmental post. Matilda had already spent several days with the two elegant ladies—mother and daughter—and had arrived home in the evening with the most exquisite clothes, some of which were to be altered, others 'disposed of', which was a way of making my mother a sumptuous gift while, to save Matilda's susceptibilities, pretending not to. We had thus discovered a dress that if Mother took it in a little would suit Gabrielle, who never had time to go shopping, admirably. As for me I had seized upon the loveliest tartan skirt of pure wool which I could never have afforded to buy and which fitted me perfectly. I had longed to own a tartan in this superb material of which only the Scots themselves possessed the secret, and I was not a little proud to reflect that it had belonged to this wealthy girl who had earlier in the year been presented at Court and who was now to accompany her parents to India.

My mother had rather enjoyed this novel experience. Several black metal trunks had already been filled with shoes, hats and clothes and these would doubtless be taken down to the docks during the course of the day. The dresses mother and daughter had worn at Ascot could, refreshed by my mother's needle, be worn at Delhi. The daughter, said Matilda, was extremely pretty —slim, with lovely shoulders, small hands and feet and auburn hair. Later, of course, she might become a bit skinny like her mother, but, after all, one had to be slim to be fashionable. I resented it when Matilda spoke enthusiastically about another girl of my age, and without being precisely aware of it I was jealous of this pretty, elegant English girl I had never seen and presumably would never set eyes on. I may also have envied the long sea journey, the dancing with rich young subalterns in the ship's ballroom, the glimpses of the desert when they passed through the Suez Canal, the sight of camels and all those other wonders that were so colourfully portrayed on the picture post-cards that Wendy sentimentally kept in a cigar box to mark her husband's brief stay in a foreign port.

I was here in my daydream when the Czech barber made a sign to me that his customer wanted a manicure. I collected my instruments, put soap and water in the bowl into which he would dip his fingers, and sat on a stool by his side. He was middle aged, wore a brown suit and passed some trite remark about the sound of passing feet on the frosted glass pavement of Coventry Street. 'Why are they all in such a hurry?' he asked. 'Because it's Thursday,' I answered. 'People walk faster in the middle of the week than at the beginning or the end.' 'You have invented it,' he said. 'I would never have thought of that!' He laughed and I rather liked his laugh. Mr Y had told me that I must always say something to make the customer feel at his ease—and not to allow the conversation to die. He had all sorts of theories on such mat-ters. In practice it was quite easy. Most men started by asking me my age, did I live with my parents—'Oh! With your widowed mother! And where do you live? Right here in the heart of London, a stone's throw from the Palace Theatre? How roman-tic!' Yes, it was as easy as that.

Mr Y claimed that most men when they talked to a girl were

shy. 'It's up to the girl to do the talking,' he would say. So in this particular case I told my client about Matilda's lady of Pembroke Square and how I had inherited a tartan skirt from her rich and beautiful daughter who was on the point of sailing with her parents on a P & O liner bound for Bombay. 'Isn't it romantic?' I exclaimed. 'It sounds like a film.'

'I don't often go to films,' he said, 'but listening to you I have the illusion of being in the front row of the stalls at a play. Is that really what you would like to do? To go to India?'

'I would like to go to India because of the elephants—and the maharajahs who wear diamonds and emeralds in their turbans, but I would just as soon go to any other part of the world. Most girls dream of moonlight on the deck of a liner under tropical skies.'

'My dreams are not like yours,' he said. 'I have done all the travelling I want to do. I am tired of trains and ships and foreign lands. But then I am no longer twenty. It is not so easy at my age to view life as an exciting film.'

'I have so many dreams,' I said, 'I would need a dozen different lives.'

He smiled. 'It sounds tiring,' he said, 'but you are enthusiastic, and that is nice in a girl.' I fell to speculating on his age. He must have been at least forty, perhaps even forty-five? We parted at the foot of the stairs.

'I am staying to go through the accounts,' said George. 'Have a nice half-day, Fräulein, and be on time in the morning.' Matilda had made me a cloche of black taffeta which suited me because I was so blonde. I put it on and ran up the stairs.

In the tobacconist's shop my client was talking to Wendy, who was selling him a box of cigars. 'Hallo!' he said, turning round. 'I was waiting for you.'

'For me?' I asked. 'Why?'

He laughed. 'Because,' he said, 'who but I will give you lunch if your mother is in Pembroke Square?'

Wendy, who was delighted to have made an important sale, broke in: 'You are right to take Madeleine out to lunch. At least, you won't have a dull moment. She will probably talk her head off!'

All this commotion brought Frenchy from his secret hide-out. He had taken off his white coat and was dressed smartly in grey. 'I haven't had a single customer all the morning,' he complained, 'and this afternoon, when presumably I might have one, or even two, I am required by law to close the salon. Isn't that a crazy law?'

My customer took out his wallet to pay for his box of Havana cigars, and having picked up the change offered a cigar to Frenchy to make him feel that he had not entirely wasted his day. Then, turning to me, he asked: 'Are you ready?'

We joined the hurrying crowd in Coventry Street, passing over the frosted glass that formed the ceiling of my subterranean alcove. It felt wonderful to be on top of it instead of underneath, and as I quickened my step to keep up with my tall companion I exclaimed: 'You must admit that I was right about people walking faster on Thursdays! It is hard to keep up with you!'

He laughed. 'That is something I shall have to remember in future,' he said.

Here at the end of the street, only a few yards from where I worked, was the London Pavilion, the theatre that dominated Piccadilly Circus and whose plays and revues seemed to mirror the gaiety and mood of the moment. My companion crossed Coventry Street and Shaftesbury Avenue and led me into Regent Street where we stopped in front of the Café Royal. Was it possible that he was taking me to lunch in this palace of crimson sofas and gilt ceilings in which all Bohemian London met; writers, painters, musicians, men and women whose names figured every day in the gossip columns of the London newspapers, whose foibles and adventures were recorded on the placards that newsboys held in front of them as they ran through the streets calling out the latest sensation? My happiness was mixed. A feeling of apprehension came over me. I had never before been in such a place, and when the head waiter showed us to one of those corner tables with sofa seats, the crimson of the upholstery reminded me of Marion's pretty hat; and this, by an association of ideas, recalled my own in black taffeta which could well in such an elegant place look home made and which was so tight upon my head that it felt like a vice. My throat became quite parched. The restaurant was crowded and the women all wore hats as beautiful as Marion's.

44

The room, like some garden full of flowers, seemed too much like a film to be quite real. Even the older women appeared with their pearl necklaces and the rings on their fingers to be playing a part. But if it were really a film then I was in it, and somebody should have warned me so that I could have had the time to make myself up. Our entry had not passed altogether unnoticed and I felt eyes being turned in my direction. Were they looking at me or at my hat? Did I appear to them like Cinderella robbed of her ball dress?

The menu dancing in front of me added to my confusion, but I need not have entertained the slightest fear. My companion brushed it aside, ordered everything, made it clear that I would have nothing to do except to look round the room and allow the warmth and colour of my surroundings to fill me with a glow of wellbeing. Slowly I felt myself regaining my composure. My companion had made use of my silence to talk about himself. He was vaguely married and doubtless wanted me to understand that by some common accord they both went their own ways, but in fact this detail had no importance in my view. I was accustomed to living in a world of women without men, and it struck me as being merely the corollary that there should be men who could get on perfectly well in a world of their own. Everywhere in this beautiful, animated room the two sexes intermingled in the most picturesque and charming manner. I was charmed, intimidated, and I would not have wished to change places with any other girl. I chuckled at the thought of what Matilda would say when she learnt that I had lunched at the Café Royal, she who must just now be imagining me drinking warmed-up coffee in our room in Stacey Street, alone with Nanny the cat. Nevertheless I did also find my thoughts straying to Pembroke Square and wondering just what Mother was doing with her elegant client and her debutante daughter.

'You are smiling,' said my companion. 'What exactly are you thinking about?'

'I am wondering whether the girl I told you about, the one who is going with her parents to India, is as spoilt as I am today.'

'Does that mean that you consider yourself spoilt because you are lunching with me at the Café Royal?'

'Why, yes,' I said, 'and also because of the fresh salmon and the Chablis. It will mark a turning point in my life.'

He seemed pleased by what I had said, but answered gently: 'Alas, my child, it requires more than fresh salmon and a glass of wine to make a person happy in this world, but oh how I envy your enthusiasm!' I think I must have talked more than I should have done, and perhaps I laughed too often. My cheeks were flushed and my legs began to feel heavy, but I was happier than I had been for a long time. Life was unfolding its potentialities in front of me. When the wine waiter, obsequious though aloof, was preparing to refill my glass with Chablis, my companion placed a hand over it, saying: 'No, you have had enough!' His words were paternal. He obviously had no intention of being seen in this elegant restaurant with an over-ebullient girl. 'Besides,' he added, 'you must reserve yourself for the next course.' This came in a silver dish—lamb cutlets, the bone decorated with paper frills, with fresh garden peas—and instead of the Chablis a deep red Pommard, smooth to the tongue and heart warming. Finally coffee, no liqueur for me, but for my companion brandy in a balloon glass, gleaming in the soft light like liquid topaz.

'You have been very kind to come and share my lunch,' my companion said to me as he lighted one of the cigars he had bought from Wendy. 'Imagine how bored I should have been had I been obliged to come here all alone. I love this place so full of London's history. Whenever I come here, I tell myself that there is no other place in which I should prefer to be. You should not feel too jealous of your young friend in Pembroke Square. Something tells me that you will do no less well than her in life. Gaiety in a girl counts even more than beauty, and you are fortunate enough to have your fair share of both.'

The black coffee brought me back to earth. The restaurant was beginning to empty. The head waiter brought me two deep red carnations and a pin so that I could wear them on the lapel of my coat. My companion had taken out his wallet to pay the bill which he carefully hid from my eyes. Nevertheless, from the high denomination of the note with which he paid it, I knew that it must have represented much more than I could earn in a month. As we rose to leave the restaurant my companion took my chin in his hands and murmured: 'That pretty little nose of yours needs to be powdered. Give this florin to the woman in the powder room. Don't hurry. I shall be waiting for you in the lounge. I have no doubt that you will come out looking even prettier than when you went in.'

His tact and thoughtfulness filled me with gratitude. I would never have dared do such a thing on my own. The powder room was as luxurious as the restaurant, and after I had bathed my wrists in cold water the woman handed me a small linen towel. I gave her the florin. 'Oh, thank you, madam!' she said. I had never been addressed like that before.

On emerging into the lounge I saw two long legs protruding from the side of an armchair from the top of which curled puffs of the Havana cigar. My companion got up as soon as he caught sight of me and we passed from the foyer into the glare of Regent Street in the hot afternoon. It must have been just after three. 'This is the most wonderful day of my life!' I told myself. 'I have started to live.'

The newsboys came rushing along the pavement with the evening newspapers they had collected from the yellow vans. They were shouting the latest sensation at the top of their powerful young voices. Mostly they called: 'Two-thirty winner! Paper! Paper! Two-thirty winner!' but on this occasion they were bawling out something else and gradually, as my eyes caught the four words printed in huge letters on the placards, the printed words and their voices synchronized: 'Death of Rudolph Valentino.'

Inexplicably I stood still and burst into tears. 'What on earth are you crying about?' asked my companion, shocked.

'Can't you see?' I murmured. 'Can't you read? Rudolph Valentino is dead!'

I think my companion was ashamed of me. He had thought better of me than this. He kept on saying: 'Listen, little girl, you mustn't cry about something so unimportant. What on earth can it matter to you that a film star should be dead? You didn't know him, did you? You could only have seen him on the films.' I was shocked that this man for whom I felt a sudden affection could be so indifferent to the death of my dream hero. My own wonderful film had come to an abrupt end. I was making an exhibition of myself in the middle of Regent Street on a crowded summer afternoon.

My companion showed signs of impatience. He said: 'Goodbye, little woman, I'll come and look you up next time I am in Town.' Then suddenly he was gone and I was all alone on the pavement— lost in the crowd.

It would be best to turn into Shaftesbury Avenue and make my way home. My make-up had run, and in order to pull myself together and regain my assurance I stopped to look into the windows of Jack Jacobus, the shoe shop. Shoes were a constant problem. Dresses, coats and hats, with Matilda's help, could be manufactured at home, but shoes had to be bought. Not only did I wear shoes out at an incredible rate, but they were my passion. The Tall Louise occasionally brought me some of her employer's elegant shoes, and I was fortunate enough to be able to wear them. As the Tall Louise's 'Mine' was very proud of her small foot and spent a great deal of money on her shoes this was very satisfactory, but by the time they reached me they needed to be re-heeled and often re-soled, with the result that they cost me nearly as much as new ones. Quite apart from this I wanted the fun of having new shoes which I had chosen myself in a shop, not merely re-heeled or re-soled shoes, however elegant, that had beaten the pavements of Bond Street or Conduit Street night after night till the approach of dawn. I did not want to spend my youth parading in 'Mine's' shoes.

Jack Jacobus was different from any other shoe shop. Its immense windows were infused with a magical quality that set a girl dreaming. Matilda and I came here on occasion when they had a sale in the hope of finding a size 4 or even a $3\frac{1}{2}$ amongst the extremes of very large or very small. Rainy days were hardest on the light, high-heeled shoes we wore and mud streaked my silk stockings. Matilda blaming me for this claimed that I walked like a nanny goat and, though I had no idea how a she-goat walked or why I should resemble one, Matilda's reproof worried me so that I feared more than ever those days when I was forced to set off for work in pouring rain. Silk stockings were expensive and had to be darned. We would set off on Sunday mornings for White-chapel in the hope of finding bargains, but on our return home we invariably discovered that no two stockings were alike. They would differ in shade or in length. As these expeditions amused us no great harm was done, but the Tall Louise would exclaim:

'When will you both learn that there is no such thing as a bargain? Business is business and what is cheap is seldom good.' It was Matilda's naïveté that principally shocked her. I was too young to be wise. But to Matilda she would say:

'I just can't understand how a woman who has spent half of her life sewing blouses of hand-made lace or dresses of exquisite silk could be taken in like that.'

On one such occasion, having snorted sarcastically, she ran into her own room and came out again a few moments later with a china teapot. 'See, madame!' she exclaimed, putting it down on the table. 'I will give it to you. I am so furious that I can't stand looking at it a moment longer. I bought it from a salesman who rang at the door. As it was late I didn't want to let him in. You know what it is when one is a woman alone. We stood there arguing about the price in the light of the street lamp. He said it was a bargain, real bone china, which indeed it is, and I planned to take it back to Belgium. But when he had gone and I examined it more closely in my room I discovered that the spout was cracked. I felt like throwing it against the wall. Instead I will give it to you.' Fortunately the Tall Louise had a sense of humour. She was able to laugh at her own stupidity.

My mother was satisfied with her week's work. Thanks to the four or five days she had spent at Pembroke Square she could give herself a short rest, which meant that she could look after the 'house' as we called our single room. She had rubbed beeswax on the big table, shaken the carpets and dusted the furniture. The linen had been ironed and put away. On the table was a small pile of stockings, all of which had unmendable ladders. 'Unless they are thrown away,' said Matilda, 'I shall be tempted to go through them all once more in the hope of finding one or two I can mend. I thought I might persuade you to make a parcel of them and go out and deposit it in the rubbish bin outside the milkshop. Once they are out of sight I shan't think about them any more.'

I did as she told me, ran downstairs, leaving the front door open, and thence into the street. On my return who should I find with my mother but Marion. 'What on earth are you doing here at this hour?' I asked her rather coldly. 'And how did you get in?'

'The door was open,' said Marion. 'I know it's late but I feel terrible. I have had a bad day and if I can't talk to somebody I shall go mad. Don't be angry. I've brought a cold chicken and a bottle of beer.'

'But we have had supper,' I objected.

'Then we'll have a late-night snack like the after-theatre crowds in the Strand,' she said. 'It will be amusing and Nanny will be delighted.'

I glanced at my mother, wondering how she was taking it. Marion must have noticed my anxious look. Turning to Matilda she said pleadingly: 'You understand, madame, I would never have dared come had there been a man in the house, but as you and your daughter are alone——' She paused. 'Please say that you forgive me.'

I could feel my mother relaxing. 'Lay the table, Madeleine,' she said. 'Your friend is right. We will have an after-theatre snack.' The cold chicken smelt delicious and Nanny, who had hidden herself in a hatbox under my couch, came creeping out to sniff the unexpected meal. She arched her back against our legs.

My mother's obvious sympathy, the white cloth on the table, the cold supper laid out, Nanny's purring and the homely atmosphere put Marion at her ease and she lost no time in unburdening her heart.

'Everything went wrong this morning from the moment I got up,' she began. 'I had a terrible quarrel with my lover and, doubtless because I was upset, on arriving at work I wrote down the wrong time for a permanent in the appointments book, with the result that one of our most important clients, the wife of a foreign ambassador to the Court of St James's, was kept waiting.'

Matilda looked up innocently.

'Then you don't live alone?' she asked.

'Why yes, of course. I was wrong not to tell you from the start that I live with a man. Oh, I'm not in love with him. It's not even that I like him particularly, but he possesses certain qualities. He pays the rent.'

'Well, at least that's something,' said Matilda. 'I take it that he is married?'

'Yes. He hasn't lived with his wife for over ten years, but as he is Italian neither he nor his wife can get a divorce. The fools went and got married in Italy. It was tantamount to putting their heads in a noose. If only they had married in England it would have been easy. At all events, she has gone back to live with her parents in Milan.'

Marion had now plunged into her tale. She was less febrile.

'I first met him at the house of some friends where I occasionally went to play bridge. He still plays. In fact last night when I got home from work he was angrily waiting for me. He had invited some friends to come and play bridge and was vexed because he had not found me waiting at home like a good little housewife.

'Before even I had time to take off my hat or my coat: "Here!" he said, throwing a carrier bag full of Italian food he had bought from a shop in Old Compton Street on the table. "Make a cold buffet for my guests and see that it's good because I have invited one or two people who can put me in the way of making some money."'

Marion looked at my mother.

'Believe it or not,' she said, 'during all the years I have lived with this man I have never been able to discover what he does for a living. At times I have a vague feeling that his business has something to do with cars; at other times that it concerns the sale or letting of apartments. At all events, every Sunday morning I find the week's rent and enough to run the house in an envelope on the table. After this I don't see him again until Monday evening. I don't know where or how he spends his Sundays. I merely take advantage of his absence to spend the day in slippers and a dressing-gown cleaning the place out. It's delicious. I have the illusion of being married and owning a place of my own.'

The beer was cool, the chicken excellent. If it had not been for Marion's worried expression the meal might have been very gay.

Now suddenly Marion exclaimed: 'I don't dare go back to the apartment tonight. I'm terrified!'

'But where will you sleep?' asked Matilda.

'Oh!' said Marion. 'You wouldn't be so cruel as to make me spend the night on a bench in the Green Park! I could curl up on a chair in the corner of the room.'

'No!' said Matilda. 'That is just not possible. But as the Tall Louise has entrusted me with the key of her room, and as Gabrielle is not spending the night there, I fancy there would be no great harm in allowing you to sleep there. Of course I shall have to tell her next time she comes. She will probably be furious, but she has a heart of gold under a rough exterior—and she has a quick understanding and a streak of genuine pity for women in trouble.'

While my mother had been speaking I became aware that Marion had dissolved into tears. Tears filled her eyes and bathed the powder on her cheeks so that she had the features of a woman no longer young, but on the point of growing old. The phenomenon struck me so forcibly that I looked furtively into the mirror to see if during the same moments I also had aged.

'I think you should explain,' said my mother.

'Yes, of course,' said Marion. 'Well, I unpacked all the food he had bought from that Italian store in Old Compton Street and I made mountains of sandwiches. His friends started to arrive while I was still in the kitchen. I never join in their card games now. I am not really good enough. Besides, they play for money and their cigarette smoke gets into my eyes. After a while I went in with the drinks on a tray, and it was at the precise moment when I was putting it down on the table that I felt a pair of eyes drilling into me with such insistence that waves of fear ran up my spine. I didn't dare raise my head to look. I kept on wondering how I could manage to leave the room without betraying the panic that had come over me. By now the man had turned his gaze on my face and I could not help seeing him, recognizing the query that was rushing madly round and round in his brain: "Where have I seen that woman before?" Then all of a sudden the explosion—the discovery, the pinpointing, the look of triumph!'

Marion paused.

'I felt my legs go limp under me, but I acted as if I had never seen the man before. Unfortunately the man I live with, jealous and suspicious like all Italians, had intercepted his guest's look, and loss of pride rather than love made the veins of his forehead stand out in suppressed rage. If there is one thing that an Italian can't stand it is the slightest impression that his dignity is impaired. He was witness to a scene that concerned me, and by consequence himself, yet without quite understanding what it was all about although guessing the worst: that it concerned his honour. Tonio's expression became so menacing that everybody at the table stopped playing.'

'Are we to understand that your friend's name is Tonio?' asked Matilda.

'Why yes, of course,' said Marion. 'I should have told you before. I am so upset that I hardly know what I am saying.'

'So what did Tonio do?' asked Matilda.

'At that moment he did nothing,' said Marion. 'It was I who did something. I put the tray down on the card table. I was in such a state that I could hear the glasses tinkling. Then I ran back into the kitchen feeling so faint that I had to cling against the door. I would have locked myself in, Madame Gal, but there was no key. Whoever needs to lock a kitchen door? I was paralysed with fear. I did not want to lose Tonio. I have never been madly in love with him. I have told you that already, but he is correct with me, punctilious, a typical Italian from the north with a reddish-brown beard and dark eyes, not unduly exigent sexually, which has always led me to suppose that I am not the only one, but in a way that reassured me. In short he treated me like most men treat their wives. That's why I am so sore at the thought that I have almost certainly lost him.'

'Oh, come,' said Matilda. 'You are not the first to see a ghost out of her past stalking uninvited into the present. It is my experience that the more such scenes are violent, the quicker they are forgiven. What you need to do now is to spend a good night in the Tall Louise's bed and tomorrow when you go back to the apartment you will find that he has calmed down. If you are really frightened to face him I'll go with you. Two women together are always more impressive than one. I'll tell him I have been making you a dress. It's partly true, isn't it?' Matilda waved her arm in the direction of some newly cut-out material.

'You never told me!' I exclaimed, peeved. It revolted me to think that my mother might have unshared secrets.

Matilda looked at me rather curtly and said:

'Since when have I been obliged to ask your permission to make a dress for a customer?'

'It was I who first brought her home,' I said. In truth I was tired and the entire business was beginning to annoy me. Besides, I had quite changed since my lunch at the Café Royal. I had glimpsed a little piece of blue sky and I now dreamt of the day when I could move in a stratum of society closer to that of my worldly-wise host. Matilda did not often rebuff me. She may have sensed that I was developing a swollen head. Sleep was beginning to steal over me, to close my lids. How I wished that like so many other girls, like the girl who was going to India, I had a room of my own. A girl of twenty (or nearly) who must share a room with her mother longs for privacy and freedom.

An air of dissatisfaction, of constraint and annoyance, hung over the room. We all three felt it. Marion wanted, and yet did not want, to tell the truth, or at least not the whole of it; and if Matilda and I were really to have any sympathy for her we must be treated with more consideration. Nobody had asked her to tell us her story and by now it must have been past midnight. The supper crowds were beginning to leave Gennaro's and the other restaurant in the neighbourhood. At last Matilda exclaimed, without great originality but opportunely: 'Only mountains never meet!'

This seemed to reassure Marion, who started off once more:

'Well, there I was in the kitchen when Jo suddenly came in——'

'Ah!' cried Matilda. 'At last you have given him a name! So the ghost out of your past is called Jo?'

'Yes, of course,' said Marion, annoyed to have been interrupted. 'Didn't I tell you?'

'Hitherto,' said Matilda, 'your men have been singularly lacking in names.'

'One cannot expect to tell everything at once,' said Marion. 'Jo came into the kitchen and said to me: "I am looking for the cold-water tap. I need a glass of water." Such an obvious lie made matters even worse. Besides, hot on his heels came Tonio

54

who, having looked at us searchingly, said: "You two have something to tell each other. I could see that just now." He faced Jo and added: "I don't like to be made a cuckold in front of my friends in my own home." His voice was trembling. "Get out!" he said.

'Back in the living-room his other guests had become impatient or perhaps they wanted to avert a scene. One of them called out: "Come on, Tonio. We have come here to play poker."

'Now Tonio's pride was being buffeted in another way. He must not show his anger openly or give the impression that what had happened was of sufficient importance to interfere with his role as host. He steeled himself and went back into the living-room, leaving Jo and me alone. Then it was, Madame Gal, that the awful thing happened. Jo, who is tall and powerful, raised his right hand and smacked me so violently on the cheek that my nose started to bleed. "Bitch!" he cried. "I have been searching for you all these years!"

'Oh, can you imagine, Madame Gal!'

Poor little Marion! I glanced at her cheek, half expecting to see the mark of the man's hand. Had it needed this act of brutality to reawaken my interest? Why has violence such a morbid attraction?

'What is he like?' I asked, trying to picture the scene.

'Tall, slim, extremely elegant!' Marion exclaimed as if to excuse his act. 'The sort of man every girl dreams about. He had only one fault—he preferred motor-cars to women.'

'With some men it's drink,' said Matilda philosophically.

'I first met him in the ground-floor apartment of a French couple in Pimlico, a quiet square not far from the Thames and the Tate Gallery. Like most of the men in my life I never discovered much about his antecedents. Impossible to persuade him to talk about his parents. As far as I was concerned he might have grown up like some untended weed in those Pimlico streets of which he appeared to know every inch. What struck me about him were his marvellous good looks. He and a friend owned a dilapidated shed off Lupus Street in which they spent most of their time putting together racing cars of their own invention which they tried out at Brooklands. I didn't realize at the time that some men who are born charmers count women as merely secondary to their cars and their fellow racing drivers. He delighted in the company of other men, who looked up to him as a sort of pole-star. His thoughts turned to women almost by accident when he had nothing better to do. He had noticed me at the house of these friends and given me a lift home in his car. Stupidly I fell in love with him.

'This romance which at first was all on my side was complicated by the stupidest misadventure. I have told you about this French couple at whose apartment in Pimlico I first met Jo. At the risk of complicating my story I must come back to them. There was the man, his wife Irma and a little girl I was very fond of. They rented the whole of the ground floor of a Victorian house and there was quite a pretty garden at the back, with a lawn, flowerbeds and some tall trees. My friendship with them provided me with the family life I sorely missed, and I particularly liked Irma, who had never been strong since the birth of her child, and who had a gentle, affectionate nature. We became close friends.

'Then one evening the husband, who had accompanied me to the front door, his wife having gone up early, suddenly put an arm round my waist and, throwing my head back, planted a kiss on my lips. I am no prude, but I dislike such tactics and the man had no attraction for me physically. On the contrary, especially of late when I had surprised his glances in my direction, I had become frightened of him. I recall him, in answer to my remonstrance, muttering something to the effect that Irma had refused since her difficult childbirth to sleep with him any longer and that nobody would ever find out if we embarked on an affair. I told him that it was unthinkable and that Irma was my friend, and that his behaviour was not dignified for a married man with an adorable wife and a little girl. With these parting words I rushed out into the street, determined never to set foot in the house again.

'I had not gone a hundred yards before a car drew up beside me. I was in no mood to be picked up by a stranger in a dark street after midnight and hurried my step in the hope of reaching the bus stop at the end of road where I might just be in time to catch the last bus home. Then I heard my name being called out: "Marion!" And there he was, my beautiful, good-looking

Jo at the wheel of his latest motor-car! "By what act of providence are you here just when I need you most!" I cried. "I was waiting for you!" he said simply. "Jump in."

'"Why? And how?" I was burning to know. Was it possible that my feeling for him had been reciprocated? I had not met him since the evening he had driven me home. "I hoped I would meet you again at the home of our French friends," Jo explained as we roared noisily towards Victoria. "I asked our host to tell me your name and where you lived. I know you merely as Marion. Marion what? Marion who? He refused. He said he had forgotten. I guessed that he must be in love with you himself." "Forget him!" I answered. "I never, whatever happens, want to see him again."

'Well, Madame Gal, the inevitable happened. Jo told me that his mechanic Fred with whom he shared a mews flat had broken a wrist when cranking up a racing car and was in Westminster Hospital with the result that he, Jo, was lonely and bored. Would I allow him to call for me in the morning so that we could have lunch and he could show me the new racing car they were building? Alas, I didn't hesitate a moment. I accepted.

'His mews flat had none of the spacious comfort of the ground floor of the Victorian house in which lived Irma, her husband and their little girl. There was no garden. There were no flowers, no trees. Nevertheless I injudiciously moved in to share these confined quarters over a noisy, unhealthy garage, first with Jo alone, later with him and his mechanic Fred when he came back from hospital. There I passed no fewer than four years. At the beginning I was so happy that I felt this must be heaven. I did not need to go out and work. When a girl is in love she is blind to everything else. I refused to face the truth that Jo had a violent temper, had no real interest outside his racing cars, and that life for a girl with two men in the same flat is doomed to failure. Fred never did approve and small wonder. My presence menaced the quiet understanding that had previously existed between him and Jo. The two men were much happier by themselves than with me. A woman could merely sow discord. When I became pregnant the beautiful dream came to an end. Jo was superbly indifferent and found a thousand excuses to postpone the idea of

57

marriage. I forgave him of course. I forgave him everything, even those first signs of physical violence that I felt certain would abate, if not disappear altogether, as soon as my child was born; but once again an unforeseeable incident came to complicate my life.

'The two men, during the last months of my pregnancy, had been spending more and more time together. They were working on some mechanical invention that was going to make us all rich. There was nothing unlikely in this. More than one great discovery has been made by artisans working in a mews garage. We all three continued to believe in this myth until just after my baby was born—a boy whom I named Jeremy. I had a difficult time with him, and I myself had been cruelly torn during the forceps delivery. At this critical moment for all of us the invention that was to have brought us happiness failed. There was no more money in our mews flat and an ailing baby to look after. I was not even able, because of my still unhealed wound, to give Jo the sexual satisfaction that might have revived his affection for me. I found myself in the same situation in which Irma had found herself after the birth of her little girl—unable to sleep with the man I needed to draw closer to me.

'One night Jeremy fell ill. Jo fetched a doctor and an ambulance was called to take Jeremy to hospital. I was able to bring him back a few weeks later, but by then life was no longer possible for any of us in the mews flat. Jo in adversity had become violent. Fred said sneeringly: "I told you from the start that he was only gentle with motor-cars—not with women." One afternoon when they were both at Brooklands I gathered my son up in my arms and left the mews for ever.'

Matilda, whose infinite compassion for women in distress came from a perfect understanding of what it meant to walk the streets penniless with an infant in arms, had listened attentively to Marion's tale.

'I found a job as a waitress,' said Marion, 'and for a month or so all went comparatively well. I had been fortunate to find a landlady willing to let me a room. Most of them won't let to a woman with a child. Nevertheless I was alone—alone with the baby but alone in every other sense. No mother, no father, not a

58

friend. Then suddenly I developed phlebothrombosis. I must no longer be on my feet. What would happen to Jeremy?'

Alas, at this point I fell fast asleep. Matilda, having seen my head tilt forward, decided that even her interest in Marion's story could not justify a night for all of us in such conditions. I must be awakened and put properly to bed. Matilda would take Marion into the Tall Louise's room. She would find her spare sheets and warn her to be up betimes so that if by chance the Tall Louise did arrive unexpectedly in the morning she would not find a stranger in her bed. During the few moments before Matilda shook me out of sleep I had been dreaming of the Café Royal, of Valentino and of the tall, good-looking man who had hit Marion so savagely on the cheek. Matilda looked annoyed with me as if it were my fault that all this had happened and that it was past one in the morning.

3

As usual the smell of freshly ground coffee awakened me to the excitement of a new day. 'What day of the week is it?' I asked my mother.

'Friday.'

'What will happen if the Tall Louise comes back tonight? Can't Marion go back to her own place?'

'She will have to,' said my mother.

'Do you think she's awake?'

'I doubt if she ever slept.' Matilda went to the door, opened it softly. 'I hear her moving,' she said.

She put out an extra cup, laid another place and a few moments later Marion came in, her large dark eyes swollen with tears. She looked forty.

'I hardly slept at all,' she said, sitting down. 'What a noise those pigeons make. Where on earth do they come from?'

'They congregate amongst the tombstones in St Giles's churchyard,' said Matilda. 'We rather like them.'

'Oh, and the clock in the tower,' said Marion. 'The din it makes when it strikes the hour. It's enough to send one mad.'

My mother did not relish these remarks. I could see a cloud passing across her lovely forehead. She said tartly:

'I thought you wanted to spend the night on a bench in the Green Park. Perhaps the chimes of Big Ben would have annoyed you less than the bells of St Giles!'

I smiled. Well done, Matilda.

'Your coffee is delicious,' said Marion. 'Mine is not nearly as good as this. If Tonio agrees to take me back I shall learn to make his morning coffee like you make yours.'

She had brought in with her the sheets my mother had lent her. They were carefully folded. She said to Matilda:

60

'I have left the back room in perfect order. Please tell your neighbour that I spent the night on her bed. It would not be honest to hide the fact from her. Tell her also that I am most grateful to her. She did somebody she had never met a great kindness.'

'Try to put things right at work this morning,' said my mother to Marion. 'It's not the moment to lose such an excellent job.'

Marion turned to me: 'Can I come with you half way?'

We walked to the top of the street, across Cambridge Circus and into Shaftesbury Avenue. Marion left me by the bus stop opposite the fire station. She said she would ride as far as the Ritz in Piccadilly, cross over by Devonshire House and run down the steps of Lansdowne Passage into Curzon Street. I waited till her bus came, waved goodbye to her and set off on my usual route down Wardour Street. Unlike Marion I had spent a refreshing night, and felt that this new day was full of promise. What a nice feeling it was not to have a past. I was beginning to enjoy a vague but heady foretaste of liberty. Liberty was something to dream about. But I planned to be much stricter with myself than Marion had been—more vigilant. Ever since Marion had begun her lamentable story I kept on telling myself how terrible it would be to fall so suddenly, so injudiciously, in love with a man who had so little to give a girl.

Here I was in Coventry Street. Wendy was not in the shop and the stairs leading down into the barber's smelt of Bluebell brass polish. The char looked up from her kneeling mat and said: 'Good morning, miss.'

'Where's Miss Wendy?' I asked.

'Downstairs,' she answered without removing the cigarette from between her lips. 'Boiling the water in the kettle, she is.'

Wendy had come early. The people who owned the tobacconist shop were sending a young man to do the stocktaking and Wendy had wanted to be there before he arrived. 'I didn't want him to put his nose in my drawer,' she said, laughing. 'I had left some chocolate and a half-finished packet of biscuits in it, and when I opened it this morning a mouse ran out. Fortunately the char was there. I nearly fainted. I have put the kettle on. You don't mind, do you? George says that he would like a cup too. We are taking advantage of the fact that your Mr Y is not back yet from his holiday in Ostend.'

'Good morning, Fräulein!' said George. The Hungarian and the Czech were also there. Marion must have made me late.

'I have been looking at the appointments book,' said George. 'You have a booking for 4 p.m. And a facial also, I perceive.'

'I could dispense with the facial,' I said. 'I am nervous about them.'

'Maybe you could,' said the Hungarian, 'but remember the commission. If you fail to make enough commission, you risk losing your job. It proves that your skill as a salesgirl is nil. I, for instance, was fortunate enough only yesterday to sell a real badger shaving-brush to an Australian for two guineas. On Monday when we cleaned out the show-case I was careful to place it in an advantageous position so that my customers could not fail to see when I was giving them a haircut. My foresight worked. When Mr Y comes back from Ostend he will notice that this expensive item has been sold and I shall certainly gain in his estimation.' He drew himself up proudly and added: 'The handle was real ivory.'

The Czech put in: 'I'm not all that keen on going out for the odd commission. Who makes the worth-while profit? Your Mr Y. If I push a customer into buying something expensive he doesn't particularly want, nine times out of ten he'll try to save on the tip. So where is the advantage to the barber?'

The Hungarian, shocked by this nonconformity on the part of the Czech, exclaimed: 'Maybe that's the reason why you never seem able to stay long in the same job!'

'Oh, but I have no desire to!' answered the Czech. 'I would die of boredom if I remained more than a few weeks in the same barber's shop. The trouble with men like you is that you lack imagination.'

I wondered which of them was right. The Czech looked sure of himself, and I sympathized with his desire to tramp backwards and forwards across the map of central London, eternally seeking the fulfilment of a naïve dream, but the other day when I had watched him go off home, melting into the busy crowd in

Coventry Street, I had been struck by his tired, aged features, the poor quality of his clothes. The barbers' white coats at work give them the same illusion of elegance as do those of the doctor or the medical student within hospital walls.

Wendy came down to make herself the much-desired cup of tea. I caught her examining herself carefully in the large mirror against the side of the stairs and, as if to explain her preoccupation, she said to me: 'I shall have to end by having my hair cut short like everybody else, but I shall wait till my sailor husband arrives home from his latest sea voyage. He sent me a postcard from Marseilles. Five more round trips to India and they will find him an office job at headquarters, or perhaps in the docks. My own dream is to have a small shop of our own.'

'Yes,' agreed George, who found it impossible to retain for any length of time his important air of temporary manager. 'That is my dream also—tobacconist in front, hairdressing salon in the rear—ladies and gents. What always frightens me is the rent.' He turned to Wendy. 'When one considers how much Mr Y is obliged to pay your company for the rent of this stuffy basement!' George had already spoken of his desire, and I was not altogether surprised, therefore, to hear him add: 'If I were Frenchy for instance . . . Frenchy has a way with women.'

Wendy answered: 'Frenchy also has his little dream. He would like to acquire one of these new machines for permanent waving, but he says that it is too great a responsibility at his age. He fears that something might go wrong. That he might burn a customer's hair and be sued for damages. His dyes are dangerous enough as it is. He is never quite sure how they will affect his delicate-skinned customers.'

'People don't sufficiently realize,' said George, 'that we hair-dressers, whom people are apt to despise, run the same sort of risks as a doctor or a dentist.'

Now here is Mr Appenrodt stepping slowly down the steep stair, taking off his hat and overcoat and going towards George's barber's chair!

'Oh, good morning, Mr Appenrodt!'

Both men, typically German of the pre-1914 era, had the same

63

waxed moustaches and close-cropped hair made famous by the Emperor William. All of us in the barber's shop paused a moment to look at them. George, whose features shone with affectionate sympathy, literally coddled his compatriot. All George's gentleness and goodness of character were visible in the way he arranged the clean white linen napkin under this customer's chin. Though they spoke English to each other, yet one had the strong feeling that it was in German that their thoughts and sympathies met. A mass of conflicting emotions descended upon me during this short but touching scene. Appenrodt's delicatessen store was as much a part of Piccadilly Circus as the London Pavilion, the flower girls with their black hats and laden wicker baskets on the steps below where the statue of Eros, just now removed to a safe place while the Underground station was being rebuilt, normally stood—the coloured lights that sparkled and ran across the tops of the buildings, the open-decked red omnibuses, and the occasional horse-drawn brewery vans. So, in my naïve girlish mind, I had the impression of part of Piccadilly Circus itself coming down into our barber's shop to talk to George.

After Mr Appenrodt had gone, George said to us:

'Mr Appenrodt and I were in the same internment camp in 1914. Bands of angry patriots hurled bricks into his famous store and broke all the glass. They looted the contents, and Mr Appenrodt himself, who loved England as much as I did, only just escaped with his life. He was saved by two London policemen who gently took him into custody.'

The Hungarian barber tapped me lightly on the shoulder:

'Your customer for a facial is in my chair, miss.'

He was extremely young, and this puzzled me. The Hungarian barber had just cut his hair and I wondered why at his age he should need a facial. He was very fair and might easily have been mistaken for a Norwegian or a Swede. His shoulders were wide and his legs seemed to stick out everywhere. Before silencing him with a hot towel I asked him what he did in life. It seemed to me to be natural that I should know.

'I had a serious accident,' he said, 'and I have spent the last five weeks on my back in a London nursing home. I'm all right again now, but life frightens me. I don't know how to take the plunge or make up for lost time.'

At this point I clamped the hot towel down on his face, giving him merely the required opening to breathe. He did not move and I was touched by the faith he appeared to have in my uncertain art. After the usual ritual I tossed the towels aside and began to massage him with cold cream.

'I'm tired of being looked after by professional nurses,' he said. 'It's nice to be pampered by a young girl who is just her normal self.'

'Did they bully you?' I asked. 'The nurses?'

'Whether they bullied me or not,' he said, 'I have decided that from now on no woman will again impose her will on me. But first I must steel myself. I must overcome this fear of returning into the world.

"He that would govern others, first should be
The master of himself."'

'Did you write that?'

'No, a poet born during the reign of Queen Elizabeth—Philip Massinger.'

'Is that what you have been doing on your back in the nursing home, reading poems?'

'Perhaps. What else could I do?' He paused. 'When you have finished my facial, I would like you to do my hands.'

'Is it to impress the girls you want to govern?'

'Yes and no. For a few days I am going to do just what I please. Next week I shall have to go home to my parents who live in the Midlands. I dislike the idea, but there is nothing I can do about it. My father is in textiles and one day I shall have to take over the mills.'

'"He that would govern others . . ."?' I had a good memory and the words came easily off my tongue. I wanted to see him blush. 'For the moment it's Dad who holds the purse strings?'

'I would not mind that so much,' he said, 'if it were not that my mother appears so anxious to marry me off to a Bradford girl. You would be surprised how many of her women friends have daughters of marriageable age.'

'I imagined it was only in novels that young men with money

65

had marriage problems,' I said, laughing. 'I also want enough time to enjoy my liberty. I kept on telling myself on the way to work this morning (walking down Wardour Street to be exact) how terrible it would be to fall in love with the wrong sort of man. A girl really can't get out of marrying young, can she? But if I were a man I would be in no hurry at all.'

By this time I was on the stool with my bowl of soapy water and the instruments on the table. 'Your nails are brittle and far too long,' I said. 'It was time you did something about them.'

'You don't seem to realize how ill I've been,' he said. 'I turned a somersault on my motor-cycle at sixty miles an hour, and injured my spine. Will you come out with me tonight? We could go to one of those Italian restaurants in Soho. You could choose.'

'No,' I said. 'I'd be no fun at all. I'd probably fall asleep before the end of the meal. I was up half the night.'

'Doing what? Dancing, I bet?'

'No,' I answered, 'listening to some young woman discussing the seamier side of love. She rather put me off the whole business.'

'You're extraordinary,' he said. 'We could have tea somewhere —with cakes.'

'There!' I cried. 'With a new face and a new pair of hands you'll find lots of girls to take out both to tea and to dinner.' Leading him to the cash box, I made out the bill—facial and manicure—half a guinea. The Hungarian barber gave me a sly look, as if to tell me that it was he who had arranged it all in order that I should get the commission and impress Mr Y on his return from Ostend.

'Are you sure you won't let me take you out to tea?' asked the young man. 'There's a Belgian pastrycook's in Old Compton Street?'

'There least of all,' I said.

Already in my young head I had written him off and the entire affair as injudicious. What could I do with a young man going to his parents in Bradford the following week? As for his tea and cakes in Old Compton Street, alas, I saw no romance in that.

I went to tell Wendy about my commission and the various tips I had collected. It enabled me to breathe a little of that invigorating street air that my poor lungs demanded. I was beginning to earn enough to impress Matilda, and what I liked particularly was this continual coming and going, this perpetual change of scene, every one of them like a film sequence. I felt the blood flowing faster in my veins. I wanted to jump, to dance, to shout my zest for life.

Wendy was not very happy. She had quarrelled with her aunt and was not looking forward to a week-end with her. Just now all her anger was directed against her sailor husband who was never there when she needed him. Men were outrageously selfish. What did he care, washing down the decks of a P & O liner in the Bay of Biscay, that his wife's nerves were on edge and that she was sick to death of living with a tiresome aunt. 'Besides,' she cried, 'the silly woman has a new dental plate that clicks like mad every time she opens her mouth. And another thing. Why am I the only person who never goes off for a holiday?'

'One doesn't really need holidays,' I said, 'when one is in the very heart of London with all these thousands of people going round and round. All the world comes to us. Why should one ever leave it? What seaside resort, what foreign land could be half so wonderful?'

'How can you understand at your age?' asked Wendy. 'Besides, take no notice of me. I'm having one of my bad days.'

Her words sobered me. Had I been selfish? Was my exuberance ill placed? I had begun to notice that often when I felt deliriously happy some other woman, my mother or one of her friends, showed a face bathed in tears. 'I'll go down and make you a pot of tea,' I said to Wendy. It was about the only thing I could do to comfort her.

I brought three cups up on a tray—one for myself, one for Wendy and one for Frenchy. We knocked on his door: 'Do you want a cup of tea, Frenchy?'

'Oh yes!' he shouted. He had a customer under the drier. 'I'll be with you right away.'

A moment later he arrived stealthily and said:

'She's a dresser from the Garrick Theatre, been driving me mad all day with a dye that won't take on her hair. Trouble is she knows as much about dyes as I do. It's her business, don't you see? Mind you, there are compensations. Her hair is grey but her heart is

67

tender and she tells me love tales that would send shivers down your spine.'

A deep voice came out from under the drier:

'If you people are drinking tea in the shop, can anybody tell me why I shouldn't join you in a cup?'

'Coming! Coming!' said Frenchy.

'About time too, Alfred!'

Alfred! Why did she call him Alfred? Why did nobody else call him by his name? This was something that had not struck us up to now. As soon as he had gone to take her the tea, Wendy whispered:

'Maybe it's his name? Everybody has a name. It is I who first called him Frenchy. Everybody followed suit.'

We peeped into the salon—Monsieur Alfred's tiny salon—and there was his customer sipping her tea, so strong that it was nearly black. At her feet was a moleskin bag in which was half concealed a very small white terrier whose eager little face was turned devotedly up towards his mistress. 'There!' she said, taking a half-drowned cube of sugar from the saucer. 'Good little dog.'

'Why yes,' said the dresser in answer to my look of commiseration. 'The poor thing has been in my bag for over two hours, but she doesn't complain. She has been with me since our last show folded up a week ago. Between ourselves it hadn't been exactly a success. Towards the end we played to half-empty stalls almost every night, but as we had leased the theatre until the end of the month we were also hoping that some miracle would happen like the leading lady becoming suddenly engaged to a good-looking young peer. The company was to tour the provinces after the final performance and already everybody was busy packing. But not me. I'm no longer young enough to spend my life in trains and theatrical lodging-houses, though, mind you, I'm not saying I didn't experience a pang of regret when the others came up to me and said: "We envy you staying in Town, Judy. Some people have all the luck."'

'And I who dream of some quiet town by the sea,' said Wendy.

'For me it's Covent Garden,' said Judy. 'Far from Drury Lane and the smell of rotting cabbages life has no attraction, if you know what I mean. Of course it's not given to everybody to lodge above a wholesale fruit merchant in Long Acre, but that's where I find all that makes life worth living. The ghosts of Garrick and Kean, the ballet dancers arguing outside the Stage Door of the Royal Opera House and the newspaper vans racing to catch the night expresses at Euston and King's Cross. The company held a farewell beano in a pub in Bow Street. Some people drink to celebrate success; we drank to drown the sorrow of a resounding flop. I slept it off on a sack of potatoes in Floral Street, and just before dawn, to enjoy the sweet morning air, rode on the top of a workmen's bus bound for Battersea.

'"Where to?" asked the conductor, seeing that I was still half asleep. "The Dogs' Home?"

'"Why, yes," I said. "That'll do me fine. The Dogs' Home." Funny, because between ourselves I was born in Battersea, and know most of the streets as well as the lines on my right hand, but the fact is that none of us when we were kids ever thought to go to the Dogs' Home. On Sunday mornings we used to come into the West End to fish for minnows in the Serpentine. Now here I was going back to Battersea on the top of a bus by accident, so to speak.

'My dad was a scene shifter at Drury Lane and for several summers Mum got a job shelling peas in Covent Garden, but as she was obliged to start work just about the time Dad was getting ready to go home, they quarrelled whenever they were together. After my kid brother was born Mum went out charring, mostly across the river in Chelsea, and as soon as my brother was old enough I took him to play with the other children in the street. In those days we would go down to the mud flats at low tide and watch the barges being tied together. The posters were all about Gertie Miller and the Gaiety girls. There were second-hand clothes shops down by the tug wharves where dresses and furs and coats were hung in the open across the front. What I longed for most was a pair of shoes with pointed toes, high heels and diamanté buckles, but I never had the shilling they cost. However, I can see now how my love for the theatre began.

'I wasn't sure passing over Chelsea Bridge on top of the bus if I would even recognize the house in which I was born. Mum and

Dad were both dead and my kid brother was killed at Ypres. I think of him every Armistice Day when they sell poppies in the street. Well, Monsieur Alfred, that's how I came upon the Dogs' Home.'

'And you bought this white terrier?' prompted Frenchy.

'I didn't buy him. If anything the dog bought me. Just as soon as I walked in an attendant asked me:

'"You lost a dog, Madam?"

'I didn't want to tell a lie. I said:

'"There's no harm in looking, is there?"

'"Why no," he answered. "You're welcome." I hadn't walked a dozen yards before this little bitch took one look at me and began barking the place down, wagging her tail as if she had known me since she was a puppy. Oh, she wanted me all right. That was clear.

'"I've never seen the likes of that!" said the attendant. "No need to ask if she's yours. They brought her in early this week without a collar." He opened the trap and she sprang out into my arms and ten minutes later we were on top of a bus on our way home to Long Acre.'

'I wonder how she'll take to life in the theatre?' mused Monsieur Alfred. 'That is, when you become dresser to another star. It's your intention, I presume, to continue in your profession?'

'Would I abandon it at my age?' cried his client. 'Now, get me out of this infernal machine and let me see how the dye has taken.'

In fact it had taken rather well and we could see that Frenchy was relieved. His customer announced that she would take her terrier for a walk in Green Park. Emerging from the salon into the tobacconist's shop, she tapped Monsieur Alfred on the back, laughingly pulled his little beard, which as usual he had smeared with dye, and said to Wendy:

'I'm going to give up smoking till my next West End engagement. I'm lucky. I can give up smoking just like that!' To illustrate the point she snapped her fingers with the noise of castanets, and with a happy laugh left the shop.

Wendy had by now recovered all her usual gaiety. Was it the miracle of the pot of tea, the vagaries of theatrical life as seen through the eyes of an aged dresser, or the frisky joy of the little bitch terrier so determined to live the life a complete stranger had suddenly accorded her?

'Her tale about the dog shows she has a heart,' said Wendy.

'Those women have stolid qualities,' said Frenchy. 'They keep their heads cool while the temperamental actresses who employ them lose theirs. Good with the needle and experts at make-up. I charged her less than I should have done today. Tugging at my beard was her way of saying thank you. But mind you, when she's back in a job I'll charge her a bit more than the tariff.'

During the lunch hour I hurried round to the Haymarket Stores. I had fallen in love with an English bone china teaset decorated with cornflowers. I had a passion for cornflowers— and poppies. I found myself waking up in the middle of the night fearing that somebody with more money than I had would buy my beautiful teaset—with the teapot, the milk jug, the sugar bowl, the cups and saucers and the plates—and that when I next went to the Haymarket Stores it would not be there any more. Innocently I asked the attendant how it was that such a pretty teaset remained unsold for so long in spite of the fact that it was prominently displayed. The young salesman, who never failed to smile at me when I passed through his department, answered:

'Because, you goose, every time we sell that line we replace it from the stock-room. There are mountains of bone china sets with cornflowers down there.'

I blushed with shame. There was nothing I disliked so much as being thought a fool, but my youthful sales attendant must have taken pity on me. He queried:

'Do you like it as much as all that, mamzelle?' Then, to stress his own importance: 'When I get married I shall give my true love the set with water-lilies.'

The idea of waiting for what I wanted until I was married repelled me. I wasn't all that sure that marriage would prove the unmitigated blessing that my young assistant made it sound, and I wanted the cups and saucers for immediate use—for the coffee Matilda made so fragrantly in the morning, and even for the hot chocolate we sometimes drank last thing at night. My mother with her lovely copper-coloured hair gave me all the happiness I presently needed, and I adored her company in spite of her occasional bouts of ill temper, her sarcasms being nearly always the result of sciatica caused by bending over her antiquated German sewing-machine with the heavy pedals. My young salesman, taking advantage of the fact that nobody was in sight, whispered into my blonde hair: 'If ever you were serious about wanting to buy it, come and tell me. The staff gets a reduction of 11 per cent. I would have it packed and bring it round to you.' It was a great relief for me to know that the store-room was full of these delightful teasets and that the young man who had taken a sudden fancy to my blonde hair was willing to buy it at a cut rate as if for himself. I would have to ask Wendy what 11 per cent of forty-five shillings amounted to. I was in no immediate hurry. My idea had been to give it to Matilda for her fortieth birthday, which would fall on 12th December.

George had asked me to buy a quarter of tea for the staff, and because I had been fortunate with my tips I decided to buy a packet also for Matilda. Pay day was on Friday and the money went towards the rent, food, stockings and shoes. But tips were manna that fell from heaven. Wendy claimed that the sad part about her job, which was quite well paid, was the uniformity of it. She missed the sudden happiness of the unexpected. Marion said the same thing. It made her mad to see the hairdressers, and even the girl apprentices who did the shampoos, receiving silver coins or crinkly notes from a society woman or the wife of a foreign ambassador, whilst she got nothing but polite smiles. In the hierarchy of female jobs I, of course, had been going steadily downhill ever since I had ceased to be a shorthand-typist first with that silk merchant in the City and later at Gaumont. Shop girl and manicurist were very low in the scale of angels in spite of the occasional rumour of a manicurist becoming engaged to a peer of the realm. Alas, I was unrepentant. I was deliriously happy and I was never tired of seeing the world pass by between those magical points of Piccadilly Circus and Leicester Square.

On my return I found all three barbers busy. George signalled me that I was to stay by the cash box and, hiding my purchase of tea, I sat there prim and quiet. The Hungarian barber whisked the white covering from his customer and started to brush him down vigorously as if he could extort a larger tip by this encircling movement. The Czech barber was also disposing of his customer. Two new ones were seated on the bench waiting for their turns, and I suddenly realized to my horror that one of them, if not both, must be sitting on a beautiful dress that had belonged to Matilda's young debutante from Pembroke Square and which she had given her for me on the eve of her departure for India. As I was a little shorter than the girl for whom it had been made my mother had shortened the hem, just tacking it down so that I could stitch it by hand carefully, taking all my time, when I had a spare moment in the barber's shop. This dress, most cunningly cut, had a sort of pleated apron in very light material that swayed from the waist down as one walked and made the most delightful effect. Navy blue with a narrow red braid, it was elegant and yet so simple that I could have worn it at work. How unwise I had been to leave it in its tissue-paper wrapping on the customers' bench. After all, the pleated part was extremely fragile. With George keeping an eye on me I could not risk leaving the cash box to fly to the help of my dress. I would have to wait until the bench was vacated. The Hungarian's client, having retrieved his coat and hat, went to the stairs, tripping over the bottom step, uttering a low oath at the sharpness of the brass border.

'Next! Please!' said the Hungarian.

'Next, please!' said the Czech.

The two waiting men, one after the other, rose to take their respective places, and I hurried to the rescue of my dress. The package was warm from close contact with the seated men, but there was no damage either to the dress or to the pleating. As all the lights were on I could even, not being wanted, start work. Matilda had warned me that my stitches must be small, tight and *hidden*. Hidden. That was the operative word. They must not show through the material. Matilda's eyes were implacable. She was without pity for the slightest suspicion of thread visible in front. Personally I was not quite so fastidious, but I was an obedient girl. I was brought up to believe that a girl should not cheat. The feeling remained with me.

I smiled to myself, remembering an incident that had taken place one summer evening not long before when a woman came up to see Matilda after supper. 'A bit of mending,' said the woman, 'but it doesn't need to be done carefully. It's for my eldest girl who is at school. You'll do it in no time.'

'Oh no, I won't!' said Matilda with her pinched-lips look. 'Nothing with a needle ever goes quickly. Work that is well done takes a long time.'

'You don't need to do it well.'

'I wouldn't know how to do it any other way,' said Matilda, smiling.

The woman drew herself up and looked at my mother with scarcely hidden contempt.

'You'll never make a fortune, Madame Gal!' she said. 'With ideas like yours you will remain poor all your life.'

'I fear it greatly,' said Matilda.

It never struck me that Matilda might be wrong. If she had remained poor it was for other reasons. I never for a moment blamed her integrity. Women often remained poor for no other reason than because they were women. I would therefore make my stitches small, tight and hidden. The work would take the time it needed, and to relieve myself of the boredom of putting in the needle and taking it out, and peering down closely each time to see that I had not traversed the material sufficiently for the stitch to show in front, I thought of the fun I would have looking into the shop windows in Wardour Street on my way home with the tea.

George had finished with his customer and was brushing him down. The Hungarian barber said of George that, when he brushed down a customer he liked, he did it gently and lovingly like the Aga Khan stroking the Derby winner, but then, of course, the Hungarian thought of everything in terms of horse-racing. But there was truth in the fact that George's gestures were full of touching affection. There were moments when I wanted to throw my arms round his neck and kiss him. Though Matilda is apt to offer the opinion that life is easier for her without the complications of a husband I am occasionally surprised by the situation in which through no fault of hers I find myself—a world without men. With the exception of a vague uncle in Paris there is not a male relation left in the family—not a father or a

grandfather, a brother or even a cousin. George's natural goodness opens my mind to the thought that there can be something
adorable, strong and protective about a man. Also I was still
under the spell of the man who had taken me out to lunch at the
Café Royal—intelligent, courteous, wealthy, the sort of ideal
older man romantic girls dream about. In this case he was not
fiction but truth. The curious thing was that he had not even told
me his name.

George beckoned to me with his little finger. It was his way of
telling me that he had something to tell me in private. The barber's
shop was suddenly empty of clients. All the lamps except the
pilot light had been extinguished. George looked very tired. I
suddenly thought he must be older than I had at first taken him to
be. I found it difficult to gauge men's ages. With women it was
easier. There were so many tell-tale marks.

'I think I shall go in your cubby-hole and take a short nap,'
said George, 'but you must promise me, Fräulein, that if I begin
to snore you will immediately give a little tug on my sleeve. So!'
He added in an amused, confidential whisper: 'It appears that
I'm terrible. My poor, dear wife complains of it bitterly, but I
have never dared tell her that she also snores. It's a funny thing
about women, but they are all convinced that such a thing never
happens to them. And, of course, what man would have the
heart to tell the woman he loved that she snored!'

'Go and have your nap,' I said, 'and be assured that at the slightest sound I will very gently tug at your sleeve. Meanwhile I'll
put the kettle on and make you a strong cup of tea so that when
you wake up it will be waiting for you.'

His tired features had frightened me. I did so hope that nothing
would happen to him. He looked so blissfully happy.

I sat on our bench under the pilot light between the Hungarian
and the Czech and, as the light was not strong enough for me to
sew the hem of my dress, I listened to the two men talking. After
a while George began to snore, first a rumble, then louder.
Remembering my promise, I was about to go over to him and
tug gently at his sleeve when the Hungarian put a hand on my
shoulder, saying: 'Let him be, miss. The poor man is quite worn
out by his responsibilities as interim manager. As there are no

customers he is doing nobody any harm. A few moments of deep sleep will do him all the good in the world.'

The three of us, therefore, seated on our bench kept watch over the German's sleep.

The Hungarian said: 'Think of it! We could run off with the cash box! Poor George.'

'We all need a holiday,' said the Czech.

'Not I!' said the Hungarian. 'I never need a holiday. The work is not hard. The hours are reasonable. I'm alone in life. What I earn suffices and best of all I can spend it just as I please.'

The Czech smiled. 'Perhaps you have discovered the secret of true happiness,' he said.

'It's all a question of appreciating what one has,' said the Hungarian. 'We foreigners who live in England sometimes realize more than the English themselves the beauty of this land. I have relatives in Budapest, but I don't want them coming over here. From time to time I send them a pound note with a postscript: "Life in England is very hard. Stay where you are." He laughed. 'I wouldn't care to see England overrun by foreigners. The country would lose its charm.' There was a silence except for George's steady snoring.

The Hungarian, remembering what the Czech had said, asked him suddenly: 'And what would you do if you had a holiday?' We looked at him expectantly, supposing he would say: 'Oh, I'd go to Brighton!' But the Czech answered:

'I'd stay right here of course. Were I to live fifty years in London I would never get to know it as well as I would like. You don't need to go anywhere different in order to enjoy a holiday. The streets of London are good enough for me.'

Steps could be heard descending the narrow stair. We all jumped up. I flew across to George and tapped him lightly on the sleeve. 'Wake up!' I whispered. 'I hear a customer.'

'Did I snore?' he asked guiltily.

'Not once!' I lied. 'People only snore at night—never when they have a nap in the middle of the day.'

'Are you sure?' he asked. 'Are you really sure?'

'Quite sure,' I repeated.

'How kind you are, mamzelle.'

When he called me mamzelle it was a special compliment, like a German soldier trying to flatter a French girl in an estaminet during the war. Normally he called me Fräulein or Miss.

Rather to my consternation, the new customer had come not for the barbers but for me. I suddenly recognized him, the tall, dark man with the grim features whose fingers curved inwards. Mr Y had carefully noted the appointment in the book, but I had forgotten to look at it.

'And how are you, young lady, since my last visit?' he asked genially. 'Was the boiled bacon a success?'

I assured him that it had been, and added gaily: 'Fancy recalling a thing like that. Is it possible that I made an impression on you?'

'More than you think!' he exclaimed. 'And what's more every time I walk down the Haymarket your story comes back to my mind.'

Though the fact of holding his maimed hand in mine sent an uncomfortable shiver up my spine I was intrigued by his personality. I found it less easy than usual to introduce a suitable subject of conversation, but my client, doubtless because of the happy impression I had made upon him at our previous meeting, began to talk about himself and soon, while I was bending over his hand, my mind absorbed in the task of pushing back cuticles, I became aware that he was describing a tiger hunt in India. The very word India sent my thoughts flying to the young debutante, the hem of whose dress I was stitching, and who, in my imagination, was at this very moment in a P & O liner somewhere on the blue waters of the Mediterranean. Would she already be surrounded by good-looking young officers anxious to flirt with her? Did she dance in the ship's ballroom every night? Tigers were a different matter altogether. There was a magazine called *The Wide World* in which tales of manly adventure in various parts of the Empire were vividly illustrated. Tiger shooting and the short stories of Rudyard Kipling passed before my mind. Was I filing the nails of one of those legendary empire builders who every so often returned to Piccadilly Circus to feel the pulse of the heart of the Empire beat?

'My mother knows a girl who is on her way to India,' I said. 'I have a dress of hers.'

77

'I spent twenty years in India,' said my client. 'I was one of the best shots in the army till this happened.' He shook his poor hand. 'Arthritis. It ended all my *joie de vivre*.'

How could I comfort him?

'My mother has sciatica,' I confided. 'She works for too long at a time at her sewing-machine. She is terrified that one day she might lose the use of her hands.'

'She has all my sympathy,' said my client.

The Hungarian barber had been trimming his hair. Our conversation flagged. In a moment this tall man with his sad features and nostalgia for India would climb the narrow stairs and disappear into the evening turmoil of Coventry Street. I remembered some hackneyed quotation about ships passing in the night. I was immensely sensitive to this daily contact with men whose achievements and travels left me unsatisfied and guessing. Men had aims and purposes that a girl could only admire from a distance.

My client slipped a new half-crown into the pocket of my white coat. When he had gone the Hungarian, laughing, held up a shilling between index and thumb: 'Nice fellow!' he said. A shilling tip for a hair trim was considered generous. Sixpence was the coin most often handed to the barber. At the end of the day they sought to change their sixpences into coins of larger denomination—or even into notes, but they shrouded this operation in understandable secrecy. They disliked the idea of Mr Y knowing how much they had received by way of gratuity and so they emptied their pockets in front of Wendy's cash register. They knew she would not talk.

Now that I was free again George, informed that there were no more clean towels, asked me if I would mind ironing a batch that his wife had washed overnight at home. He had brought them wrapped up in brown paper and as soon as I undid the parcel I exclaimed at their whiteness.

'They smell of sunshine and good country air!' I said.

'Of course,' said George. 'German women are renowned for their skill at homely tasks. My wife would have been glad to iron them herself, but I knew you wouldn't mind. She hung them on a line in our garden to dry.'

'Your suburb must be very pretty!' I said.

'Oh yes!' he beamed. 'It's magnificent.' He had enunciated every syllable, adding: 'Inside also the house is beautiful, real German furniture shipped from Potsdam after my parents died.'

'Who looks after the garden?' I asked.

He smiled. 'We look after it together,' he said. 'My wife buys the seeds and plants and I dig the ground, sometimes in the evenings or on Sundays when it's not my turn to come to work.' George and Mr Y took it in turns to be at the barber's shop on Sunday mornings.

At home that evening Matilda was eagerly awaiting my return. There was that particular expression on her face that told me she was just bursting with news.

'Your Marion came here at lunch time,' she exclaimed. 'She wanted me to go back with her to Tonio's place so that she could pack her things and leave him.'

I smiled. Why was she 'my' Marion? Did this denote a faint undertone of disapproval on my mother's part? I put down my handbag, took off my hat and shook out my blonde hair. 'Go on!' I said impatiently. 'What happened?'

'There was nobody in the apartment,' said Matilda. 'It's comfortable and well situated, and I'm not a bit surprised that Marion is broken hearted at the thought of having to leave it. She took me into Tonio's room. I just can't tell you how luxurious it was— a wardrobe full of expensive suits and hand-made Italian shoes. I had no idea that men could be so extravagant about their clothes. And all those silk shirts with his initials embroidered on them and his ties—scores of ties in every colour hanging up as if they were in a shop. Your Marion was quite proud to show me all this. She even forgot to be afraid. It's terrible to have such a slavish admiration for a man who isn't even your real husband.'

'How about the rest of the house?'

'The ground floor is occupied by a solicitor,' said Matilda. 'There's a brass plate at the side. Tonio and Marion live above. The kitchen has a big window through which one can see the trees in Bloomsbury Square. The bedroom is nice but rather dark, and there is an old-fashioned bathroom. Marion showed me everything and then all of a sudden we both felt desperately hungry.

79

There were eggs and a York ham in the larder and several bottles of Chianti. We had a simply wonderful lunch and afterwards Marion made strong black coffee. I think we must have drunk more Chianti than was good for us. By four o'clock we were still at table, quite forgetting what we had come for. Between ourselves my head was still heavy. Suddenly the kitchen door opened and a terribly good-looking man with a reddish-brown beard walked in. I guessed right away that it must be Tonio. Poor Marion quite changed colour. Tonio looked at me and then at Marion and asked:

'"Who is this woman?"

'"She is the lady with whom I spent the night," said Marion, slowly recovering her composure. "She and her daughter live in Soho."

'"Oh!" said Tonio.

'He drew up a chair and said:

'"The coffee you have both made smells excellent. Is there any left?"

'Marion beamed. Her hand flew to the coffee-pot, and as we had been making fresh coffee steadily for the last two hours there was plenty left for Tonio. She laid him a place, and now there we were all three of us drinking coffee.

'Feeling that it was up to me to ease still further this delicate situation I looked out through the open window and said:

'"You have a beautiful view from here—all those trees in Bloomsbury Square."

'"Yes, indeed," said Tonio, "and once the solicitor has vacated his offices downstairs, and all the other offices are closed, the evenings are delightful. One might be in the depths of the country. One is not even tempted to go away at week-ends."

'"The solicitor has always been very correct," said Marion.

'"Oh!" exclaimed Tonio, with the laugh of a man proud of his own jokes. "You have never heard of a solicitor overworking!"

'This was the sign for all of us to feel relaxed.

'"Do you smoke?" asked Tonio, offering me a cigarette. They were fat Turkish cigarettes with gold tips. Though I only smoke once in a way I could hardly refuse this sign of amity. Turkish tobacco is an excellent accompaniment to strong black coffee. I looked at the wind passing gently through the leaves of the plane trees and wondered how it could be that we were all three sitting there like old friends. If only you knew how terrified Marion and I had been. There was a clock ticking away on the dresser. I wondered how on earth I would ever get away. As if in a dream, I heard myself say:

'"It's nearly five o'clock and sometimes my daughter has nothing but a sandwich for her lunch. When a girl is only twenty she needs a proper meal at night. I really don't know what has come over me today."

'Marion caught my eye.

'I followed her gaze and to my stupefaction saw that we had left an open suitcase in the middle of the kitchen floor. Neither of us dared to move.

'Tonio, having surprised our little by-play, said:

'"Surely the kitchen is no place for an open suitcase. Really, Marion, it looks incongruous, don't you think?"

'"Yes, it does," said Marion gently. "I must be mad. How very stupid of me."

'Stealthily she rose from the table, banged the suitcase shut and tossed it in a corner.

'"It must have fallen down," she said lamely.

'Tonio now turned to me and said:

'"Well, madame, I quite understand about your daughter. If I had a girl of my own I also would keep a close eye on her. Allow me to accompany you to the bus stop."

'"Oh, no!" I cried, leaping up. "Please don't give yourself the trouble. There's a No. 38 that passes right by your door. I shall be home in no time."

'I did not dare look at Marion. I went on talking nonsense as Tonio showed me out. I said to him: "I get off at the bottom of Shaftesbury Avenue. It's not a minute's walk from there. Everybody knows our street because of the bookmaker who stands in front of the churchyard of St Giles. It's not a very aristocratic street, but it's full of colour. Thank you so much for the excellent coffee."'

'Well, what do you think?' I asked. 'Is he going to take her back?

Or will he beat the life out of her? How shall we know?'

'We must be patient,' said Matilda, 'but at least I was right to accompany her to his place at lunch time. At least I prevented her from packing her things and running away.'

I must have caught cold during the afternoon. My eyes were running. Matilda suddenly realized that, in spite of what she had said to Tonio about the need to give her daughter a satisfying meal in the evening, she had been too busy to do the shopping. She now decided I must go straight to bed and she would make me a cup of hot chocolate.

I undressed and slipped between the cool sheets with Nanny purring on my pillow. I had a novel to read, a love story in which I could be reasonably certain that everything would finish well. Matilda had read it before me. We read prodigiously and nothing prevented us from dreaming the same dreams.

'Gabrielle came to see me this morning,' said Matilda as she poured the milk into the pan and lit the gas. 'She was worried about that daughter of hers, the one who is in a smart convent on the south coast. The Mother Superior wrote to say the girl is pale and off her food. Everybody is so busy impressing the poor child with the importance of having a particle to her name that she probably misses all the fun in life. Gabrielle didn't look any too good herself, but she was very pleased with the dress I gave her from those I brought back from Pembroke Square even though she says that neither her husband nor her mother-in-law will ever believe that I gave it her as a present.'

On summer evenings the noise in the street came right into the room. A youth who worked as an apprentice cook at the Cecil Hotel in the Strand had just bought himself a motor-cycle and all the girls were crowding round him while he revved the engine up. If it had not been for this stupid running cold I might have been tempted to slip out and join them, but Matilda, closing the window, said:

'Silly girls. They look like a lot of flies buzzing round a piece of sugar.'

I knelt up on my bed and looked behind the lace curtain. There was another young man a few yards away with a superior expression on his face. He had found himself a job in the City and came home one day to everybody's amusement wearing a bowler hat. None of the girls went over to talk to him. The apprentice chef of the Cecil Hotel had let it be known that he was buying a side-car and all the girls were wondering whom he would choose to take to Richmond Park on Sunday afternoon.

The chocolate was delicious and I kept on trying to read my novel, but the thought of the motor-cycle, the sidecar and Richmond Park became confused with the narrative. The truth was that I wished to be everywhere at the same time. Though I had been tired when I arrived home, I now felt an urge to open the window again and to fly out over the roofs of London.

'Tomorrow you'll feel better,' said Matilda. 'What you need is a good night's rest.'

4

IT LOOKED LIKE BEING another lovely day. As the front door slammed behind me I felt again the incredible joy of setting forth through the streets of London. Though the sun was already high, a fresh wind blew across my legs. The fronts of all the little houses, alike as peas, were wet where the pavement had been scrubbed. What a mania these women had for polishing door-knobs, putting whiting on their steps, scrubbing a semicircle in front of their entrance doors. They all stopped to look at me as I passed on my way to Cambridge Circus. I found it very disagree-able to be stared at in this way, examined from head to feet by these mothers, stepmothers and grandmothers, as they all were. Nothing escaped their sharp, intelligent eyes—the dress that wanted ironing, the coat that had been altered, the silk stocking that had a ladder, the shoes with the worn-down high heels. How easy it was for them to pick one's appearance to pieces, they whose lives were drawing to a close. Nobody could give them the sack if they arrived late at work. The problems of being twenty no longer concerned them. There they were, like figures on a stage set, all along the street, waiting until I had passed to tear my repu-tation to pieces.

Almost as soon as I turned from Wardour Street into Coventry Street I saw that something was wrong. There they all were—George, the Hungarian, the Czech and even Wendy—forming a little group in front of the iron shutter of the tobacconist's shop. The char had not arrived and nobody had the key to unlock it and draw it up. Somebody had gone to fetch the spare from the bank. George looked at me with a touch of reproof in his honest eyes. I had arrived late. If there had not been the *contretemps* of the missing char and the absence of a key I would have arrived after the day's work had begun.

Ah! Here was the man from the bank. The iron shutter was solemnly drawn up and we all trooped in.

The barbers donned their white coats; I filled the kettle and put it on the gas ring; all the lights were switched on and soon the hive was throbbing with life. Mr Appenrodt came down for his shave and George began to strop his razor with that supple rhythmic movement of the wrist which was a joy to watch. The two Germans exchanged a few kindly words, and soon it was the hot towel on the freshly shaved face, the invigorating lotion and, after each had bowed to the other, Mr Appenrodt went up the stairs ready for his day's work at the delicatessen shop on the far side of Piccadilly Circus.

Frenchy came down to have a word in the ear of the Hungarian barber. He wanted his hair cut short at the back. 'I can manage the front and the sides myself,' he explained, 'but it's difficult to cut one's own hair at the back.' As he took his place in the Hungarian's chair he added:

'It wouldn't matter so much if my hair wasn't turning white. If I let it get straggly I should be dyed in front and at the sides and white at the back, and that would never do.'

The scissors clicked professionally and speedily, a small kindness between friends.

George, looking at his own hair in the mirror, said to the Czech: 'I could do with a quick trim myself. Fräulein, post yourself at the bottom of the stair and warn us if you hear a customer.'

These preliminaries to the day's work were quickly over. The salon was tidy once more and the water in my kettle was boiling. I served the men and ran up with a cup for Wendy. Frenchy was already in his own department busily engaged with a client. He had left the door ajar and I peeped in. She was very young with a rather sweet, innocent face and auburn hair, lots of it, thick and luxuriant, and Frenchy at her request was cutting it short. As the tresses fell her eyes became filled with tears.

'Oh, the poor girl!' I exclaimed. 'I know what she must feel like. I also wept when they cut my hair short.'

Frenchy, looking round, put a finger to his lips. What had I said that I should not have said? A little later, on some excuse, he came out into the shop, where Wendy and I stood on either side of the glass counter on which I had placed the tray with the cups and the pot of tea. 'She is in terrible trouble,' whispered Frenchy. 'She asked me for an address, but alas I don't know of one. She imagined that because I am French I ought to know the name of a doctor willing to perform an illegal operation. In fact I know of none. If I did I would not tell her. Most of these men are caught after a few months and end up in jail. They move all the time. It's not for a foreigner like me to meddle in such things. They would deport me. That's what I told her. So she burst into tears. It seems she had pinned her last hopes on me—and I failed her. I hate to see a young woman sobbing her heart out, especially one as young as she is. She tells me that she is not quite twenty.'

'Then we are the same age,' I said.

'Well, then, imagine it had happened to you!' said Frenchy. 'Don't you suppose I would be miserable?'

I peeped through the half-open door again.

'Don't you think you had better go back to her?' I suggested.

'She's all right,' said Frenchy. 'I gave her a shampoo and now she's under the drier. She told me she was a secretary to some important man in the West End. He took her out to supper and she had too much champagne. She said it was the first time she had ever done it and this is the result.'

'She certainly appears to have opened her heart to you,' said Wendy. 'Did she tell you all this while you were bobbing her hair?'

'Women always spill out their troubles at the hairdresser's,' said Frenchy. 'You should be aware of that by now.'

I went down to the barber's shop feeling as miserable as Frenchy and his customer. Matilda would merely call her a silly goose. My mother was far from being tender on such occasions. I had often thought about this, trying to reconcile her two different selves, the tenderness she could show on occasion towards women who had been bruised by society and her harshness towards those who got themselves into this particular form of trouble. On reflection I had come to the conclusion that her harshness was probably a way of putting me on my guard. I remembered Marion making us both laugh by saying: 'It's much easier to fall into bed than to fall downstairs!' But in retrospect her words only made me laugh on one side of my face. I was so happy this morning on my way to work to be a young girl. How could this picturesque, wonderful world be otherwise than at my feet? But now, having seen this girl of exactly my own age rocking her poor head in grief, some of my happiness had disappeared.

I had scarcely finished washing up the teacups when George announced that I had a customer. He could not have come at a worse moment. I was not feeling well disposed to men, and as I had shaken the tea leaves out of the teapot I had told myself that never under any circumstances would I allow a man to get me drunk. Especially my boss on champagne! Not that I ran any risk with Mr Y!

I picked up my stool in one hand, my box of instruments in the other and arrived with a stern face. He was young and blond with a rosy skin, and I burst out laughing at the mere thought that he could seduce any girl.

'What are you laughing at?' he asked as I put the fingers of his right hand in warm, soapy water. 'Are you laughing at me?'

'You look so absurdly young,' I said.

'You are quite right,' he said. 'I'm at the age when nobody takes me seriously. Men think I'm a fool and women consider me immature. But it won't last that way. Things will be very different when I own my father's and my uncle's business.'

'Oho!' I exclaimed. 'We are going fast, aren't we? And how old are you, pray?'

'Twenty,' he said.

'Twenty! But everybody I meet appears to be twenty today! It must be an epidemic.'

'Yesterday, to be exact. At twenty a man is nothing, but at twenty-one no girl will dare laugh at me.'

I took his hand out of the soapy water and exclaimed:

'I can't think why you want a manicure. Your nails are bitten to the quick. Have you no control over your nerves?'

'It's a habit,' he said contritely.

'I'll do my best for you, but promise you'll not bite your nails again.'

'On one condition.'

87

'Say it.'

'That you'll come dancing with me tomorrow afternoon at the Kit-Kat Club.'

The Kit-Kat in Haymarket was famous for its *thé-dansants* on Sunday afternoons. I hesitated. Where would be the harm? My prospective dancing partner was scarcely out of the nursery.

'Very well,' I agreed.

Two small boys faced Wendy across the cherry-wood and glass counter. They were asking for cigarette cards. Many customers, when they bought a packet of twenty Gold Flake or Players, tore the silver paper and tossed aside the card before removing their first cigarette. Others owned silver or gold cigarette cases which they immediately filled. These cards, beautifully coloured, ran in series according to their subject.

'Got any footballers, miss?'

'Got any wild birds, miss?'

Wendy explained: 'Their dad is an able seaman in the Merchant Navy.'

In fact everybody spoilt them. In addition to cigarette cards, Wendy gave them cedar boxes which had contained expensive cigars, and Frenchy gave them empty tins in which there had been henna. They owned a soap box on wheels which they dragged behind them by a rope, and into this vehicle went everything they collected during a day when there was no school. 'I pity their mum when they get home at night,' said Wendy, 'with all the rubbish they must bring her.'

Frenchy, still upset by the plight of the girl he had not been able to help, gave the two boys by mistake a tin in which he had hidden a number of £5 notes. But the lads were honest. 'See, mister, you made a mistake!'

'O! Mon Dieu!' cried Frenchy.

'What are you both going to do when you are older?' I asked the lads, thinking of Wendy's husband just now on his P & O liner returning home—perhaps in the Bay of Biscay or entering the English Channel.

'Costers!' said the boys. 'You know, miss, with a barrow.'

'Selling what?'

'Maybe bananas. Maybe grapes.'

Wendy was watching Frenchy counting the £5 notes in the old tin.

'Shouldn't you keep them in a safer place?' she asked. 'My aunt once tossed a cardboard box into the fire with £20 she had hidden in it six months earlier.'

But the truth was that Frenchy did not admit even to himself that business in his establishment was not so bad. He hid away the occasional £5 note and would say: 'I don't even earn enough to pay the rent.' It was a trait left over from his peasant stock.

Earlier in the week Wendy on her husband's behalf had called at some shipping office in Leadenhall Street, and she had come back from this expedition convinced that none of us had any idea of how the rest of the world lived. She now railed at Frenchy for his smallness in hiding away £5 notes in an old tin. Had we any idea of the magnificence of all those shipping offices in the City? Had we ever seen the bankers' shields in Lombard Street? Should we not break away from our little worlds of hairdressing and tobacco and widen our interests? I wondered at the time what moved her to make this strange outburst, but in retrospect I am certain that it had something to do with her sailor husband's homecoming. It seemed unfair to her that he should have seen so much of the world while she had remained eternally waiting for him beside a difficult aunt and a pile of picture postcards. Of course her job here in the shop was wonderful. The money was steady and she certainly did have this daily contact with men who travelled the world over, but on reflection was it not they, thanks to the fact that they were men, who had the good times rather than she? It seemed that she had failed to make the best of her youth just as the girl who had been in tears in Frenchy's salon an hour earlier had obviously failed to make the best of hers.

In truth this incident continued to put us all on edge. I for one had felt so sure of myself, a trifle superior because I had all the years of my life to come. I was so green and new that I could aspire to anything. Often, of late, my mother's conversation and that of her friends weighed on my shoulders. Gabrielle and Marion were in my estimation already old, and, as for Matilda, she was my mother and therefore did not count. In my youthful selfishness I denied her all happiness unconnected with myself. Having me as a daughter was in my opinion more than sufficient. I denied her the right to have a man. I would have considered it treason had she taken a lover or even thought of marriage again. I had flared up angrily when Marion one evening had said to me: 'One day you'll leave your mother all alone at the corner of the table with her sewing and that stupid black cat!' The women I brought back to meet my mother at home, not to mention Matilda's own clients, often ended by telling me unpleasant truths and, though I loved to listen to their gossip, I thought myself superior to them. For was I not different? Did I not possess all those wonderful years, like virgin sheets in a copybook, in front of me? I had not as yet made any irreparable mistake. It had not yet struck me, or at least not until this morning, that a girl of twenty was to that extent vulnerable. That doing something just once, for the first time, after drinking a glass or two of champagne, could jeopardize the whole of her future, bring her down to the level of the Gabrielles, the Marions or even eventually of women like the Tall Louise. For a girl who dreamt of reaching out to the stars this was indeed a sobering thought.

The next customer who called for a manicurist was polite but distant. I tried to be as gay as usual, but it wasn't easy. My mind was still engaged in a sort of self-analysis, and I kept on remembering remarks dropped in the past by Matilda and to which I had paid scant attention at the time. I had been painfully aware, for instance, of the growing pleasure that Matilda took in Marion's company, of the interest she showed in her past and of Marion's slighting remarks whenever I tried to break into their conversation.

'What have I done to her that she should suddenly dislike me?' I asked Matilda one evening when we were alone.

'She doesn't dislike you,' said Matilda. 'She is merely bitter because she has made a mess of her youth and she secretly fears that you may make a success of yours.'

'And what do you think?' I asked Matilda.

'Oh, I!' exclaimed Matilda. 'If you could guess but a thousandth part of my constant concern about your welfare! Night and day I never for a moment stop worrying.'

'Do you believe I shall leave you, as she claims, all alone at the corner of the table?'

'Why yes, of course,' said Matilda. 'But she was wrong about Nanny. Nanny is not a bit stupid. Nanny is no ordinary black cat!'

We had laughed, and the memory of that laugh brought a smile to my face, but the man whose finger-nails I was filing appeared perfectly oblivious to my presence. He had thrown his handsome features back and was talking to himself. What was he saying? I tried to hear, but though his lips moved very little sound emerged from his mouth. And yet all his handsome features were taking part in this silent pantomime and now and again a humorous glint appeared in his eyes. At first I had thought that his lack of interest in me might have been due to the fact that I was a foreign girl. One has to be prepared for anything. Now, a more sinister idea crept into my mind. 'There must be something wrong with him,' I thought. 'Only madmen talk to themselves. It is said to be a sign of disequilibrium.'

Just as I was finishing my work my client threw up his handsome head and exclaimed: 'Hurrah! I've got it now.'

'Got what?' I queried.

He inspected his fingers and said:

'Very good work. Thanks a lot, little blonde girl. You have been an excellent influence.'

Diving into his pocket he produced half a crown.

'That's for you!' he said, and paying his bill he ran lithely up the stairs.

A moment later Wendy came down, her features flushed with excitement.

'What did he say, Madeleine?'

I looked surprised. So did the barbers.

'Didn't any of you recognize him?' asked Wendy.

'No!' we all answered, shaking our heads.

'Why, that was Jack Buchanan!' she said. 'He's rehearsing at the Hippodrome.'

'Oh, that explains it!' I murmured, rather ashamed of myself.

'I thought he might have escaped from a mental hospital. He must have been learning his part.'

'You are lucky!' said Wendy. 'Sitting at Jack Buchanan's feet while I had to stay up there all alone.'

She ran lightly across to where I was standing and whispered in my ear:

'Do you remember Daisy, that lovely young woman with the dark eyes who told us about her adventures in a Brussels hotel? When she innocently walked into the job of a call girl?'

'Yes, of course,' I answered. 'Frenchy's client.'

'Well, she's with him now, having a shampoo and set. Come up if you're free.'

Ten minutes later I found an excuse to run up to the shop.

'Hallo,' said Daisy when she caught sight of me. 'It appears you have been helping Jack Buchanan to learn his part. Did he offer you a role?'

'I didn't even recognize him,' I said.

'All right,' she said, 'I was only pulling your leg. This week I feel on top of the world. I've got a job in a chorus. And that's not all. I'm understudying a famous West End star.'

'Who is she? June? Alice Delysia?'

'I can't tell you her name. One has to keep it a secret. It would bring me bad luck.'

'Bad luck to you or to her?'

'To me. I have to hope she catches influenza or breaks a leg!' Daisy laughed a wicked yet most ingenuous laugh. 'Imagine! A telegram or a simple phone call to say she is indisposed. I put on her dress, her jewels, walk on to the stage and start reciting her lines, the manager tells his friends in Fleet Street, the critics arrive and the next morning I'm famous! Don't laugh. It could happen. I'm keeping my fingers crossed.'

Frenchy had managed to turn her into a stunning peroxide blonde. She was delighted and danced round the mirror on her high heels. 'And I haven't told you all, Madeleine,' she exclaimed, calling me for the first time by my Christian name. 'You don't mind my calling you Madeleine, do you? I've found a vacant room in an extraordinary house in St Giles Circus. Who do you think I have as a neighbour? You wouldn't guess in a thousand years. Grock, the Clown. Isn't it simply too inspiring! I've never had such a run of good fortune. Mind you, I'm prudent. I know by experience how quickly one's luck can turn. So in order not to invoke the anger of the gods I haven't unpacked my trunks. Often in the past when I arrived in some wonderful new place, expecting to stay there for at least six months, I have been obliged to leave at the end of the first week. I noticed that it all had to do with my trunks. If I started to unpack them the show folded up, or my money ran out, and I had to leave. If I didn't unpack them all went well. I stayed. To give you an example. I once spent an entire year in a room in which I never unpacked a thing. One day I got tired of seeing those two great osier theatrical baskets parked in the middle of the room with all my things inside as if I lived in the middle of a railway station. I emptied both of them and arranged my clothes in the wardrobe and the tallboy. At last my room looked like home. This happened on a Saturday evening. On Monday morning I received a letter from the management giving me the sack. I swore it would never happen again. Since then, whenever I rent a room I hang a line from one wall to the other and on this I suspend what I'm most likely to need. But all the rest, my small personal belongings like the vanity case I was given in Shanghai and all the hand-made lace I bought in Cairo and the silver and tortoise-shell brushes and combs, remain packed in my trunks. It's not my fault if I'm superstitious. At my age one can't afford to take unnecessary risks. And I've spent so many years with theatrical folk that I have picked up their bad habits as well as their good ones. Don't you think that Frenchy has done a magnificent job with my hair?'

'Yes,' I agreed. 'It's terribly effective, but your hair looks so thick. It almost looks like string.'

'Of course,' she said, not in the slightest put out by my criticism. 'It's meant to. To appear at its best it needs stage lighting. I shall be a real hit in the chorus. Girls with natural fair hair like yours pass unnoticed on the stage.'

'I have no desire to become an actress,' I answered, 'unless on the films.'

I was not exactly vexed, but her words might well have been meant to hurt. I was so much younger than she was. Nevertheless

I was prepared to believe that, with her huge dark eyes and that peroxide blonde mop of thick hair, she must make an impression in a theatre.

'By the way,' she said suddenly, 'Wendy tells me that we have become neighbours. Is it true that we live on opposite sides of the church of St Giles?'

'It's very likely,' I answered, 'if you lodge in St Giles High Street.'

'At least we heard the same church clock strike this morning,' she said. 'That makes us neighbours, doesn't it? Why don't you come and look me up on Sunday morning? I don't work Sundays and stay in bed most of the morning with a mud pack on my face and cold cream on my tummy. It doesn't help a woman to have had two children.'

Daisy was waiting for me when I ran up the stairs after saying good night to George, the Hungarian and the Czech. 'I thought we might walk part of the way home together,' said Daisy. Obviously I was on the point of making a new friend. I wondered what my mother would think of her. Wendy was counting the money in her till. Frenchy had removed his white coat and was preparing to lock the entrance to his sanctum. Outside in Coventry Street the traffic growled and the newspaper sellers were calling out the Late Night Final—All the Football and Racing Results.

One point about Daisy intrigued me.

'The first time we met you told us about your job in that Brussels hotel, and that you possessed all the qualifications, including a British passport,' I said. 'But I can't quite reconcile that with those lovely oriental eyes of yours and the way you appear to speak at least two languages without the trace of an accent. And then again, what were you doing in Cairo and Shanghai?'

Daisy laughed.

'One thing at a time,' she said. 'My father was Egyptian. From him I inherited these dark eyes. He met my mother when he was a student at London University, but he wasn't much good at exams. He said he always knew the wrong things—things that other students didn't know. He was clever, cleverer than most, but in his own way. Besides, a person can be clever in the affairs of his own country and not in those of another. He probably didn't fit in. The young woman who was to become my mother allowed him to cry on her shoulder. She consoled him. She paid dearly for her admiration for this romantic descendant of the Pharaohs. He married her, took her to Egypt and put her in a harem.'

'I don't believe you!' I exclaimed.

'Nobody ever does believe what I tell them,' said Daisy. 'In the end I have to hide so many things that I get muddled. Where was I?'

'About your mother being put in a harem.'

'He had introduced her to two lovely young girls as being his sisters. Actually they were his wives. She took it all very badly, and after a year or so managed to escape. From my point of view she would have done better to stay. I have no doubt at all that I would have had a far better life. When much later I went back to Cairo, and tried to get into touch with my father, the British authorities had me deported. They didn't want women of my kind making complications with the Egyptians.'

I still did not believe her. I thought she might well be trying out on me some role in a play. It sounded the sort of stuff that could be offered to small provincial audiences. She must have guessed what was in my mind because she exclaimed:

'You think I'm crazy, don't you?'

'Not entirely. Only yours is not the sort of story I'm accustomed to. You might not believe some of those that happen in my mother's world. How did your mother escape from the harem?'

'She was afraid of being poisoned. She used to tell me when I was a little girl that the other women cut cats' whiskers into tiny pieces which they mixed into the food of those they wanted to do away with. The victims in due course died in atrocious pain. Their stomachs were perforated.'

'Why should they have wanted to murder your mother? Because she was not of their race?'

'Presumably.'

'You mean that if they hadn't want to murder her she would have been content to remain with the other wives in the harem?'

'I have already told you. She took the whole thing badly.'

'What happened?'

'I think the marriage must have been annulled. She was shipped back to England. Only the right kind of Englishwomen were tolerated by the British authorities in Egypt. Like Caesar's wife, no scandal must be attached to them. As my mother was still young and determined to have a good time she handed me over to her mother in Nottingham. At sixteen I ran away, took a train for London and found myself a job.'

'What sort of job?'

'At the hostel where I got a room for the night I heard that a repertory company was auditioning girls for a musical that was to tour the Provinces. I could sing, and was tall and slim with the right kind of legs. I went to the audition and was hired on the spot. The next day I found myself the youngest girl in the chorus.

'We had been touring for about twelve weeks when one night in Liverpool a young man sent me flowers and was waiting for me at the stage door. His name was Harry. He was a bank clerk, and he was rather sweet. As he took me to meet his family and offered me marriage, I stayed behind that following Saturday night when the rest of the company was packing to play in Glasgow the following week. Harry took me home with him. They could not have been nicer, but they were unbelievably poor with brothers and sisters sleeping indifferently in the same bed. None of them seemed to worry that I was another mouth to feed. When there was enough money we all ate Lancashire hot-pot, fried fish and chips or sausages and mash. Somebody invariably managed to bring home a bottle or so of beer. I sang the songs they had taught us in repertory, I danced and clowned. I had brought my trunk from the lodging-house and everybody dived into it and the girls tried on my dresses. Our wedding was stupendous and personally I would have been quite happy to go on like that indefinitely. Lancashire people have the warmest hearts in the world.

'But Harry had other ideas. "This is all new to you," he said, "but it has ceased to be good enough for me." Mostly when men get married they want to settle down. With Harry it was the opposite. Before marrying me he was afraid to let himself go. No sooner was the wedding over than he felt liberated from his family.

I had told him about Cairo and how my father was a Bey. The travel bug had bitten him. He wanted to see the world, and when he married me had not been saddled like most men with in-laws. I was virtually alone in the world. Grandmother had gone into a home shortly after I ran away to London, and one night when we were playing in Birmingham I got a telegram to say she had died. I'm not saying that I did not have a short stab of conscience, but what could I have done? As for my mother, I had no idea where she was. So, you see, Harry was free—free to do just what he liked.'

Daisy had dragged me into a Lyons. She had ordered poached eggs on toast and tea and I hadn't the heart to refuse. Besides I had wanted to hear her story. The teashop was warm and noisy and in my opinion there was nothing more succulent in the whole of England than poached eggs on buttered toast as served with a cup of tea in a Lyons. I was very English in my taste in food. I was almost childishly surprised by the superior quality and the modest price. It was no good talking to me about the marvels of French cuisine. The yellow of the poached egg when one burst it with the knife was like sudden sunshine. I could have wept with joy. She wanted to pay for my share as well as hers but I was too proud.

'Well,' said Daisy as we resumed our journey down Charing Cross Road, 'as I practically have to pass your street on the way to mine, I'll accompany you as far as your mum's.'

But rather as I had feared Matilda could be seen peering out of the window above my bed anxiously awaiting my return. The little lines round her mouth which made her look hard and stern presaged one of those angry scenes, caused by worry, that I was constantly forced to calm down by soft words. I was late. I had wasted my time with Daisy in a Lyons. I might have been run over in the street. The supper she would have made me had perhaps lost its savour. And I had blunted, with that delicious poached egg on toast, my appetite. But, as the Tall Louise used to say, 'if you treat your daughter like that, Madame Gal, how will she ever make a life of her own? She is going to be twenty this coming August. You are lucky that she comes obediently home to you every night. At her age life held no more secrets for me'. Matilda on these occasions would look at the Tall Louise in a superior way and say: 'You appear to forget that Madeleine is my daughter!' How did the Tall Louise dare to compare herself to Matilda's daughter!

'Well,' said Daisy, unaware of what was waiting for me upstairs. 'This is where I say good night. Don't forget. I shall be expecting you tomorrow morning at my place.'

She turned off sharply in the direction of St Giles.

In spite of having had to pay for my poached egg and toast, I was bringing home not only my week's pay but several silver half-crowns that my customers had slipped into the pocket of my white coat. These I poured out on the table to wipe away from my mother's forehead the little clouds of anger that had been gathering there. Also without waiting for any explosion on her part I burst forthwith into an account of Daisy's tale.

'Come!' said Matilda, making a neat little pile of the heavy silver coins and visibly relieved that at last her daughter was safe under her roof. 'Your Daisy sounds to me like a prodigious liar. Are there harems in Egypt?'

'At all events a Bey can have several wives,' I said. 'And after all it happened a long time ago. Even supposing Daisy isn't more than twenty-seven or twenty-eight she would have been born before the turn of the century.'

'That's true,' said my mother. 'See what I've made for supper. Are you hungry?'

'Not very,' I admitted. 'She took me into a Lyons and we had a poached egg on toast.'

Matilda said nothing. I could see that she was anxious to soften her resentment. As she bent over the gas stove, she said:

'Oh, it's not that I mind you having a little fun on your own—only that I get so anxious. I was watching all those people stepping out of cabs to dine at Gennaro's. Every other woman was draped in a Spanish shawl, but the men are very elegant in their white waistcoats and tails. I have always claimed it needs a Britisher to look at ease in evening dress.'

At heart I agreed with Matilda, but Daisy had said: 'Make no mistake about it, Madeleine. All these men who take their fiancées and their wives to dinner in Soho restaurants on Saturday nights are little men who believe that Soho represents the last word in cosmopolitan sophistication. Never be taken in by them. They are no good to a girl. You would only waste your time.'

I had felt inclined to answer: 'But didn't you marry a bank clerk?' But I held my tongue. She had obviously told me only a small part of her story. I must not judge until I had heard the end. And where in the main did these clever evaluations lead a girl? How much wiser would I be when I had listened to the often hair-raising experiences of the Tall Louise, of Gabrielle, of Marion and now of Daisy? What had I learnt of any value to myself? I wasn't even vaguely in love with a man. I did not even cut out photographs of film stars and keep them in my handbag as Wendy so often did. There had been Rudolph Valentino, of course, but I had never translated my admiration for him into anything personal. But tomorrow might prove to be an important day in my life. Not only was I to call on Daisy in the morning, but I had not yet dared tell my mother that I had been invited by a client to go dancing at the Kit-Kat in the afternoon. What would I wear? Matilda would have to help me choose something suitable. But tomorrow was tomorrow.

We both slept so late that we missed the milkman's second round, and this was a pity because Matilda had intended to make me whipped eggs with cream, a sweet at which she excelled. There was a milk shop at the end of our street which remained open until one o'clock, but I avoided it, having had words with the owner's son, a lanky youth with straw-coloured hair. The other girls in the street eyed this spotty-faced individual with interest. As father and son owned the business the mothers with daughters of marriageable age thought it might be worth while cultivating them. The young man had been invited to tea in almost every house in Stacey Street except ours. Quite apart from my personal dislike of him my mother would have considered that we were too modestly housed to receive any member of the opposite sex save the rent collector, the coal-heaver or the man who came to inspect the gas meter. Some of our neighbours, married women with families, had basement flats in which on Sunday afternoons they made a big spread with bread and butter, cucumber sandwiches, watercress, home-made cakes and jam. The table in our room was always cluttered up with material for a dress, or a blouse or a skirt. At meal times we merely cleared a corner of the table and laid a linen cloth on it. But, as Matilda reminded me, there was another milk shop in St Giles High Street which would be on my way to Daisy's place.

In point of fact the milkman in question was Daisy's landlord, and when I arrived Daisy was actually in the shop wearing slippers and a green kimono with a golden dragon embroidered upon it. Her peroxide hair was piled on top of her head and in her arms were a loaf of bread, a carton of eggs and a bottle of milk. Daisy rented the room previously occupied by the owner's son who was newly married and had gone to stay with his in-laws. Delighted with her lodging, which was cheap and conveniently situated near to theatreland, Daisy hoped that the arrangement would last as long as possible.

'Come!' she said.

I followed her out of the milk shop to a narrow brown side door with a brass knocker leading to the maisonette. Her room was on the first floor immediately above the shop, and as I looked out of the window I remember seeing a No. 38 bus emerging from Shaftesbury Avenue followed by a No. 19. It was fun finding oneself on the same level as the passengers on the open top deck. It had been raining and the conductor had fastened the small covers of waterproof sheeting over several of the unoccupied seats to save them from getting wet.

In the middle of the room were Daisy's famous trunks, tall oblong osier baskets lined with rather gay chintz. The lids were thrown back to reveal the contents in colourful array. Daisy, plunging a hand into all these treasures, exclaimed: 'I am going to give you all this beautiful real lace made by Chinese girls in Hong Kong. It comes from the same shop in which I bought the kimono I'm wearing. I had the loveliest kimonos in Shanghai and I would put one on as soon as I got out of bed in the morning. There is something regal about this one, don't you think? When I look at my reflection in the mirror while I'm doing my hair I dream that I am a princess.'

The princess looked a little *passée* in the grey light of a London Sunday morning, and her hair, after its massive application of peroxide, lacked shine, but her eyes were as usual immensely effective. 'Why do you give me all this lace?' I asked. 'You must have carried it with you half way round the world.'

'That's the whole point,' said Daisy. 'In the end somebody is bound to steal it from me, and as I shall never make use of it myself I may as well give it to you. It's incredible how people steal my treasures, but I have learnt to take it philosophically because the more they steal the lighter become my trunks, and when they have both become half empty I'll pack all my remaining things into just one trunk and throw the other one away. I shall thus travel lighter because, believe me, something is bound to happen to send me off on the road again.'

The dress Daisy had worn the previous day hung over a clothes line. I went over to examine it. 'I bought it in Chelsea,' she said. 'I buy most of my dresses and coats at a second-hand dress shop near Chelsea Town Hall. I have discovered a way of renewing my wardrobe at frequent intervals at low cost. This is what I do. I go into this shop, choose what I want and leave the clothes I am wearing in exchange. The result is that I go in with one ensemble and come out with another without having to open my purse.'

'I think it's a horrible idea!' I cried. 'I could never bring myself to wear the clothes of some woman about whom I knew nothing.'

'That shows you have never been on the stage,' said Daisy. 'In the theatre one learns not only to be in another woman's clothes but in her skin. One exchanges the whole of one's personality for that of a stranger. Thus one has more than a single existence. What am I saying? One has a dozen different lives—a hundred different lives. Isn't that more exciting than living your own small dull little life?'

The clock of the church of St Giles struck midday.

'Didn't I tell you we were on opposing sides of the churchyard,' said Daisy. 'I to the north, you to the south. We shall have to see a lot of each other.'

'Mother is to make whipped eggs with cream for lunch,' I said, 'but we missed the milkman on both his rounds. I promised to buy both the eggs and the milk here. I must be running or I shall be late and Mother will scold me. Thanks for the lace. By the way, I'm going dancing this afternoon. I'll tell you all about it next time we meet.'

I bought the eggs and the milk and hurried back to Stacey Street. Then I showed Matilda the roll of lace that Daisy had given me. My mother, who knew more about lace than anybody I had ever met, and who, when I had been a baby, had made those exquisite lace blouses in Paris, took up the roll of lace and said, with a rather pinched expression: 'Your Daisy has indeed given you a regal present. This lace is genuinely hand made and is very delicate and beautiful. You will be able to make yourself a magnificent lingerie set—if not two.'

Lingerie was a constant subject of conversation between Matilda and myself. She would never have allowed me to wear any but of lawn or *crêpe de Chine*, hand made and embroidered with real lace. Under her tuition I had learnt to sew, like those girls in French convents, the most complicated of stitches with the finest of needles. Matilda used to say that what was hidden must be even prettier than what was visible. So I spent hours sewing rose, sky blue and jade green *crêpe de Chine*.

I chose this moment to break the news to Matilda that I was going to dance with a customer at the Kit-Kat Club. Not only did she take it very well but she added: 'As a matter of fact I was wondering how to tell you that Marion had invited me to go to a film with her this afternoon at that cinema in Tottenham Court Road. She is coming to fetch me at 3 p.m. Unless of course, Tonio objects. If by 3.30 p.m. she is not here I shall know that Tonio, whatever he had previously planned to do, has changed his mind and wants her to stay with him. They have patched up their little quarrel, but their relationship is fragile. She told him a part of her story and, because he has a past of his own, with a wife and possibly children, he agreed to allow things to go on as they were, at least for the moment. Marion has made a resolution, however. From now on she is going to put money aside just in case he changes his mind. Ah! That reminds me, Marion wants you to make an appointment for her with Frenchy. Her hair is turning grey again at the roots. She suggests next Saturday afternoon.'

I looked at Matilda's golden helmet of hair and my own, so vigorous and honey-blonde, and reflected that we were indeed fortunate never to have to go to a hair stylist. There had been a time when I envied girls with lustrous dark hair, but, now that I realized how quickly it passed, I was grateful to nature for having made me as I was.

'I suppose,' said Matilda, 'that you won't be satisfied until you have brought that girl, Daisy, round to meet me?'

'Naturally,' I answered.

Matilda laughed. 'As if we had not a mad enough collection of women as it is,' she said. 'But never mind. I shall look forward to meeting her. I'm glad you brought Marion here. She has a mystery and I haven't solved it yet.'

As soon as lunch was over I began to get ready for the *thé-dansant*. What I most feared was that it should start to rain again. Because the Kit-Kat was a fashionable club I would not be able to arrive with my dancing shoes wrapped up in brown paper as most girls did when we went to the Italian Club off Tottenham Court Road or to the Palais de Danse in Hammersmith. My partner would doubtless be waiting for me outside the entrance in the Haymarket. I must therefore arrive looking fresh and relaxed. Ever since I had accepted his invitation I had been wondering which of my dresses to wear, and, though I was delighted by the importance of the occasion, I felt certain that whichever dress I chose, unless my mother helped me, would prove wrong.

Matilda, guessing my dilemma, said: 'If I were you I would wear the navy blue, the one that belonged to my client's daughter in Pembroke Square. Now that you have shortened the hem it suits you admirably. The pleated apron will swing from your hips as you dance rather like a ballet dancer's tu-tu.'

At this moment Marion, having arrived early, could be heard calling Matilda from the street below our window. We threw her the key and I changed into the navy blue dress. 'Oh yes,' said my mother as the door opened, 'nothing could be more elegant than that for a *thé-dansant*.'

Marion took in the situation at a glance. She exclaimed:

'So Mother's little girl is going off to a *thé-dansant*!'

I looked at her angrily, but Matilda answered proudly: 'Yes, and isn't that dress just perfect on her?'

'The dress is perfect on her,' said Marion, 'but not to go dancing in. That pleated apron, so light and pretty, would be rumpled in no time by her partner holding her tightly. What others has she got?'

Marion quickly picked out my little black satin, and said: 'This is the one she needs. You should keep the navy blue for a much more special occasion.'

She was right and my mother was delighted by her friend's sagacity—for Marion was increasingly becoming her friend rather than mine. At all events they were both by now in high good humour, and having changed my dress I took advantage of the situation to hurry away.

I followed the same route as if I had been going to the barber's shop, across Cambridge Circus, along Shaftesbury Avenue as far as Wardour Street and thus to the Haymarket. The streets had their Sunday afternoon appearance with slow-moving crowds and the Sunday newspapers on overturned soap-boxes at street corners.

My young man, just as I had expected, was waiting for me in front of the club. I took an instant dislike to his brown suit, and neither his tie nor his shirt found grace in my eyes, but as we entered the club and the sound of the orchestra began to electrify all my youthful limbs I was delighted. First, however, there was the tea ceremony, and to my embarrassment I was supposed to pour it out and inquire if he took milk or sugar. But after a while I heard him say: 'Shall we try this foxtrot?' And to my relief we took to the floor. Here I encountered another deception: his manner of dancing. Instead of leading me as he should have done he danced for himself. I looked round the room. Some of the girls' dresses were pretty, extremely so. This was not the clientèle of my Italian Club, still less that of the Palais de Danse. My partner appeared to know a great many people. He exchanged politenesses with them and appeared much more concerned to impress them than to bother himself with me. I recalled with a touch of nostalgia the excessive consideration that older man had shown me during lunch at the Café Royal, and I was beginning to make comparisons that would almost certainly make me a difficult girl to please. I was becoming bored. The club was elegant, but this Sunday afternoon clientèle was clearly different from that which frequented it on weekdays. The whole of this area from Leicester Square to Piccadilly Circus took on quite another appearance on Sundays. 'Shall we go back to our table?' my partner asked.

No other man would dare to cut in on us in this place. I was saddled with him for the afternoon. The cakes were delicious and it would have been wonderful to steal a chocolate éclair and take it back to Matilda, who would have had a good time at the pictures but no tea and cakes. Several young men at adjoining tables had begun to smile encouragingly at me and I noted with pleasure that the girls they were with had already noticed their behaviour. Had my partner noticed it also?

He was beginning to be aware of my presence. 'Can you Charleston?' he inquired in a low voice as if he wanted it to be a secret.

'Of course,' I answered. 'Can you?'

'It's not allowed here,' he said, 'but we could dance our way into a corner and defy them. What do you say?'

'Let's!' I agreed enthusiastically. Alas, it had taken all this time for me to realize that I was enjoying myself.

We danced the Charleston so successfully in our corner that soon other couples followed suit and even the orchestra sympathized and warmed up. 'Will you come again with me next Sunday?' asked Michael. Yes, he was called Michael. This was the first time I had learnt his name.

'I'll think about it,' I answered as we emerged into Haymarket.

'I'll call a cab,' he said.

'No, don't do that!' I pleaded. 'I can walk home. It's only a hundred yards away. Just leave me here. I assure you, that is what I would prefer.' I did not want him to see the street in which I lived. So like Cinderella I said goodbye to him and disappeared down Wardour Street.

Marion and Matilda were not yet home and I felt sick, having eaten too many cream cakes. Nanny jumped up on the table to arch her back under my chin. She also felt lonely. What could we do, Nanny and I? It was far too early to go to bed and I did not feel like reading my novel. Sunday was always an unsatisfactory day. It struck me that I was only really happy on working days.

Half an hour later Matilda arrived home alone. She and Marion had not been to the cinema after all. They went to eat ices at the Corner House and there they met a middle-aged gentleman with whom they laughed and joked like two little girls. 'He had come up to Town for the day,' said Matilda, 'and he confessed that he had been very bored until he met us.' 'But how did he meet you?' I asked. 'We were enjoying our strawberry ices,' said Matilda, 'and you know how amusing Marion can be. We started laughing, and this gentleman, who was sitting at the table next to ours, was so intrigued that he inquired about the subject of our conversation. Something Marion told me must have been devastatingly funny.'

'What had she been saying?' I asked, slightly piqued.

'I forget,' said my mother. 'But it's not often that either she or I have the chance to be gay.'

'What did your gentleman friend talk about?' I asked.

'His four years in the trenches,' said Matilda. 'The Battle of Mons, the British retreat, the Marne, the Aisne, Arras and Lens and heaven knows what. You should have heard how he pronounced all those French names. As Marion said, if only Tonio hadn't been in Town we could all three have gone back to supper at his apartment. But it wasn't the moment to make him jealous again. Did you have a good time?'

'Fairly,' I said, 'but obviously it was not so hilarious as yours!'

5

BACK FROM HIS SUMMER HOLIDAY at Ostend, Mr Y had put on weight and was so burnt by the sun that the skin was peeling off his forehead and his nose. He had prolonged his vacation by a week in order to go to Luxembourg where he had relations. His presence had a sobering influence on his little staff. One felt instinctively that the boss was back. George, divested of managerial authority, was back at his own barber's chair and so was the Hungarian. The Czech had doubtless made his way on foot to some other temporary job. Up in the tobacconist shop Wendy was dusting her cherry-wood counter with a yellow duster. 'How did the *thé-dansant* go?' she asked. 'Guess what Aunt and I did on Saturday afternoon? We hired a row boat at Richmond and tied up against a clump of willows by Kew Gardens. There is no river so lovely as the Thames. Have you ever seen the lion on top of Sion House? Afterwards we had tea at an hotel and ate maids of honour.'

'Who are they?' I asked, my thoughts wandering.

'What are they?' she corrected. 'Delicious little cakes that date from the days of the Georges. George the Third, I think.'

'Where's Frenchy?'

'He must have got up late this morning. He must have had no early appointment. Monday morning is never a good time for him. Did you notice your boss's nose? He is so sunburnt that the skin is peeling off. Well, now he is back it is a sign that the summer is nearly over. I shall have to think about buying a winter coat. What a bore!'

Strangely enough, Matilda had also at breakfast been talking about winter coats, not for us but professionally. Women who bought themselves autumn or winter clothes invariably found as soon as they got home that they needed altering and that, as one might say, brought grist to the dressmaker. The approach of autumn had also reminded her that she would need to order a sack of coal. The operation consisted of opening the window and waiting for the horse-drawn cart to make its appearance at the corner of Stacey Street with all those sacks of coal stacked one against the other under a notice on which was chalked the price per hundredweight. The driver, an empty sack all stiff and shiny with use cunningly placed over his head, the end part falling against his back, would then descend and, having thrown the reins over his horse, walk slowly the length of the street calling out: 'Coals! Coals!' as he looked up at the houses on either side. Matilda would then have to make signs that she had an order to place; but as all the other women in the street would be leaning out of their windows to do the same thing, my mother would become self-conscious and the little veins in her forehead would stand out at the thought of her humiliation. It was terrible to be so shy—and so proud.

I was to have a taste of this feeling during the morning. A customer whose hands were in a terrible state called for the manicurist. After several feeble attempts to interest or amuse him I relapsed into silence. So did he. In the end, unable to stand this mutual suspicion any longer, I asked him what he did for a living. He said that he was a solicitor with offices in Lincoln's Inn, but that his car had broken down on Wimbledon Common and that he had tried to mend whatever was wrong with the engine. He then asked rather aggressively:

'What's happened to the girl who did my hands last time?'

'I haven't the slightest idea,' I said.

This was perfectly true. I knew nothing about my predecessor —not even her name or the colour of her hair or why she had left. My solicitor became even more inimical. Clearly he didn't believe me. When it came to paying the bill he said to Mr Y: 'Why did you get rid of that delightful girl who did my hands last time?'

Mr Y smiled in a non-committal way and added: 'I hope, sir, that you were none the less satisfied with the services of my present young lady?'

Judging by the tip he gave me, the solicitor from Lincoln's Inn obviously was not. On my return home I would seek sympathy from my understanding mother, but I knew in advance what she would say: 'None of us has the universal popularity of a Louis d'Or!'—an old French expression that meant exactly what it said.

In fact I never did tell her. I had not been home a couple of minutes before I heard the postman's rat-tat-tat on the street door. This gay noise was seldom heard in our house, but when it was, excited by the thought that there might be something for us, I would rush downstairs hoping to arrive before the wife of an Italian chef who lived in the basement. I seldom won this race. She merely had her own door to open. I had a long flight of steps down. At best I would only collide with her, which made us both furious. But I persisted. I hated the idea of a stranger looking at a letter addressed to Matilda before I could snatch it away. This, I repeat, happened very seldom. We did not receive many letters.

As usual, hearing the postman's rat-tat-tat, I rushed down.

'For Madame Gal,' said the postman, handing me a letter with a Paris postmark.

I returned breathless to my mother. She tore open the envelope, read the letter and looked pensive.

'It is from my dear sister Marie-Thérèse,' she said. 'The one who is married to your Uncle Louis. Do you remember how her sister-in-law (Louis's sister by the same occasion) went off as a young woman with their mother to Buenos Aires?'

'Of course,' I answered. 'The one thing that sticks in my mind is that she became very rich. You used to call her jokingly the Fabulous Aunt from Buenos Aires. And the old lady was said to have been quite a beauty in her time. Is that not right? Then later she developed a dangerous passion for expensive period furniture.'

Matilda laughed.

'Exactly,' she said.

'Is the letter about the Fabulous Aunt?'

'Precisely. The Fabulous Aunt and her mother have arrived back in France and Marie-Thérèse, in spite of the fact that they are still probably quite wealthy, is not at all pleased to have them on her hands. One can hardly blame Marie-Thérèse, ill and tired as she is. I pity her having her husband's sister and her husband's mother both foisted on her without warning. It would be enough to make any woman mad.'

The Fabulous Aunt had become something of a myth in my mind. The Argentine was a place of pampas grass, the tango and Rudolph Valentino in *The Four Horsemen*. My geography was hazy, but I liked fairy stories.

'What was her real name?' I asked Matilda.

'Maria,' said my mother. 'At least that's what we always called her. She and her mother went to the Argentine in the hope of becoming rich. The old lady had distinguished features but expensive tastes. Her daughter Maria became the mistress of one of the wealthiest men in the Argentine. I know little more than that. Marie-Thérèse doesn't tell me in her letter if they have returned penniless or with bags of gold.'

My mother was amused. Personally I had little interest one way or the other. I was secretly vexed because there was never a letter for me. My resentment was ridiculous because I knew nobody. But that was just it. It felt sad to be twenty and have nobody from whom to receive a letter. For my mother a letter from her sister in Paris was an event. There was excitement all over her features as she kept on reading and re-reading the words written in violet ink. Her customers seldom wrote to her, except now and again to cancel a fitting. They invariably paid her in cash. Or occasionally with a money order which we would take to the post office. Cheques never came our way. The very sight of a cheque would have filled us with panic. Marion, who managed to laugh at all our harmless inexperiences, had said one day:

'Well, at least if you never receive a cheque you don't have the problem of having them bounce back.'

On the Tuesday morning I got up so late that after swallowing my coffee I raced down the stairs putting on my coat and hat as I went.

'You'll break your neck on those high heels one day!' Matilda shouted angrily after me.

'I must look awful without make-up,' I thought, 'but I can do it in the barber's shop.' For no known reason I found myself modifying my usual route. In Newport Street I was greeted with the heady odour of newly baked bread. As I had been far too late to eat a thing at breakfast I went into the shop and bought a fresh roll. There were hundreds of crisp hot rolls in wooden baskets waiting to be delivered to all the restaurants in Gerrard Street and Wardour Street. The heavenly smell made me feel quite faint. 'One penny, dear,' said the woman handing me the roll in a paper bag. 'I'm going to eat it now!' I said.

Waving amicably to Wendy I raced down the stairs, removing my hat and my coat as I went. I had become adept at dressing and undressing on stairs. Mr Y pretended not to see me. What in fact had happened to my predecessor? At the beginning I had merely been asked to take her place while she was away. I was engaged on a temporary basis, but as she never reappeared I stayed on. I would never have given the matter another thought had it not been for the solicitor making inquiries about her.

George pointed to a pile of linen serviettes that needed to be dampened and ironed. I put the iron on the gas stove, set up the board and decided to compensate for my lateness by a great show of zeal. In my hurry I forgot to raise the hot iron to my cheek to gauge its temperature. Slamming it down on a serviette I recoiled in horror at the charred hole and tell-tale wisp of smoke. With all these mirrors at different angles somebody was bound to have seen me. What was Mr Y doing? Fortunately he was at the far end of the room. But the Hungarian, though he had his back to me, had seen my dilemma in the mirror. He left his customer with lather all over his face and quickly took the burnt towel which I saw him bury at the bottom of his own pile. He would find a moment later in the morning to destroy it.

I had been ironing for at least half an hour when the Hungarian managed to slip behind me a second time. 'It's supposed to be lucky to burn something,' he whispered into my ear. 'At least that's what my mother said when I was a child in Budapest and she burnt a napkin or the goulash for our supper.' I smiled at him. How kind these men were to me.

Here again was the man in the dark suit and the hands with their turned-in fingers. Seeking me out, he asked:

'Are you free, miss?'

Mr Y, appearing as if by magic on the scene, answered:

'You are fortunate, sir, my young lady has just this moment finished manicuring a customer.'

Blushing slightly at the sound of this abominable lie, I collected my instruments, filled a finger-bowl with warm soapy water and went to sit beside my client. 'Tell me what you have been doing since we last met,' he asked. I told him that a young man had invited me to dance at the Kit-Kat Club on Sunday afternoon, but that it had proved much less amusing than I had hoped.

'Ah?' he asked, interested. 'How was that?'

'In the small Italian Club where I often go, the men change their partners all the time,' I explained. 'It's more fun for the girls. If one happens to be invited by a bad dancer, a better one soon comes along.'

My client laughed. 'It doesn't portend well for your future husband,' he said. 'I'm afraid you are going to give him a difficult time.'

'I expect it will be different when I am married,' I said. 'At least I shan't have to get up so early in the morning. This morning I was shockingly late. Mr Y hasn't said anything to me yet, but I am expecting a lecture at any time.'

After a moment he asked:

'Wouldn't you like to know what I did on Sunday?'

'It never struck me that men did anything,' I said, 'except read the paper or play golf. What else is there for a man to do on a Sunday morning! With me it's different. I practically never stop. I sew, I mend my stockings, I help Mother make lunch, I make a hat. I find that if I can make a becoming new hat on a Sunday morning it helps me to look my best during the whole of the rest of the week.'

'How extraordinary!' said my customer. 'How does one make a hat? I confess I have never thought of such a thing. No, really, you are right. What is there for a man to do on a Sunday morning? I can't quite see myself making a hat so that I should face a new week with fresh courage. Imagine my handsome features under a home-made bowler hat!'

He laughed and I saw the Hungarian winking at me. There were moments when it did us all good in this airless basement to relieve the boredom of a long day. When I had finished, and he was paying his bill, I heard him say to Mr Y:

'That little French girl is a born actress and she manicures splendidly. The place is quite changed since her arrival.'

Two good marks. One bad. As long as Mr Y did not find out about the burnt towel I might get through the day without too much trouble. It was my lunch hour, but I would be wise to watch the clock.

'May I go out to lunch, Mr Y?'

'Yes,' said Mr Y, consulting his watch. 'Mr Darley appeared very satisfied with your services. He is a charming gentleman.'

'Is that his name—Mr Darley?'

'Why yes,' he answered. 'You should acquaint yourself with the names of your customers. It's an American habit which is immensely important in business.'

So the man in the black suit was called Mr Darley, and as I turned into Wardour Street there he was looking into the windows of Mr Willy Clarkson. 'I suppose you have never heard of *La Princesse Lointaine*?' he asked, turning round to greet me as if our meeting was the most natural thing in the world.

'Of course I have,' I said indignantly. 'You have been looking at Edmond Rostand's letter to Willy Clarkson, and the photograph of Sarah Bernhardt in the role of Mélisande. What are you doing in Wardour Street? I mean, how did you know that I would be going home by this route?'

'You told me,' he said, 'the very first time we met. It's amazing how much you have revealed to me about your private life. "I pass along Wardour Street every day on my way to lunch," you said, and so it struck me that as you also complained about the speed with which your pretty light shoes wear out, we could look in at Jacobus and buy you a pair.'

'You are unkind to tempt me,' I laughed. 'Girls should not accept presents from strangers.'

'It is you who are unkind to call me a stranger,' he said. 'By now we are almost old friends.'

We crossed Shaftesbury Avenue and as we entered the shop he asked me if there was any special model to which, when lately I had been passing this way, I had lost my heart. I could not very well tell him that there was hardly a model that did not enchant me. I could easily visualize buying the entire contents of the shop, but as we sat down to be greeted by an obsequious attendant I said:

'Yes, what I would like most are patent leather with slim heels.' I tried on half a dozen different styles, telling myself perhaps for the first time in my life that I had no need to worry about the price. This was an experience so new to me that I remember having no qualm at all about accepting this munificence so gallantly offered. The assistant suggested a pot of special cream with which to clean the shoes and a little velvet pad with which to make them shine.

'Yes, yes,' said Mr Darley. 'Of course we will take the accessories which no doubt will prove very useful.'

'May I wear them now?' I asked.

The assistant took a pair of scissors that hung by a tape from her waist and scratched the soles. 'I'll pack the old ones in a box,' she said.

We came out into the sunshine, but by now so much of my lunch hour had flown away that I would never have time to lunch at home. I dared not be late twice at work the same day. 'Oh, thank you!' I said to Mr Darley, looking up at him as we stood on the kerb. 'You are wonderful. I have seldom felt so happy!'

'You are fortunate to find happiness so easily,' he said, 'but it must be contagious because I also have enjoyed myself enormously. Be discreet in your barber's shop but tell your mother, of course, and give her this evening my kind regards.'

I watched him hail a cab and drive away. As for me, I arrived back at work nearly a quarter of an hour too early. Mr Y was filling bottles of hair lotion and arranging them in front of each barber's chair, discussing the while with George how they could satisfy a mail order from a customer in Cape Town without the packing and postage costing nearly as much as the article.

'No doubt,' said George with his German good sense, 'but when the customer in Cape Town opens the parcel he will have the impression of receiving a fragrant breeze from Piccadilly Circus. He will be grateful.'

As nobody was taking any notice of me, not even to note the fact that I had returned a quarter of an hour early from lunch, which could only be a mark of my zeal, I allowed my thoughts to wander to Matilda's coming birthday. She would be forty. Exactly twice my age. I must go to the Haymarket Stores and buy her that teaset with the blue flowers. It would be the first time that I had been able to buy her so considerable a present or to contribute usefully to the adornment of our small lodging. Almost everything of modest beauty within those four walls had been due to Matilda's skill with the needle. Having been the object of Mr Darley's munificence, my heart was bursting with a desire to make somebody else happy.

That evening as I hurried down Stacey Street on my way home the organ-grinder at the corner of Phoenix Street was playing 'Valencia'. Generously I threw a penny into the greasy cap artistically disposed on the pavement. The brute did not even say thank you, but the money might help to feed the little monkey in his red pullover and blue shorts grimacing on top of the organ. From the direction of Shaftesbury Avenue came the sudden clanging of bells as two fire-engines raced out of the red portals of the fire station.

At home I found Marion sitting on the edge of my couch. She had brought the dress of some former colleague before whom she had unwisely sung the praises of Matilda's dressmaking skill. 'She's a bitch,' she was saying colourfully, 'and I refused to give her your address, but what could I do when she brought her dress asking me to bring it to you. The hem needs shortening.'

Matilda's eyes went straight to my new shoes and then to the box with the old ones in it that I put down on the table. Doubtless she also noticed that the new ones pinched. One could not hide anything from Matilda. It was best to tell the two women everything. So I burst enthusiastically into my story, hoping to make a sensation. When at last I stopped to take breath it was as if I had thrown a stone into a pail of water. There was the noise of my voice and then a terrible silence. Marion said sententiously:

'My poor girl, it always starts like that. An innocent present. Next time he will want to help you put them on. The time after that you will go to bed with him.'

'I don't believe a word!' I exclaimed angrily. 'He is not that kind of a man.'

'And I don't believe in male generosity,' snapped Marion.

'Men merely pay for what they can get out of a girl. Some are so mean they don't even pay.'

My eyes began to fill with tears. I hated Marion at that moment. All the infinite happiness I had carried home with me had suddenly disappeared and I stood like some wounded bird in my new high-heeled shoes that pinched and made me wince.

But what was the matter with me? Was I really as stupid and as naïve as Marion was trying to make out? I looked at her searchingly. The gas mantle softly illuminated her features as she sat there on the edge of my couch, one arm resting on a pile of cushions. Turning to Matilda, she said:

'You must admit that I'm right?'

Matilda said nothing. She wore her thinking expression, the unmistakable sign that she was weighing the pros and cons carefully in her wisdom. At last she said very slowly:

'Well, at least she has got a lovely pair of shoes out of him, maybe half a size too small, but extremely elegant. As for the rest, my daughter will have to learn to fight her own battles in life. There are moment for distrust, and there are moments for generosity.'

Marion laughed bitterly. 'If really you believe that anything can be learnt like a lesson at school then you are more naïve than I supposed! Could I, for instance, have anticipated what happened the other evening at Tonio's place? And the brutal way in which Jo slapped me? Could I have anticipated that?

'With men, however much you think you have learnt, the unexpected happens, and you have to start learning all over again.'

Her bitterness seemed to fill the room.

Matilda sensed that Marion's outburst was due to something much deeper than the sight of my new shoes. She asked pointedly: 'Why do you never tell us what happened to the child you had with Jo? A boy, if I remember rightly, called Jeremy?'

'Shall I tell you why Jo, on that famous evening in Tonio's apartment, slapped me on the face? Because he was certain that I took the child away from him out of spite. He probably loved the boy in his own manner but he did not think it worth while to show it. He thinks I stole the baby! Alas, neither of us has it.'

She paused, trying to put her thoughts in order. She had reached the stage when she was willing to tell us everything.

'When I had to quit work because of that attack of phlebitis, I could no longer afford to pay the woman who looked after Jeremy, and when I brought him home the landlady refused to have us in the house because Jeremy cried so much. He cried incessantly because he was ill, so ill that after one night worse than the preceding ones I had to take him back to hospital. I doubt if any woman has endured worse suffering than that which became my lot from that moment onward. I was penniless, my legs were swollen to the point that I could scarcely walk and my child was in a critical state in hospital. I spent an entire week trudging the streets between St Giles Circus and the Euston Road looking for a cheap room where I could keep a baby. When at last I found one near Goodge Street, sordid in the extreme, the rent payable in advance, the hospital informed me that Jeremy's condition had taken a turn for the worse and that he had been isolated.

'"It is your duty to inform the father," said Sister.

'"He wouldn't care," I answered. "Motor-cars are his only interest." I simply had to find the money for my first week's rent, and it struck me that if I could get myself employed as cashier in the pay box of a cheap cinema in the vicinity of Oxford Street I would at least spend my working hours seated.

'Now it so happened that I had a friend who occupied the pay box in just such a picture house near Waterloo Bridge. It was a ramshackle place that dated from pre-war days and they used to show the films of Charlie Chaplin and Mary Pickford. She sat in her narrow pay box in front of stiff rolls of different coloured tickets—6d., 9d. and 1s. I felt sure that she would have acquaintances in the trade, ways of discovering if there happened to be a vacancy for that kind of post in some West End cinema.

'She was not there when I arrived. Could I come back in half an hour? So I walked up Craven Street and across Trafalgar Square as far as the stone ramp of the National Gallery, where a lot of people stood basking in the sunshine, watching the fountains playing and the pigeons being fed. They spoke all sorts of different languages and looked prosperous and happy. Many had cameras slung over their shoulders. They were certainly delighted to be in London and this was a high spot in their stay—something they would want to talk about for years to come. I must have been the only really unhappy person in this small crowd, and I began telling myself how gladly I would have changed places with any other woman within sight—even though she might be secretly ill. The world was full of infuriating imbalances. I was youthful and still pretty but cursed as if I had been a leper. How had all this happened? Was it a reward for my friendship for Irma, whose husband's advances I had refused out of loyalty to her?'

'Out of loyalty to her,' said my mother, 'but also because he held no attraction for you physically.'

'Maybe,' conceded Marion, 'but he would have set me up in a nice little apartment of my own and I might have lived happily ever afterwards. Why yes, Madame Gal, I was a fool if ever there was one. Honesty doesn't pay. I was seriously thinking of suicide when a distinguished-looking man, impeccably dressed, removed his hat and asked me if I was alone on this sunny day, and if this were indeed the case, might he suggest that we should go to a charming little teashop he knew about off St Martin's Lane. As I had not eaten properly for more than a week and was faint with hunger I saw no harm in accepting the invitation. As your daughter Madeleine has just said of the gentleman who bought her those lovely shoes, he didn't look the kind of man to behave otherwise than as a gentleman. He was right about the restaurant. It was one of those cosy places with false oak beams and gay chintz curtains run by efficient spinsters who make delicious home-made cakes stuffed with chocolate cream. The tea was piping hot and I said no more about myself than that this was my afternoon off and that I had come to see a girl friend who worked in a nearby cinema.

'"What a wonderful idea," he said, "if the film is any good we could stay and watch it. I haven't been to the cinema for a long time."

'We walked slowly down to the river and already some of my despair had begun to lift, but when we reached the cinema and my friend was not in the pay box I was doubly distressed—firstly because she had been the only source of information in the trade, and secondly because her apparent non-existence made it look as if I had invented her to impress the man who had taken me out to tea. A girl appeared holding a torch in her hand. I asked her what had happened to my friend. My insistence appeared to embarrass her.

'"She has left," she said.

'"But why? She liked the job."

'"Personal reasons," said the girl.

'My escort had listened from a polite distance but now he said:

'"Oh, don't worry. She probably walked off with the till!" This was no moment to make jokes of so questionable a taste.

'"Don't say that," I said angrily. "The girl will overhear you and I shall be made to look ridiculous."

'What would I do now?

'"Do you want to see the picture?" he asked.

'I looked at the poster. The film was Pola Negri in *Bella Donna*!

'"Oh, yes!" I cried. How could I resist such a passionate, tragic love story. I had read several of the books of Robert Hichens—*The Garden of Allah, The Call of the Blood*. We had all read them.

'"Then perhaps you will be kind enough to give us two tickets," my escort asked the girl. "We may as well stay and see the show."

'"Ninepence or a shilling?"

'"A shilling—if those are the best."

'Guided by the usherette's torch we were shown to two seats at the back of the house. Before long I felt a hand squeezing my arm, but I had other preoccupations. Tears were flowing down my cheeks and I wanted to take a handkerchief out of my hand-bag and discreetly wipe them away before my companion became aware of the depths of my tenderness. The story of this woman on the screen so passionately played by Pola Negri kept on merging in my troubled mind with the thought of my poor baby in hospital, my predicament without a penny in my purse, the sordid room for which I could not even pay and the dreary, terrible night ahead.

'When the film was over even its tenuous joys could no longer sustain me. I dared not go to see my baby again at hospital. I shuddered at the thought of facing a furious landlady without the money she had demanded of me.

'"There is a grill-room in Leicester Square," said a voice, "where they serve excellent steaks. What do you say?"

'Night had fallen and the West End was crowded and romantic. Taxis were depositing men in evening dress and women in fabulous cloaks outside Daly's and the Alhambra. After supper the man, having paid the bill, began idly playing with the crinkly white paper of a £10 note. "I know a place where we could spend the night," he whispered, folding the note and placing it discreetly in my handbag.'

'After all, I wasn't a virgin,' said Marion. 'What was all the fuss about? I had been Jo's mistress, hadn't I? I had a baby to bring up as soon as I could bring him out of hospital. I needed the money, didn't I? Besides, to be honest, I had seen it coming right from the start, and the man was rich and agreeable to look at in his way. It might even lead to something—something that would change the whole of my existence.

'So we registered as husband and wife and were given the key to a comfortable room. Suddenly I was utterly relaxed, but in spite of the gentle pressure the man had kept up on my arm during the film, in spite of his occasional incursions in the direction of my breasts or my legs, here in bed in spite of all his efforts, not to mention mine, he remained incapable of making love to me. Personally I had all the hours of the long night ahead of me. I was in no sort of hurry, but the man worked himself up into such a frenzy of anger at his continued impotence that he began to swear at me, and after he had sworn at me he started to hit me and finally, taking up a poker from the old-fashioned fireplace, he set upon me like a madman. My cries only increased his rage. He stuffed a pillow in my mouth and went on assaulting me with the poker until I lost consciousness. When they discovered me lying prostrate on the bed an ambulance was called and I was taken to Charing Cross Hospital with two ribs broken. The man who had disappeared into the night would have done better to kill me. Alas, he was no more capable of that than of making love to me. In order to save myself from having to go back to a sordid lodging

I had ended up with two broken ribs in hospital. The police had found nothing in my handbag to reveal my identity or my address. "Don't worry," a young doctor passing one evening through the ward said to me, "at your age a couple of broken ribs heal quickly. You'll be out dancing again in a month." But what I most needed to know was if my child was better. I persuaded the almoner of the hospital to make inquiries. It was then that the tragedy of my miserable misspent youth unfolded itself in all its horror. My baby, Jeremy, had died. The hospital notified me at the address in Goodge Street to which I had never returned, and the authorities believing that I had abandoned the child did what they usually do on such occasions. I never dared inquire what that meant. My youth ended on that dreadful day.'

My resentment against Marion had subsided by now. Nobody spoke for a few moments. Then Matilda, who was visibly moved, said: 'To be honest, I felt sure that you must have abandoned your baby, and that it was for that reason you never spoke about him. I was intrigued by all you told me about your past, but though we had quite a lot of fun together my friendship was tainted by disgust. It's curious how sympathy and even hatred can go together. What you have just told us increases my sympathy and I feel a bit ashamed at my former mistrust.'

'Does Tonio know?' I asked.

'That afternoon at the apartment after your mother had left us I tried to tell him the story. He appeared relieved on the whole to think that our relationship did not risk any sudden complication. Before long his interest flagged. On the whole he's a simple man with problems of his own. The incident with Jo had been a matter of his honour. I could see that he was happy to forget it on the condition that I also agreed to consider the flare-up closed. I hate to admit it but I have become selfish. I need Tonio's protection and the semblance of a quiet married life.'

'So nothing has changed,' said my mother.

'Fortunately for all of us,' said Marion. 'For Jo, for Tonio and for me. Jo is certainly married. He probably has children. Tonio is all for a quiet life—as for me . . .' Her lips were thin and white with resentment. 'As for me, what happened merely confirmed the inescapable fact that my life is a total failure.'

She laughed bitterly.

'I still don't know how Tonio makes his money. I shall certainly not ask him. We have become partners in a business in which each of us finds a certain profit. I keep house for him. He provides me with food and lodging, even a modest degree of luxury. This makes no difference to the bitterness that lies hidden in my heart. Bitterness against myself? Against others? I'm not sure. Tonio knows a wealthy widow who lives in a charming house in Green Street, Mayfair. She is extremely elegant and beautiful, but people say that she is only really happy when doing calculated harm to others. A strange thought came over me the other day when she called on Tonio. I told myself that I would almost like to be her personal maid so that we could unite our desire for revenge on society.'

For some days after hearing Marion's story I began to have moments when I felt sick. Yet I may be wrong about the date of the first symptoms. They might even have begun following my disappointing *thé-dansant* at the Kit-Kat Club. One evening I left my mother bending over her sewing and ran down into the street to fill my lungs with fresh air. At that moment I saw the Tall Louise emerging from the direction of Phoenix Street, and this surprised me because it was only Monday, or perhaps Tuesday, at all events the beginning of the week and the Tall Louise seldom made an appearance until the week-end. She said: 'Mine is having dinner and I stole out of the house knowing that she would not discover my absence for half an hour or so. I have come to see if there is a letter for me. The Belgian mail generally comes by the evening post. Mother went to hospital for a serious operation and my sister Leona promised to write and tell me how she is. If anything went wrong she would send a telegram.'

'Yes,' I answered. 'A letter from Belgium did come for you by the evening post. I took it up myself. Mother is keeping it for you.'

'Oh, thanks!' she exclaimed. 'But tell me, what are you doing all by yourself in the street at this hour?'

'I felt sick and I came down for a breath of fresh air.'

'You feel sick?' cried the Tall Louise. 'And does your mother know?'

'No, why?'

'Heavens!' exclaimed the Tall Louise. 'That would be the end of everything!'

She grabbed me by an arm and hurried me back along the street. Upstairs Matilda was pinning up in tissue paper the dress that Marion had come to fetch for her former colleague. My mother had shortened the hem and was now glad to be rid of it.

'The Tall Louise has come for her letter!' I exclaimed.

Before my mother even had time to give it to her the Tall Louise exclaimed angrily, looking daggers at Matilda:

'How can you stand there fiddling with that tissue paper while your daughter has to run down into the street because she's feeling sick? What on earth has come over you?'

Marion, who was sitting on the edge of my couch waiting for her parcel, shot me a searching glance. An extraordinary expression had come over her.

'Feeling sick!' she cried. 'So soon after those new shoes!'

The unfortunate Matilda, who for once had been perfectly relaxed, was suddenly transformed into a statue of petrified horror. Three pairs of eyes were now concentrated on my small person. By this time I understood.

'What's the matter with you all?' I cried. 'Here we are, three women in a single small room on a hot night, and you are all surprised that I turn faint with the lack of fresh air.'

'So you are not pregnant?' asked the Tall Louise suspiciously.

'No,' I answered. 'I am not.'

'Then,' she asked, turning defiantly to Marion. 'What is this story about the new shoes? You must have something in your silly mind!'

My mother, thinking that it was high time to take control of the situation, gave the Tall Louise a sober account of the incident in question. We waited for her judgment as if her vast experience in such matters gave it special importance. After a few moments she said: 'I don't think that Madeleine did any harm in accepting the shoes. She is a very balanced young person.'

'Ouf!' said my mother. 'That takes a load off my mind.'

The Tall Louise, ripping open the envelope Matilda handed her, swiftly read the contents. 'There are no complications,' she announced, relieved. 'My sister Leona says that the operation appears so far to have been a success.' She folded the letter and put it in her handbag. 'I must run,' she declared. 'Mine will be going out to work at any moment now. I shall read Leona's letter more carefully later on in Mine's kitchen while I do the washing up. Good night, everybody.'

'Good night,' said Matilda.

The Tall Louise gave me a backward glance.

'Don't dare give me any more shocks like that!' she said.

Marion remained silent on the edge of my couch. I wished she would take her parcel and disappear. I was tired of seeing her there, monopolizing my mother's attention. I resented having been judged by her and by the Tall Louise. Both women, Marion whose past was so stormy and the Tall Louise who lived in the shadow of those beautiful but cynical women who trod Bond Street and Conduit Street after dark, watched over me as if I belonged to them. I wanted to go to bed, but first I would have liked to take a steaming hot bath with bath salts in the water so that I could wash out of my body and of my thoughts all these impurities that floated around me. I wanted to feel clean and to smell good, to put on a beautiful soft silk nightdress and wrap myself up in a kimono like Daisy's with a golden dragon all about me to protect me from the dangers that beset a girl at twenty.

'Well, I must be going!' said Marion.

My mother handed her the dress tidily pinned up in tissue paper.

'Good night!' she said.

We listened to her steps descending the stairs, passing into the street. The front door banged. There I was alone with Matilda who, as if some miracle had happened, stood before me with her happy face—the face of her good days. Out in the street the pubs were beginning to close and the French, the Italians and the Irish started to sing.

Rain was falling in sheets when I woke up the next morning. I had slept badly with the same recurring nightmare. A man was beating me about the head and shoulders with one of those Victorian pokers one still saw in certain London houses.

'You woke me up twice in the night,' said Matilda, 'and I had to calm you. You should learn not to be so sensitive.'

'It's all these women!' I said. 'They are driving me crazy.'

'My livelihood depends on women,' said my mother, pouring out the delicious hot milk and coffee. 'I admit they can be tiresome, but it's even worse for a woman when she has to depend on men.'

Wendy with a feather duster in her hand was singing 'Tea for Two'. Her husband had arrived in his liner and had sent a telegram from the docks. 'My problem now is how to get rid of Aunt,' said Wendy.

Frenchy was also in high spirits. The last few days had been difficult, but his appointments book was filling up. In spite of this his voice sounded muffled. He had caught cold waiting for a bus in the rain.

'You shouldn't go about with holes in the soles of your shoes,' said Wendy. 'It's amazing how careless some men are.'

Frenchy shrugged his shoulders. Shoe repairing was expensive and he had reached the age when he disliked spending money on anything that was not imperative. Every now and again he would pop a peppermint camphor lozenge in his mouth so that this repugnant smell added to that of green soap and Havana cigars made me feel sick again.

'I continually feel sick,' I said to Wendy.

'You're not pregnant?'

'Oh, for heaven's sake!' I entreated. 'Don't start that. I had it from my mother and her friends all evening.'

'Then it's your liver,' she said. 'Run across to the chemist and buy yourself a box of little liver pills.'

'I will,' I said, 'but not right now. I must go down and report to Mr Y. He'll think I'm late again.'

Mr Y was also busy dusting. He had one of those dyed yellow dusters in his right hand and he used this to flick off imaginary flecks of dust from his beautifully labelled bottles of hair lotion. As he appeared to be well disposed I asked if I might run across to the chemist. He nodded assent, and added:

'I don't feel too good myself this morning.' He put a hand in his trouser pocket and brought out some small change. 'I have one of those sick headaches. Buy me a bottle of aspirin. There's a good girl!'

'It's probably your liver,' I suggested.

At least Mr Y could not be suspected of being pregnant!

'You may be right,' he agreed. 'It may be all those sandwiches I eat during the lunch hour, but all the same what I need is an aspirin.'

Since his return from Ostend he had become more friendly in his dealings with me. Or perhaps it was I who feared him less. In retrospect I realize that all of us in the barber's shop were afraid of losing our jobs and Mr Y impressed us. This did not prevent us from having our individual dreams. George had several times told us how he would have liked to own a little hairdressing place in the suburb where he lived. The Hungarian would have liked to work in one of the very fashionable places in the West End, like the one in Bond Street frequented by smart young officers in the Brigade of Guards. It would have given him status.

Some while before, the representative of a Lyons silk firm whom I had known when I worked as a shorthand-typist in the City had given me several yards of *crêpe georgette*, and now Matilda promised to make me a beautiful new dress to go with my patent leather shoes. It was her way of showing me that I was in no way to blame.

Narrow pleats were much in fashion and, in spite of the fact that I already owned the dress that had belonged to the girl who by now must be nearing India and which had that pleated apron, Matilda was in favour of again using pleats but in a different way. She would place them at the sides.

'It will be extremely pretty,' she said, 'and the dress will only cost you the pleating.'

On these occasions my love for her overflowed. She understood so perfectly the immense pleasure I found in a new dress, and it was a matter of great joy to her that her skill with the needle could compensate for the fact that she could never afford to buy me expensive clothes. She had cut out two pieces that I was to take to a firm in Great Pulteney Street off Broadwick Street in

Soho where they specialized in pleating. 'Go during the lunch hour,' she had said. 'I am going to be terribly busy and shall need the whole table for cutting out.'

She hated to be disturbed when she had something complicated to do, and on such occasions it was no good my trying to go home for lunch. She would have her worried face. The material would be spread all over the table and Matilda would hover over it with her cutting-out scissors—calculating, hesitating, measuring, miserable because if she made a mistake there might not be enough material left over to rectify it and everything would suffer, her reputation, her purse and the confidence she had in her skill. She was like a swimmer hesitating on the edge of the springboard before executing a deep-water dive. If ever I happened to be in the room on these occasions I would hold my breath and keep absolutely silent. I who knew and understood her so well because I have inherited both her timidity and her force of character, her devastating modesty that hid a grim determination to succeed, could tell by the little lines round her eyes that she had remained awake most of the night planning every detail of the following day's work. These crises lasted nearly a week, during which our meals would be reduced to the minimum and, of course, no cooking with onions or celery whose odours seep into delicate material, even into the thread with which one sews, clinging for days to the fibre.

Although my mother had advised me to have a sandwich and a glass of milk before going to Great Pulteney Street, I would have neither. I would wait till the afternoon when I could have a cup of tea with the barbers or with Wendy. Daisy used to say that it was her habit not to eat during rehearsals. 'The smallest mouthful of food,' she said, 'and I find myself dancing like a sack of potatoes.'

At midday, which was my lunch hour, Piccadilly Circus was at its busiest, most scintillating. All the flower girls, seated in a colourful circle with their osier baskets full of flowers, were busy wiring button-holes for sale in the evening when gentlemen in immaculate tails would be going to their clubs, to the theatre or to the fashionable restaurants of the West End. The sun caught the windows of Mr Appenrodt's delicatessen on the opposite side of the circus. Now that I saw him every morning when he arrived to be shaved by George I took an interest in his shop and would have liked one day to go inside, but this was something that I would never dare do. This shyness I had also inherited from my mother. There were so many things we did not dare do.

My first impulse had been to approach Great Pulteney Street by way of Regent Street. This would have allowed me to pass the golden portals of the Café Royal and to admire the many-sided windows of the Galeries Lafayette where once I had worked as a salesgirl. But having absorbed the sights and sounds of Piccadilly Circus with its constant roundabout of taxis, cars, vans and red omnibuses, I turned my back on the flower girls with their osier baskets and hurried up Shaftesbury Avenue as far as narrow Denman Street which would lead me into the labyrinths of Soho—Sherwood Street, Brewer Street, Great Pulteney Street. Here in Denman Street I trod well-remembered ground. After leaving the Galeries Lafayette at the age of seventeen I had worked first in the City with that silk merchant in Aldermanbury Street as a shorthand-typist, then with Gaumont, the film people, in Denman Street, before spending several weeks in Paris with Matilda in order to learn hairdressing and manicure. Gaumont was fun and to some extent satisfied my inquisitiveness about certain angles of the film business. The administrative offices were on one side of Denman Street, the cutting-rooms and pro-jection theatre on the other. Over all these reigned, when he was in England, the already legendary figure of sixty-one-year-old Léon Gaumont, one of the great international names in the film world. With a little white moustache à la Pétain, a slim figure and delicate hands and feet, he not only had a most distinguished air but possessed what is sometimes described as old-world courtesy. My immediate boss was a charming Frenchman whose business it was to run over the German and French newsreels and choose from them any items that he thought might be included in the British Pathé news. Conversely we chose English items for the German and French Gaumont newsreels. Enthusiastic and im-petuous I ran hither and thither from projection-room to cutting-room, from one office to another in a round of perpetual delight.

All the world's events came in pictorially to us in these offices situated only a few yards from the heart of the Empire. One heard three different languages—German, French and English—and I came to be thought of as a sort of volatile mascot who could be used to type letters or run errands for anybody.

Thus it happened that one afternoon my immediate chief in the administrative office sent me with a pile of documents to M. Léon Gaumont himself in the cutting-rooms on the opposite side of the street. Gathering them up, I sped down the stairs and into the street. Here on the pavement I collided with the great man himself and landed in a crumpled heap at his feet. Unknown to us he had just left the laboratory and was on his way back to his office.

'O mon pauvre petit lapin!' he exclaimed, bending down to pick me up. I can still see the affectionate look in his grey eyes as he peered into mine. As for those words: 'Oh, my poor little rabbit!' they were precisely those that Matilda (who practically never made use of affectionate terms when she addressed me) reserved for moments of extreme crisis when, for instance, I ran a fever and she would anxiously bend over my bed wondering if she was going to lose me.

Passers-by helped pick up the scattered documents and Léon Gaumont doubtless never gave me another thought, but on reflection it now struck me that George, the good German barber, had something of that immense interior kindness that I had perceived in Léon Gaumont's eyes. Strange also that with the exception of my short job in the City these streets round Piccadilly Circus had proved the scene of so many adolescent emotions. I think I could have made my way to Great Pulteney Street blindfolded. What unsuspected crafts were to be found behind dusty, untidy shop windows, almost relics from Victorian days. These people specialized in covering buttons with the material to match that upon which they would be sewn. They did the complicated pleating used on our short dancing skirts. Tomorrow they would hand me back the squares of *crêpe georgette* my mother had cut out, narrowly pleated with the white paper that had backed it in the machine pressed into similar pleats. The tiny premises were always full of women who, like bees, buzzed around this hive of industry. On my way I would pass through the busy street market lined by small dress shops into which one was almost dragged by competing barkers determined to sell one a skirt, a coat or a dress. On the barrows cluttering up the centre of the street was all the produce of a great empire, so abundant and cheap that Matilda, when she had first arrived here from Paris, had the impression of having stepped into a land overflowing with milk and honey. Never did I hear her evince the slightest desire to return to the country whence she came.

The next day I returned to the shop and my pleating was ready. The Hungarian barber, seeing me arrive back in the barber's shop with the pleated material rolled in a short tube, exclaimed:

'Why the field-marshal's baton?'

I untucked an end so that he could examine the pleats.

'I would never have guessed,' he said, suddenly interested.

'If ever you go down Great Pulteney Street,' I suggested, 'go in and have a look. Half the street is devoted to small industries that produce the things we women need. It shows that lots of you spend your entire lives trying to make us women beautiful!'

I made him a mock curtsy. This was the first time I had been successful in drawing him out on any subject except the turf, and it amused me to try out my feminine charms on him.

Curiously enough he took my banter seriously. 'Oh, I'm not denying it,' he conceded.

'But secretly you feel there is something degrading for a man to spend his whole life working for women? Isn't that the lot of most hairdressers?'

Swiftly he answered: 'I'm a barber. I would hate to mess about with women's hair. And frankly I find no charm in a woman with her dyed hair in curls under the drier. Where I was brought up as a child, some thirty miles from Budapest, women dried their waist-long hair out in the sunshine in some flower-scented meadow or by the river. I used to dream of kneeling at their feet and burying my head in their long, straight blonde hair. I like tall women with supple movements like those of a young mare.'

It surprised me that this short man had such a preference for tall women. I pictured him dancing round a maypole with his tall, blonde Hungarian peasant girl. What curious but enthralling secrets men bury in their hearts! This evening he would merge into the crowd passing along Coventry Street, and who would guess his innermost thoughts?

My clientèle was increasing, and as most men gave me at least half a crown I suddenly made a stupendous discovery—that I could make more in tips in a single day than Matilda could make after all the strain and eyesore required during the six or seven days she took to design and sew a single dress. The thought filled me with shame. How inconceivable that life should be so full of such injustice. Of course it did not happen every day, but rather to my alarm I saw myself becoming the chief earner in our mother-daughter relationship.

6

AUTUMN—THE THEATRES OPENING with new shows and society returning from country estates with historically famous names or from journeys abroad; the Prince of Wales and everything he said or did being commented upon in the papers; the days shortening, the streets mysterious in gaslight; more exciting scandals of great financiers and famous actresses—autumn was when London looked and felt its best.

I discovered in me a strange fascination for older men of distinguished bearing and a general air of having accomplished romantic deeds. They invariably walked in from some distant part of the globe or were about to depart on adventures the purpose of which I was not always able to comprehend. Many stayed at the Engineers' Club hard against Leicester Square, and so it happened in the case of the man I still think of by the name I gave him at the time—'my Rumanian'.

I noticed him as soon as he came down the steps and entered the salon—a tall man wearing a Homburg hat of soft felt so light in colour that it was almost a rosy beige. Grey at the temples, he had a slight limp and a soft, agreeable voice. He went over to sit in the Hungarian barber's chair and a moment later the barber came over to tell me that his client was asking for his hands to be done. I gathered up my stool and my instruments and went to sit at his side. He looked serious and thoughtful, but after a few moments told me that he had just arrived from New York on the *Mauretania*. The arrival of these famous liners, continually striving after more speed, injected fresh excitement into the life of the West End. They brought names that automatically spelt news, names of boxers, tennis stars, theatrical impresarios.

'Did you have any film stars on board?' I asked.

'Why?' he said, laughing. 'Do they interest you?'

'Of course,' I answered. 'Don't you ever go to the pictures?'
'Oh yes,' he said. 'I certainly do when I'm busy making them.'
I almost nipped a slice of flesh off his finger.

'Easy!' he exclaimed, laughing. 'There's no reason to draw blood. I'm off to Africa in a fortnight's time.'

'What for?' I asked suspiciously. 'You have no idea how many of my clients go off to Africa just as soon as I have done their hands.'

This reflection appeared to amuse him.

'I'm going with Pearl White,' he said.

'What!' I exclaimed. 'Did you say Pearl White? You are going to Africa with Pearl White?' I sat staring up into his face. Was it possible that I was holding the hand of a man who knew Pearl White? The barber's shop no longer existed for me. I was a girl of ten, perhaps eleven, dressed in navy blue serge with pleats, clinging to my mother's arm as we hurried through the darkened streets of war-time Clichy on our way to the local cinema to watch the latest episode in the adventures of Pauline played by Pearl White. How she made us love the American scene! How we turned to her in our desperate need to forget the blood-bath of Verdun. Tied by villains to the railroad track she would struggle to free herself while one of those huge American locomotives with cow guard and clanging bell rushed towards her. I remembered exactly how she was dressed—in a skin-tight black tailor-made out of whose long narrow sleeves fell waves of frilly white lace. It would be Saturday night and I would fall asleep before the end of the episode. During the whole of the ensuing week I would ply Matilda with questions: 'How did it end? How did Pauline escape?' Oh, those fearsome expeditions to and from the cinema in a Paris suburb through dimly lit, deserted streets where an occasional dog barked and the sound of distant gunfire sent shivers down our spines. I could even still smell the blue serge of my dress which my mother had made out of material used by the P.L.M. Railroad for the curtains of its first-class carriages!

'I shall try to make a film with her,' said my Rumanian, who had been peering down at me while I was lost in my dream. What a pity that he had to go to Africa, that I should be losing him so quickly after making his acquaintance.

I noticed that sometimes when he moved his injured leg he would wince with pain. 'Were you wounded?' I asked, my mind still being on the horrors of a war that lived in everybody's mind.

'Yes,' he answered, 'but I recovered. That was the important thing, wasn't it? Any violent change in the weather brings it on, but I'm afraid that my dancing days are over. I take it that you think about little else?'

'It depends,' I said, not quite sure following my experience at the Kit-Kat Club of the right answer.

'If you don't think me too dreadfully middle aged,' he said, 'do you think we could have dinner together one evening. There are some quite pleasant French or Italian restaurants in Old Compton Street.'

'Wouldn't you find me very dull company after Pearl White?'

'I'm willing to take that risk,' he said. 'In what part of London do you live?'

Oh no, whatever happened he must not discover Matilda and me in our one-room apartment in Stacey Street with the only table cluttered up with dress material and Nanny hiding terrified under my couch. Supposing Marion were to be there? Or the Tall Louise? My mother would die of shame. What could I tell him?

'I live alone with my mother . . .' I began. 'I think she might not like you coming round. But Old Compton Street would be wonderful. I mean it's almost my home territory. It wouldn't be a minute's walk from where we lodge. Our window practically overlooks the front of the Palace Theatre. We can even watch the people going in at night.'

'What a wonderful place to live!' he exclaimed. 'I envy you. So you accept? You will have dinner with me?'

'I would love to,' I said.

Business was so brisk that it was not until tea time that I managed to tell Wendy about my Rumanian.

'He smokes real Havana cigars,' she said. 'I sold him an entire box.'

Wendy was apt to judge men by the quality of their cigars. She claimed that certain ones tried to impress her whilst others were critical judges. Some bought a cigar to celebrate a coup on the Stock Exchange, a sudden promotion or to look big with their friends. Others merely because they liked them. Frenchy was talking to a client under the drier and because of the noise he had raised his voice to such a scream that one heard him through the closed door. On such occasions Wendy would go to the door and knock on her side of it. This was a signal he understood. He would modulate his voice and occasionally open the door and emerge for a breath of air. There was no window in his tiny salon and at times both hairdresser and client began to choke.

True to form Frenchy after a while cautiously opened the door and peeped out. Seeing me he exclaimed:

'I'm glad that you found a moment to come up. I have under the drier the mother of a manicurist who works at the Savoy. Hadn't you made an application to work there?'

'Yes,' I said, 'but there are moments when I think it will happen too late or perhaps not at all.'

'Luck hangs by a slender thread,' said Frenchy. 'You must help it along. Today I have the mother for tinting. Tomorrow, Saturday, I have the daughter for a shampoo and set. I'll introduce you.' He lowered his voice. 'I understand the girls all wear black or navy blue dresses. It gives the place a more distinguished air. I must do all I can to help you.'

'Don't start putting ideas into her head,' said Wendy. 'She's lucky to be here. Originally Mr Y only engaged her to replace a girl on holiday. New ventures are always dangerous.'

'Frenchy!' cried the client from under the drier. 'It's too hot and I can't breathe. What on earth are you doing next door?'

Frenchy threw up his podgy little hands and said to Wendy: 'They are all the same. As soon as one leaves them under the drier they feel abandoned. They probably believe I've left them for ever. I don't deny it must be hot under that contraption but, as I tell them, if they were Chinese women they would have their feet bound and then they would have a right to complain.'

'That's true,' said Wendy, 'when my husband was on the China run——'

'Perhaps they don't do it any more,' I said. 'I must ask Daisy who lived in Shanghai.'

Down in the basement business had been wonderful and everybody was in high spirits. Mr Y was smiling as he counted the money in the cash box. George was radiant because his boss was happy. I had never met a man whose happiness depended so entirely on the happiness of others. 'On Sunday,' said George, 'my dear wife is going to roast a goose and I shall have goose pâté to eat in the sandwiches I bring to the barber's shop for lunch. My dear wife worries terribly about the sandwiches she packs for me in the morning. She does her best to make them varied. I fears she worries too much. I worry about her health and she worries about mine. I once had a malaise in the street and was taken in an ambulance to hospital. It appears that when I am delirious I speak German. It's very awkward because nobody can understand.'

'It's natural,' said the Hungarian. 'Take me, for example. My heart is in London, but I can't help my tongue occasionally reverting to the language of my birth.'

It was time to go home. The barbers had covered their chairs with dust sheets and Mr Y had taken the money from the cash box. I dressed, ran upstairs, said good night to Wendy and Frenchy and hurried out into the street only to find Daisy waiting for me.

'I ought to be at the theatre but I'm not going,' she said. 'I simply must talk to you. I thought perhaps you would invite me home.'

I hesitated. Though we had discussed her at length, Matilda had not yet met her and after my experience with Marion I wondered if I should take the responsibility of bringing Daisy home.

'What happened?' I asked. I had already started walking briskly in the direction of Leicester Square. I had learnt not to keep my mother waiting at night. Like the German barber's wife, she worried, continually imagined me being run over and taken to hospital. But I was also madly interested to discover what new folly Daisy had committed. Was it because she had opened her trunks? Why had she quarrelled with the stage manager?

'About nothing really,' she said. 'I merely told him that it would be better for the girls in the chorus to go on stage from the prompt side and he told me to mind my own business. I told him

136

that he ought to listen to me because I had seen the same mistake being made in other shows.

'"We all know you've danced in rep half way round the world," he said, "the trouble is it doesn't make you any younger." I turned on my heels and walked off stage. One of the dressers said: '"Why the hell can't that silly bitch keep her mouth closed."''

She looked at me with large, frightened eyes: 'Let me come home with you,' she pleaded. 'Your mother won't mind. Don't please leave me to spend the evening alone.'

'You are overwrought,' I said. 'You need a good long sleep.'

'You're right,' she said, 'I do, but as soon as I allow myself to go to sleep I don't wake up for days and I'm hoping that by tomorrow morning everything will have blown over and I can turn up for rehearsals again.'

By this time we had reached Cambridge Circus. 'Very well,' I said. 'I'll risk it. Come home.'

We found Matilda all smiles. She had cut out a dress, run it up and successfully made her first fitting. The customer was delighted and my mother looked twenty years younger.

'You look twenty!' I exclaimed. 'We are both the same age!'

She laughed her really happy laugh and I said: 'Oh, I forgot. This is Daisy.'

'I would have recognized you,' said Matilda. 'My daughter has told me all about you. Take off your things and sit down.'

'Have you noticed, Madame Gal,' said Daisy, taking off her coat and cloche hat, 'how the crowds in the street change colour from time to time? A few years ago all the men wore dark suits and the women had a liking for brown tailor-mades. Today the men are bolder. They wear light checks and the women have blossomed out into shades of rosewood or tea-rose. Everybody is much gayer. I learnt to love these bright colours when I lived in Shanghai!' Daisy's voice was as warm and bewitching as that of a snake charmer—soft, melodious but firm, and Matilda who was already, inasmuch as her dress had proved a success, in an excellent mood, listened to her attentively, a smile of approval on her lips. I who had been so afraid of the effect on my mother of this meeting sighed with relief. Even Nanny the cat, instead of hiding under my bed which she generally did at the approach of a stranger, had stealthily approached Daisy who was stroking her arched back.

'Nanny's purring!' said Matilda who was clearly impressed. 'I have never seen her take so quickly to a stranger.'

A warm, friendly atmosphere was developing under the charm of Daisy's almost tropical voice. What a change from Marion's sharp, dry staccato that so often got on my nerves. Besides, Marion was a fatalist. She no longer had any illusions about life, and though at times she could be quite amusing and even make my mother laugh, there was always an element of restraint in her gaiety. She never let herself go. Daisy was an optimist. Tomorrow was bound to be better than today. Most important of all, she was mobile—ready at a moment's notice to strap up her osier trunks and fly off to the other side of the globe. Just now she had dived into her handbag for some photographs of her two schoolboy sons which she showed to Matilda. 'You can bet my life,' she was saying, 'that I never let on that they are my sons. They are still young enough not to hinder me professionally. Later on it may prove more difficult, but by then I shall have created a position for myself. Either I shall have become a successful actress or else I shall have bought a night club or a small hat shop, or again . . .' She laughed. 'If I could find the right dancing partner we could do an act and get ourselves engaged for cabaret shows in the big West End hotels. There is hardly anything that I would not be capable of doing if only I had the right backing. If only somebody would give me an introduction to C. B. Cochran or André Charlot!'

'There are so many ifs!' Matilda sighed.

'Yes, indeed,' said Daisy. 'If I had not left that repertory company in Lancashire to get married I might have risen faster in the profession. On the other hand, I would not have gone to Shanghai, and that proved something picturesque and vitally important.'

'Tell us about it,' I asked.

'You remember that Harry, my husband, showed a sudden desire after our wedding to seek adventure in the Far East. He was offered this job with a bank in Shanghai and six weeks later we sailed first class on a liner from Liverpool, all expenses paid by the firm. I quickly settled down into a life of luxury. I mnst have had it in my blood, with an Egyptian father about whom I knew absolutely nothing but whom I liked to picture wealthy and important in his own land. Did I not inherit from him my dark eyes? In Shanghai we had servants, and whenever I wanted to buy anything I merely signed a chit. I was welcomed into the English colony and I spent long, idle days with little else to do but enjoy the exuberance of my youth. My husband fell as easily as I did into this comfortable life. He had his work, his clubs, his suits of beautiful shantung and a boy to serve his every need. Harry was never short of money. Indeed he appeared to grow richer every year, and my two sons were born into what I firmly believed would be an assured future. I had a nurse to look after them and I was free to go dancing whenever I wanted to. The streets so full of life and colour enchanted me, and if there was poverty what concern was it of ours? We, the women, left business and politics to the husbands. Unfortunately mine got into financial trouble. His ascent had been too rapid. The authorities started to delve into his accounts and our wonderful dream came to a sudden end. I was to return to England with my two children and see if his parents could come to my aid until something happened to clarify his situation. I packed what I could salvage from my former splendour into two trunks and sailed second class on a ship bound for England by way of the Suez Canal.'

Daisy laughed.

'I could not quite see myself sharing a bed with one of Harry's female relations in Liverpool,' she said. 'I thought up a plan that might have allowed me to step from one paradise straight into another. If I left the ship with my two children at Alexandria I would have just enough money to make my way to Cairo and seek out my wealthy father, who would be sure to welcome a long-lost daughter into his arms. It sounded an ideal solution. Alas, I had counted without the British authorities who impounded my passport and sent me back to England on the next ship. They did not want a penniless Englishwoman with two young children making trouble for them on Egyptian soil.'

'Did you go back to your in-laws?' I asked.

'Only for a time. I left them suddenly, as many years earlier I had left my grandmother when I was a girl. One must count on nobody but oneself in life. Besides, I had a profession. I wanted to get back into the theatre. I had dreams of making a name for myself. I would make my way back to London and see my name in lights outside a West End theatre. Something was bound to turn up.'

Daisy looked at the clock on my mother's table.

'You can't think, Madame Gal, what good it does me to talk myself to a standstill. I can't stand the idea of being alone. I was wrong to think I could influence a young stage manager. They will never learn. It's a nuisance to know so much and not dare open one's mouth in case it gives one's age away. That's where men have such an advantage over us. They boast of their experience whereas we have to hide ours. It's better for us to appear dumb but young.'

'I do hope you can put things right,' said Matilda rather sweetly.

'By tomorrow he will have forgotten all about it,' said Daisy with a merry laugh. 'All I need do is quietly to take my place in the chorus. Even if he did notice he would probably say nothing. At this time of year girls are always falling out with influenza. With any luck the chorus will be one short tomorrow and somebody will exclaim: "Thank goodness you're back, Daisy!"'

'I'll walk with you as far as the church of St Giles,' I said.

When I returned to our room Matilda said: 'I heard you talking to some man in the street. Who was it?' It was late and my mother had started to undress.

'The Italian chef who works at Claridge's,' I said. 'He was looking for his key just as I arrived back from saying good night to Daisy. I opened the front door before he had time to open it himself. He looked very pale and tired, and as there is no direct bus between Claridge's and here he walks home every night. He told me his legs could hardly carry him tonight. It comes from standing those long hours in front of the ovens.'

'It's a terrible life,' said my mother. 'It's time you also were in bed.'

I asked her what she thought of Daisy.

'I like her,' she said, 'and I feel sorry for her. What she needs now is luck. None of us gets anywhere without it.'

I was in my nightdress and slipped comfortably between the white sheets. Nanny was already curled up on my pillow. I adored her sweet, warm presence. In the morning she would be on my feet, having changed places while I slept. Matilda had put out the light. It was the moment we exchanged conversation in the dark from bed to bed. Matilda said:

'A friend of Madame Sandret's came to see me today.' (Mme Sandret, whose family came from Le Havre, had a long narrow shop in Soho where she sold coffee. She roasted it in large machines at the back and numbered amongst her customers not only members of the royal family but many of the most famous people in the land.) 'A charming woman,' my mother added. 'She has a very pretty apartment in a building next to the Holborn Restaurant.'

'Did she want you to make her a dress?' I asked.

'Yes, something very simple but in a very fine *crêpe marocain*, the kind that hangs so well and looks so very distinguished. As she was in no hurry she settled herself happily on the edge of your couch and talked.'

'French?' I queried.

'Oh, very much so, not pretty but homely, in the middle thirties as far as I could judge. A gentleman friend died some years ago leaving a clause in his will that the executors should pay her rent for the next twenty-five years. She is still attractive enough to have lovers, but whatever they happen to give her merely pays for the extras. She has no expenses except her clothes and her food. It's an ideal life but she gets bored.'

Matilda said nothing for a few moments. She was summoning up courage to express an idea that she feared might antagonize me, but, after a while, out it came.

'This lady happened to tell me,' said Matilda, 'that there are several small apartments vacant in her block of flats that might suit us if ever we decided to move. She pointed out that I could probably increase my clientèle if I moved to more commodious quarters. We could each have our own room and there might even be a spare one that could be used as a fitting-room for my ladies. Now that you seem to be earning more don't you think that it might be a good idea?'

'How much more do you suppose it would cost us?' I asked.

'I'm afraid there would be nothing under thirty shillings a week,' said Matilda. 'It would be a big jump from the ten shillings a week we pay here. An increase of one pound a week does rather frighten me. It's what I get paid for making a dress. We would have to think about it seriously before taking so grave a step. Besides, we would have to furnish it—the furniture, the beds, the hangings, the carpets. Alas, I fear it will have to remain a dream.'

The Seven Dials street market with stalls running all the way up to Cambridge Circus was already getting under way, and with a wind blowing in from the direction of Covent Garden the streets smelt of cabbages, or oranges and bananas. If, as Matilda had suggested, we lived in Holborn I would doubtless ride to work on a 19 or 38 bus, and I would miss all the fun of walking through these streets that I loved. Why did people, on the excuse that they wanted to help one, seek to change the quiet rhythm of one's life? Besides, suppose I ever did get married, who would pay the thirty shillings a week that Matilda would require for her rent! Husbands were not supposed to be so very generous towards their mothers-in-law. In spite of these considerations I was tempted by the idea of having a room of my own. Later that morning during a quiet spell in the barber's shop, during which I discovered George seated in a dark corner of the alcove eating a slice of cake that his dear wife had packed for him in a linen napkin before he left home, I laid the facts before him. 'Move to a different part of London when you both live so cheaply right in the heart of it!' he exclaimed with his mouth full of marzipan and plum cake. 'Oh, my dear little Fräulein, hesitate, I beseech you! Hesitate! Every move costs a small fortune. The removal van, the carpets that no longer fit, the furniture that you formerly lived with and now looks so broken and drab. Then again to leave Cambridge Circus and theatreland and Soho for the doubtful pleasures of far-away Holborn—all that needs a great deal of careful thought.' The Hungarian barber who had overheard our conversation put in his word: 'One's happiness, mademoiselle, is from within. Does not the snail carry his home on his back? Luck is what you need. With luck it doesn't matter what happens.'

What did Wendy advise?

'I pay twenty-five shillings a week,' she said when I ran up to consult her, 'and Aunt pays half of it. We live in the suburbs of course. That makes a difference. We have more for our money than you would have in the centre of Town. On the other hand, you might share the rent with your mother as I do with Aunt—each of you pay the same amount.'

'That wouldn't solve my problem,' I answered. 'If I were to marry I should be obliged to leave her.'

'That's true,' agreed Wendy, adding with a touch pride: 'Of course, I am married.' Though he was seldom there his existence gave her the undoubted prestige of being a married woman.

Later that same day Mr Darley made another of his now frequent appearances. As on a former occasion he appeared disappointed that I was not wearing the shoes he had bought me.

'I'm keeping them for a new dress that Mother is making me,' I explained.

'Ah!' he exclaimed, interested. 'You are going to have a new dress?' I told him that a silk merchant who had known me when I worked in Aldermanbury Street in the City had given me several yards of exquisite *crêpe georgette* and that Matilda was making it up into a very smart model with pleated sides.

He smiled. 'What would *crêpe georgette* be?' he asked with a most serious expression.

I tried to explain to him, though with a point of irony, the difference between *crêpe de Chine*, *crêpe georgette* and *crêpe marocain*.

'I never realized,' he said, 'that there existed such subtle distinctions. Fortunately when I go to my tailors to order a suit he doesn't embarrass me with a lot of names.'

'At least you are not in black today,' I said. 'At one time I called you the man in black, but I can't do that any longer. Your suit is grey, though a slate grey.'

But what was I doing wasting my time talking to Mr Darley about the difference between *crêpe de Chine* and *crêpe marocain*? Men of his kind would be good at business, and I plunged into the problem of whether or not Matilda and I should move to a new apartment in Holborn. Mr Darley, as I had expected, gave me a man's forthright opinion. 'The owners would almost certainly require a lease,' he said, 'and I very much doubt if they would give one to two women on their own, one a widow, the other a girl not yet twenty-one. One must face the fact that neither of you has guaranteed employment nor any fixed asset. Also, from your point of view, I think it would be bad business. In your present abode you pay weekly, and such a very small amount at that. Four customers like myself and you have paid the rent for you and your mother for seven days! Where else in the heart of London could you find so satisfactory an arrangement?'

'Other people have real apartments,' I said, 'with carpets and nice furniture.'

'Furniture often becomes a liability,' he countered, obviously referring to himself. 'One ends by putting it in storage where it costs money and deteriorates. As for carpets, they are useless.'

'Oh no!' I exclaimed. 'It would be my dream to have a lovely carpet!'

Mr Darley had not been gone many minutes before Wendy came down to tell me that Frenchy's client who worked as a manicurist at the Savoy was having her hair set. I had a lot less conviction than Frenchy that it would do me any good to make myself known to a girl who already worked as a manicurist at this famous hotel. My application would have to be championed at a much higher level. I have already told in *The Little Madeleine* how, during the previous year, my mother had taken me to a school of hairdressing in Paris in order for me to qualify for a job in London. On the eve of receiving my diploma—an illuminated scroll announcing that I, Mlle Madeleine Gal, had passed with honours an examination in hairdressing and manicuring—my handbag full of newly acquired treasures, a powder compact, a lipstick, a comb, a notebook with some addresses and all my savings in a pretty wallet, was stolen.

My nose shining, my eyes red with tears, I went down into the rue de Rivoli, crowded, noisy, still bathed in sun. Quite lost with nothing to hold in my arms and feeling stupid and blind to everything round me, I bumped into a passer-by who, after an angry expostulation, took me for a drink at the terrace of the Régence, one of the most beautiful cafés in Paris. He proved to be a wealthy man who was just then building an hotel of his own near the

Etoile. There would be a beauty parlour that I could take over if I wished, but meanwhile he had written a letter of introduction to a friend who might engage me as a manicurist at the London Savoy. It was while waiting for this letter to have a happy sequel that I had decided to fill in my time by working at Mr Y's barber's shop in Coventry Street, but I was well aware, of course, that something could go wrong. Nothing as yet was certain. And, according to my mother's theory, we were not as a family, at least until now, particularly singled out by good fortune.

Be that as it might, Frenchy introduced me to the girl from the Savoy, telling her that I had great hopes of one day working there. A gentleman I had met in Paris, a genuine count, had given me a letter for somebody of importance connected with the Savoy and I was waiting to see what would happen. He had told me that there was no better place for a girl to work.

'He was certainly right,' said the girl from the Savoy, 'but as the directors never dismiss a girl, there is very seldom a vacancy unless, of course, one of us leaves to get married.'

'From what you tell me,' I said, 'I would appear to have very little chance—perhaps even none at all.' She was a fine-looking girl and she was friendly though a trifle condescending in view of my very modest employment in a downstairs barber's salon in Coventry Street. 'Before going to the Savoy,' she said, 'I was employed in a famous establishment in Bond Street! It was an impressive reference.'

Her words crushed me. I reflected that it might be wiser for me to keep a tight hold on what I had rather than to chase moonbeams. Bidding her farewell rather curtly I rushed downstairs, hoping that Mr Y would not have noticed my absence. After all, this was an excellent job. I was happy and I had already created quite a useful clientèle of my own. I must strenuously oppose Matilda's vague desire to pitch our tent elsewhere. This was not the right moment to take risks. Besides, though I often criticized them I had no desire to lose the almost daily enjoyment of meeting Gabrielle, the Tall Louise, Marion and all our other friends.

On my way home that evening I wondered if Matilda realized how sad it sometimes was for me to walk all by myself night after night through these well-loved streets. If the man who had invited me to lunch that day at the Café Royal were suddenly to appear round the next corner and suggest we sup there, how happy I would be. How exciting to watch him hail a cab and hear him say: 'Get in, my dear.' How terribly I was beginning to envy the sort of life that I imagined that the girl from Pembroke Square was now enjoying, surrounded by young subalterns and members of the Viceroy's staff in India!

The theatres all along Shaftesbury Avenue had long queues at the side of them waiting to be admitted to the cheaper seats. Another disturbing thought was beginning to creep into my mind—that for a girl of twenty I was missing many of the enjoyments of a great capital. What was the good of living in the heart of London if one merely passed the brilliantly lit exteriors of these famous theatres and never went inside? This made me wonder about Daisy. I hoped she had been able to step back into the chorus of her show.

That evening the postman brought Matilda another letter from her sister. Marie-Thérèse continued to complain bitterly about her mother-in-law and her sister-in-law, saying that Louis, like all husbands, was weak. He should have made it clear from the start that they must seek hospitality elsewhere.

'Considering that the fabulous aunt from Buenos Aires and the old lady, her mother, are only just back from South America, I rather side with Uncle Louis,' I said. 'It's only natural that he should wish to welcome them home and listen to all their news.'

'Of course,' said Matilda, 'but my sister is difficult. We love each other dearly but, as you know, our quarrels can be long and fierce. She has a sharp, cruel tongue and is so madly in love with her husband that she gets on other people's nerves. Those sort of women are often downright stupid. For instance . . . I suppose you don't remember much about our sisterly quarrel at the beginning of the war?'

'Remind me!' I said. I simply adored hearing Matilda tell again those stories of which I had not forgotten a single incident, but which always charmed me, coming from her lips.

'When war broke out in 1914 you were about to celebrate your eighth birthday. I was just twenty-seven. Your father, Milou, and your Uncle Louis went off within twenty-four hours of each other—Louis on 2nd August and your father on 3rd August. Before leaving they had decided that it would be cheaper and safer for their two wives and their respective daughters to live together. You and I could leave our apartment in Clichy (which nobody could take away from us because of your father being at the war and for which we did not have to pay rent during the hostilities) and move in with Marie-Thérèse and your cousin Rolande at their much larger and more commodious apartment in the aristocratic rue de Longchamp, right in the heart of Paris. Marie-Thérèse was broken-hearted at the thought of being separated from her husband Louis. She pictured herself already a widow. Even Rolande her daughter gave her no comfort. She wept for hours on end. I, of course, as you know, felt the opposite. For me the departure of your poor father was a liberation. I spent the most delightful hours with Rolande and you in the deserted streets and parks of the aristocratic quarters all round the Etoile and the Bois de Boulogne. Everybody had gone. Rich and poor had fled. Passy, the gardens of the Trocadero, the Avenue of the Bois—all these were ours. Never had summer been more beautiful, the shade of the trees near the lake more desirable. Here and there patriots, called to the colours, had hung flags outside their apartments—the tricolour, the beautiful Russian flag of the Czar with its black eagle, the Union Jack, the Belgian flag.

'In due course both Marie-Thérèse and I received postcards from our respective husbands. Louis had not been sent to the front but was in a base hospital where he could not have been safer. Your father, back in the Chasseurs Alpins, was guarding a fort above Mentone against the Italians who were our allies! Marie-Thérèse, with no more excuse to cry her eyes out, her husband being as safe as mine, began quarrelling with me. She said the nastiest things about you, that you would never be pretty and that it was a sad pity to see a girl with such long blonde hair that had not a single curl in it. And that, compared with her daughter Rolande, you were dumb. I understood her being worried, but that applied to us both. She was a modiste, and no woman would want to buy an expensive hat until the war was over. I was a dressmaker, and who would now come to me to order a dress?

'I saw no reason to stay in her apartment to hear any more of her insults. One day, when she and Rolande had gone off to do the shopping, I made a bundle of our belongings and decided to take you back to our own apartment in Clichy, where at least we could do what we pleased and be in peace.' Matilda laughed awkwardly: 'You see how difficult she is, my sister Marie-Thérèse!'

Oh yes, I understood. I remembered the rest of the story as if it had happened yesterday. I recalled every inch of that long, long walk under a sultry August sun—the rue de Longchamp, the Avenue Kleber, the Majestic Hotel that they were turning into a military hospital, the Etoile. We started off walking gaily. Matilda was young, immensely pretty with her helmet of golden red hair, and she felt free—free as the pure, invigorating air of Paris in the height of summer. From time to time we would stop and sit on a bench under the acacia trees. My mother as usual was dressed in black because black suited her and, being coquettish, she knew that it set off to advantage her pearly skin. Between walking and sitting we had covered about a third of the distance when Matilda suddenly discovered that in her hurry to leave the rue de Longchamp she had forgotten the key of our Clichy apartment. 'We shall have to go all the way back!' she wailed. 'It's under the clock on the mantelpiece. I hid it there not to confuse it with my sister's front-door key.' We retraced our steps less joyously than when we had started on our long walk home. When we came in sight of the rue de Longchamp my mother said to me: 'I am going to stay here. Your aunt will be back in the apartment and I don't want to meet her. She would try to make me change my mind and it just wouldn't work. Be a clever girl. Go all by yourself and when you see your aunt tell her why you have come, that we are going back to Clichy but that I forgot the key.'

My heart was beating very fast. I started off very slowly. My mother had said to me: 'Don't run! Walk sedately like a girl who is very sure of herself. Don't let her think that we are afraid.'

But of course I ran. I ran as fast as my legs would carry me, so that by the time I had climbed the stairs and arrived at Marie Thérèse's door I was panting for breath. She had probably only discovered our departure a few moments earlier. At all events when she saw me she burst into tears. And all the time she kept on repeating:

'But why? But why has she done this to me?' Oh, how she sobbed. 'How could my dear little sister and you, my darling Madeleine, be so cruel as to wish to leave me all alone with Rolande in the middle of this dreadful, dreadful war?'

'Mother left the key under the clock on the mantelpiece,' I said, running into the sitting-room, and because I was not quite tall enough to reach it I stood on tiptoe, putting my hand on the cold marble. I could still feel the deathly cold of it. All this time Marie-Thérèse stared at me with wild eyes, red with tears. Rolande was not in the apartment. My aunt had left her daughter with some wealthy neighbours, and this was another thing that Matilda had never been able to stand, the idea that her sister had rich friends with whom Rolande could be left but not I—as if my mother and I were not good enough to be introduced to them. Matilda had continual crises of hurt pride that made her quite ill.

Now Marie Thérèse kept on her sad refrain, 'What have I done to hurt the feelings of my dear little sister Matilda?' As I wasn't very sure myself, I said nothing. Rolande and I never quarrelled. We had ceaseless fun together, either inventing games that we played round the Renaissance-style Musée Galliera or wandering into the shady groves of the tiny Passy cemetery where so many famous people were buried. We would try to read the poetry on the tombstones and speculate about what they did during their lives. Though I was eight months older than she was, Rolande was cleverer than me by a good three years. She could recite by heart many of the fables of Jean de la Fontaine. I, on the other hand, sang the popular songs of the moment, many of them ribald, with a seriousness that made Matilda and Marie-Thérèse forget their bickering and cry out for more.

But at this poignant moment I remained key in hand wondering how to leave my aunt. Should I throw my arms round her neck and kiss her or leave in a dignified manner, showing her that my mother and I were but one, espousing the same quarrel. At the age of eight this was indeed a grave decision to take. But Marie-Thérèse knew exactly what to do. I saw her drag a chair in front of a tall cupboard and stand upon it. I remember exactly what shoes she wore because as she stood on the chair her feet were in line with my vision. The heels had the form of a reel of cotton and the front of the shoes, which were hand made by what the French called a *bottier*, had silver buckles. Perched on this very high chair, up which she had clambered with some difficulty, she was just able to reach a hatbox stored on top of the cupboard. She brought it down very carefully, holding it at arms' length, and when she had removed the lid I perceived that it was full of waves upon waves of tulle net of every imaginable colour. A tint of lettuce green dominated this ethereal rainbow. Never had I seen a more airy tulle—like little clouds riding the sky. Paris modistes used it before the 1914 war to garnish the immense hats that fashionable women wore at garden parties or at the races. They would clump it together so that it looked like the wings or the nest of some imaginary bird. My aunt, choosing the lettuce green, measured off enough to garnish me several hats, then she did the same with some pink and some blue. She tore it easily. It was as light as a wisp of smoke. Then taking a paper hat box, the kind that were wider at the base than at the orifice, she gently pushed all these marvels inside as if she had been a magician with a wand. Never had I seen her perform gestures so filled with affection. It was my turn now to cry. She put the package in my hand, saying: 'There, my dear little darling, go quickly. *She* must be waiting anxiously for you!'

True enough, Matilda was eating her heart out at the corner of the street. 'What on earth have you been doing all this time?' she asked, anger masking her nervousness. I had left her at the end of the street. She had now come three-quarters of the way up it, convinced that I must have fallen down the stairs and broken my neck. 'Hurry!' she said. 'We have a long way to go and we must make up for lost time.' We exchanged no word until we were well past the Etoile and down the Avenue de Niel. 'Are you tired?' she asked. 'Do you want to sit down a moment?' There was a stone bench under the trees and she led me to it.

No longer able to hide my impatience, I opened the paper box and showed her the contents: 'Look what *she* gave me!' I exclaimed.

Matilda peered unbelievingly into the clouds of tulle and answered: 'You will never know what it must have cost her to give you all this. Trimmings of such beauty for a modiste represent diamonds and precious stones for a jeweller. No, you can't possibly understand!' On the contrary, I understood very well.

We had left the elegant part of Paris far behind us. The streets were becoming more crowded. We were tired and by this time I was very hungry, but I did not dare complain. The street merchants who in the poorer districts of Paris sold fried potatoes all sizzling hot over charcoal fires had disappeared at the outbreak of war, but Matilda took me into a baker's shop in the Avenue des Ternes and bought me a croissant. Having eaten I began to feel thirsty. There was one of the famous fountains donated to Parisians by that Sir Richard Wallace whose art collection is in Manchester Square. The water was deliciously cool and I drank avidly from the suspended cup.

'No,' said Matilda, 'not like that.' She put her joined palms under the running water and raised them to her lips. She drank. I drank. We laughed like children. The sparrows collected round us for the crumbs that remained from my croissant. Oh, how beautiful Paris was during that first week of August 1914.

But it was getting late, and like two pilgrims we gathered up our sparse belongings and continued our way, skirting the fortifications as far as the toll gate—or *octroi*. The high double gates that used to be opened to allow the tramways to pass through were closed, presumably because of the war, but the two side gates were open and an aged customs employee wearing a kepi that dated back to the Franco-Prussian war of 1870, his long moustaches snow white, dozed on a kitchen chair in front of his sentry box. He opened an eye sleepily, but seeing a young woman and a little girl did not even trouble to get up. We had the appearance of neither enemy spies nor smugglers. As evening fell we reached the promised land of Clichy. Well-remembered landmarks came into sight—the Protestant schools for girls and boys, the big garden which every spring was full of lilac but now was untended and had become a refuge for homeless cats. By the time we reached home I must have been so tired that my mother told me later that she had been obliged to carry me in and put me to bed.

After all the changes that had taken place since I had been eight and Matilda twenty-seven one thing remained constant. She and

I remained close together. Her great mass of golden red hair had been cut according to the fashion of the day but still shone like a copper helmet. I clung to her and in a way she clung to me. We lived in even more restrained quarters than during those early months of the war, but in our more hopeful moments we were buoyed up by the immense enthusiasm of my twenty years—all my tomorrows were ahead, waiting for me.

I was almost as tired at the end of this long London day as I had been when Matilda had been obliged to put me to bed in Clichy. The mere suggestion that we should change our abode had upset me. I was incapable of approaching the smallest problem without taking it so seriously that in the end I would often make myself ill. I was incorrigibly intense. I hovered between laughter and tears, between fear and delight.

'Mr Darley was of the opinion that it would be unwise for us to move,' I said to Matilda as I undressed. 'I laid our problem before him.'

'I was never really serious myself,' said Matilda. 'I was momentarily impressed by the quiet assurance of my client. She is one of those homely women who inspire confidence in men. Beautiful girls often do less well than the homely kind that pass unnoticed in the street. Men are put off by girls who are too beautiful. They are afraid of them. When this plump little woman in her beige coat trimmed with beaver told me about her rent being paid under a trust fund, and how money had virtually ceased to be a problem for her, I was jealous. Security is something I have never known. Your girlhood may occasionally strike you as having been picturesque, but that period remains in my mind as something of a nightmare. I don't often enjoy looking back upon it.'

'What made this woman come to England?'

'She fell in love with a young British soldier in Boulogne—the old story—and followed him to London only to discover that he was engaged to another girl. So she was jilted. Rather than return to Boulogne, where people would have laughed at her, she remained here and eventually became the mistress of the man who set her up in this comfortable flat. "Since I've known you," he told her, "I am not only happy but I have a reason for wanting to live. You have no idea how bored I was before we met." He was so madly in love with her (though she is not a bit pretty) that he trembled every time she threw a window open for fear that she would fly away like a bird and that he would never see her again. After his death she received a letter from his solicitor. She would never have to worry about her rent. It was all tied up in a trust fund.'

On the morning of my mother's birthday I went to the Haymarket Stores to buy the tea service with the blue flowers, and at lunch time I came home with my present and a bunch of violets. I was so overcome with emotion as I offered them to her that I burst into tears. Her features were contorted by annoyance and she did not even open the box. A few moments later she exploded. The coal-heaver, who after breakfast had brought up a sack of coals, had done so in such a clumsy manner that she had spent the entire morning cleaning the room. Because of this the lunch she had wanted to make me in honour of her birthday was not ready and I could not have arrived at a more inopportune moment.

'Don't worry,' I said, 'I could not have stayed long anyway. Mr Y made an appointment for me. I'll try to be home early this evening.'

I ran downstairs, opened the front door and found myself facing a rotund little woman in a beige coat trimmed with beaver. She had no need to introduce herself. I had recognized the woman from Holborn who, as my mother had already told me, was homely rather than beautiful.

'Is Madame Gal at home?' she asked. 'Yes,' I said, 'and I am her daughter, but I'm afraid you are going to find my mother in a very bad temper. The coal-heaver smothered the room in coal dust and she has spent the whole morning trying to clean it.'

By the time I reached Cambridge Circus I had forgotten all about the coal-heaver and my mother's tepid reception. There were long queues for the matinée at the Palace Theatre and the dress shops in Shaftesbury Avenue were full of flimsy dance frocks trimmed with ostrich feathers and winter coats with fur collars and fur cuffs. Jack Jacobus displayed evening shoes in silver or gold—shoes for a Cinderella to wear at a ball. How I loved London! My joy at being alive made me richer than any rich girl.

The client for whom Mr Y had made me this lunch-time appointment had some important function at the National Gallery. I had already done his hands on a number of occasions and he had invited me to look him up at his office so that he could show me round the gallery, but I was still at the age when the colourful street scene was the great attraction from which nothing could tempt me. No sooner had I seated myself on my low stool in front of him than he said: 'I am concerned by your addiction to cheap French novels. It's high time that you read the English classics. Have you ever heard of the novelist Richard Blackmore?'

'Yes,' I answered, rather to his surprise, 'there was a nun at my convent who read us portions of *Clara Vaughan.*'

'You are less ignorant than I expected,' he said, 'but I have brought you a very nice edition of *Lorna Doone.* It's printed on India paper. If I give it to you, will you promise to read it?'

'I promise that I'll try,' I said. 'It will depend how much time I get to myself at home. There is always a great deal to do and Mother's friends keep on looking in.'

My client, who could scarcely have been more than thirty, answered severely: 'I always find time to read.'

I accepted his reproof in good part. If only he could have guessed, the poor man, the immense number of novels that Mother and I had devoured in the course of our strange existence. One of us would surely read his *Lorna Doone.* He reminded me of my Protestant pastor at Clichy who used to say to us: 'You must make the time to pray. You can always find time to do what must be done.' The memory of his words filled me with a shame at the thought of how little I had heeded them. I would try to read *Lorna Doone,* or at the worst pass it over to Matilda to read. I would also see what could be done to follow more closely my pastor's advice. What strange happenings took place in the airless basement of a Coventry Street barber's shop!

Rather less than a week after my mother's birthday, and the unfortunate incident with the coal-heaver, we had just finished breakfast when a telegraph boy in his smart uniform with the belt and pouch and pillar-box hat knocked at the front door with a telegram. A telegram was so great an event that the house was soon in a turmoil. But it was for neither the Italian cook in the basement who worked at Claridge's nor for us. It was a cable from Belgium and it was addressed to the Tall Louise.

Matilda, turning the cable over and over in her hands, exclaimed: 'If it comes from Belgium it can only be from her sister, Mademoiselle Léona. But why, if their mother's operation was as successful as Mademoiselle Léona claimed in her letter, should she now want to send her sister a telegram? Whatever shall I do?' As we were in the middle of a week, the Tall Louise was with 'Mine', her lady, in George Street, Hanover Square. At this hour she would doubtless be rubbing beeswax into the furniture and polishing it until she obtained the desired shine. Her mistress, having worked half the night, walking up and down Bond Street, down and up Conduit Street, on her high heels, would be enjoying the sleep of the just. She never rose till midday. Matilda trembled with emotion at the sight and the feel of the telegram. 'I shall have to take it round to her,' she said.

Though I was as curious as Matilda to learn the contents, I bade farewell to her and hurried off to work. My mother, as she told me later, remained for several minutes longer sorely perplexed. People in her world, and in the world of the Tall Louise, never sent telegrams except to announce a catastrophe. Telegrams were too solemn and expensive to convey good news which could be dealt with in a leisurely way by post. As the Tall Louise would not in the normal way come to Stacey Street until the week-end, and as the telegram obviously could not wait until then—'Yes' said Matilda, to give weight to her decision. 'I shall have to take it round to her.'

But first of all Matilda went to Berwick Street in the faint hope that the Tall Louise might have decided to do her shopping early. The French girls' maids foregathered there almost every morning with their baskets under their arms to buy the meat and vegetables, the fruit and flowers while their mistresses slept. They were easy to recognize because they congregated in front of Monsieur Paul's French butcher's shop, all wearing elegant cloche hats that their young mistresses had first worn during their nocturnal rounds.

Matilda shyly asked one of them: 'Have you seen Madame Louise today?' No, she had not yet seen Madame Louise.

Well, it was a lovely cold, brisk November morning and Matilda, as she told me later, decided to enjoy her walk. Passing through Golden Square, she cut into Regent Street between the Galeries Lafayette and the furrier Révillon whose furs were richly exposed in the windows—silver fox, white ermine, squirrel, beaver and mink—and, crossing the wide street, made her way into Hanover Square and past the church into Conduit Street. The Tall Louise's Mine lived in a maisonette above a tailor and a solicitor. Matilda, having climbed the narrow oak stairs of this beautiful Georgian house so redolent of another age, rang very timidly at the entrance to the maisonette. She feared greatly to wake Mine. When the Tall Louise saw my mother standing with her worried expression at the door she gave a cry of terror, for she was seized by the idea that the apartment at Stacey Street must have gone up in flames and that my mother was there to announce the tragic news. Had she forgotten to turn the gas off before leaving after the week-end? Had there been an explosion? But no, my mother had the keys. She would have gone in to see that everything was in order.

When the Tall Louise saw the telegram she guessed that it must be from her sister Léona. She opened it, put it down on the kitchen table and said: 'The operation was successful but my mother is dead. The funeral is on Thursday.'

'What's the matter, Louise? Who are you talking to?' came a voice from the bedroom.

'It's nothing, madame. Merely a telegram for me to say that my mother is dead.'

'Ah!' said the voice and relapsed into silence.

'Whatever shall I do?' asked Louise in a low voice. 'I can't possibly go to Belgium in the middle of the week. Madame would be furious. I might even lose my job. And what good would it do? I'll send my sister Léona a money order. I'll pay all the funeral expenses. That's what I'll do.'

The kettle was singing on the hob and the Tall Louise started to make fresh coffee just as Matilda made for her whenever she looked in on us. 'Poor Léona,' she said. 'It is she who is most to be pitied, the youngest of the family, the one who stayed at home to look after our mother. From now on she will be all alone!'

The Tall Louise poured out the milk and fresh coffee in large bowls and she and Matilda sat facing each other on either side of the kitchen table.

'Louise!' came the voice from the bedroom.

'Yes, madame.'

'You are making fresh coffee. Bring me a cup. It smells delicious.'

'Very well, madame.'

These girls all insisted that their maids should address them in the third person. They were well aware of the prestige that their money conferred upon them, and were they not young and beautiful. The Tall Louise's Mine knew the usage in rich Norman or Brittany farms where most of them had started as dairy maids, being obliged to treat the farmers' wives with respect. 'Let them have anything they wish,' the Tall Louise would say, 'as long as they allow me to put money aside. They are partly good and partly bad, but it's a profession that wouldn't suit everybody.'

On my return home that evening I found Matilda in conversation with Marion who had brought a bottle of Chianti round. My mother had told her about the Tall Louise and now for my benefit she started all over again. Alas, I would never have time to start *Lorna Doone* this evening. Matilda described a superb grey squirrel coat she had seen in the windows of Révillon in Regent Street. Nothing was more fashionable that winter than grey squirrel, the softest, warmest, most elegant of all furs. The girls in Bond Street and Conduit Street all wore them with cloche hats of different gay colours and Paris shoes with very high heels. These glimpses into the lives of girls who made fabulous sums every week, more than a Cabinet Minister, more than an actress or an opera star, threw other women into a sort of mental perplexity—a state of mind not so much conditioned by jealousy as by wonderment. How could society be so madly ordered? It never entered my own head to pass judgment, but it struck me as surprising that with my own youth and exuberance I could do no better than pick up the odd half-crown.

All this did nothing to disturb my happiness. The barber's shop continued to give me moments of immense satisfaction. Mr Darley was anxious to learn what decision Matilda and I had taken about moving to a larger flat. I had by now dismissed this subject from my mind. As the nights became longer our room was warm and homely. What had really first put the idea in my mother's mind was not so much the suggestion by the little woman who lived in Holborn that there were vacant apartments in her building that might suit us as Matilda's glimpse of the trees from the open window in Tonio's kitchen that afternoon when she had lunched there with Marion. My mother was a queer mixture of town and country. She had inherited from my grandmother at Blois a love for country lore, and sometimes yearned for trees and green fields, for the succulent dandelion leaves that one puts into a salad and the mushrooms one gathers at dawn. But Holborn would have been no more countrified than St Giles, and we noticed that though at one time many of her customers had looked down a little on the modesty of our one-room apartment, yet these same women all appeared to find the place very much to their liking and would remain, often to my annoyance, with us so late into the night that I would fall asleep before their departure.

One evening shortly before Christmas I arrived home to find my mother bending over a large parcel wrapped in brown paper and addressed to me. Nanny, as usual, had run forward to meet me, but as soon as I was in the room she began to play with the label attached to the thick cord which secured the bulky parcel. All three of us were anxious to discover what was inside, but Matilda as usual refused to hurry.

'This cord could be very useful,' she said, 'we must not cut it.' Her nimble fingers were busy undoing the knot. She was both excited and steeled for disappointment. It might prove to be something wonderful. It was clearly addressed to me: Miss Madeleine Gal, but there might have been a mistake. We might have to send it back. We were not the sort of people to receive presents. My mother had succeeded in undoing the knot, and as we removed the layers of thick brown paper there rolled out a quantity of camphor mothballs which, scattering in various directions, sent Nanny, who wanted to catch them one after the other, crazy with perplexity. Gradually unrolling the contents we saw laid us before us a very large rug made of wild animal skins mounted on a base of soft brown felt. We had never seen anything like it. We laid it out on the floor, but it covered half the room, so deep and beautiful to walk on that the heels of my shoes sank into it. What on earth could I do with such a marvel? I could never lift it over my couch to shake it out of the window as I shook the other carpets every morning. I turned to Matilda and asked: 'Was there nothing else on the label other than my name and address?' Matilda answered that she had been too excited to look. Where was the label? Nanny had taken it and was throwing it up in the air like a mouse. The mothballs had ceased to intrigue her—or perhaps she disliked their smell. Having retrieved it we discovered on the reverse side to that of my name and address the name of the warehouse where Mr Darley had stored it on his return from India. So these were the skins of animals he had shot. What animals? We had no idea. My mother, visibly disappointed by this princely gift which in no matter fitted in with her conception of an easier existence, began to feel seriously inconvenienced by the pungent smell of camphor balls. 'Make haste and eat your supper,' she said to me, 'while I try to roll this horror up in its brown paper. As soon as the Tall Louise arrives I will ask her to lift it on top of the cupboard. Neither you nor I would have the strength, but the Tall Louise with her long arms would have no difficulty at all.'

'It was because I had told him that we might be moving to a new apartment in Holborn,' I said. 'Of course he had advised us against it, but then I remember objecting: "Other people have real apartments with carpets and nice furniture!" to which he had answered: "One ends by putting furniture in storage where it costs money and deteriorates. As for carpets they are useless." "Oh no!" I had exclaimed. "It would be my dream to have a lovely carpet!"'

'The poor man could not have guessed that we live in a single room!' said my mother, busy rolling up the sumptuous carpet. 'You can't possibly send this monstrosity back to him. It's more than princely. It's regal. But how can a man in his position be expected to guess how two women like ourselves live? One can only imagine what one has personally experienced. If only he had sent you a fur coat instead of a fur carpet! Just imagine if he had sent you a silver fox or a mink wrap?'

'But I did tell him that it was my dream to own a lovely carpet, didn't I?' I objected. I was not quite sure what in all this had gone wrong. 'Well,' said my mother, 'I'm glad you didn't tell him that you wanted an elephant. Picture the sensation in our street if he had taken you at your word and sent one round.'

Daisy had not been taken back into the chorus after all. She had hit a bad patch, but was convinced that it would not last and that she would soon be back in a West End show. Meanwhile she had found a job as hostess in a dance club in Leicester Square teaching the Charleston, the Blackbottom and occasionally the waltz. She made good money and was often invited to dinner by members anxious to display with her in public the dance steps they had learnt at the club. All London danced—at thé-dansants or in hotel restaurants during dinner and supper. Even the men who had held back longest now felt it their duty to learn, not so much for their own pleasure but to satisfy the exigencies of their wives, their fiancées or their daughters. Many were terrified when they were obliged to get up in a crowded place and invite a girl to take the floor. They found that a night out with Daisy instilled confidence. She was so light to hold, so expert in the way she cunningly guided their faltering steps. To most women dancing came naturally. They seldom needed to be taught.

Matilda had gone through Daisy's wardrobe, shortening the hems, altering the waistlines and bringing everything up to date. All these flimsy dresses set off her lovely eyes, her sparkling white teeth and that peroxide hair so effective under artificial light. Matilda had even turned a black satin kimono bought in Shanghai into a straight, tight-fitting evening dress trimmed with a narrow band of rabbit skin that Daisy had purchased by the yard at the store next to the Empire Theatre in Leicester Square, and as she wore this with her silver shoes the effect was tremendous. Mother called her the Nocturnal Venus, and I got it into my head that Daisy had something of Pearl White. Daisy was delighted by the comparison, reflecting what she would do to men if she had half the seductive powers of the great film star. She and Marion, often meeting now under Matilda's roof, struck up quite a friendship. Because of the very storminess of their lives both sought to avoid rather than seek any further adventures with men.

'I no longer have any illusions,' said Marion one evening. 'Every time I pass in front of that hospital that treats VD cases, and I see the queues of people waiting, I feel both horror and pity.'

'So do I,' said Daisy, 'and I don't need to go any farther than that place behind Daly's. I'm always reminded of those verses in the New Testament about the lepers with their bells.'

I looked at Matilda, but she was busy running up a hem and her face was closed. Was I too young or too old at twenty? I had done nothing and heard so much.

Daisy said, laughing: 'Oh, it's not as bad as all that. Lots of girls pass unscathed across an ocean of calamities.'

Marion was adamant. 'No,' she said, a little too harshly. 'If they go on taking risks, disaster catches up with them.'

Marion's pontifical voice made me feel sick. Why had I been so stupid as to invite this little woman with her pigeon's breast and short legs into our home? At least in Daisy anybody could perceive the warmth, the tenderness, the understanding in those lovely dark eyes. And yet my mother took pleasure in Marion's conversation, and Matilda, in my estimation, had far too much experience to make a mistake.

But this altercation between Marion and Daisy with Matilda as the silent arbiter had not yet finished.

'I,' said Daisy, 'drive through life at full speed. You, Madame Marion, drive with your foot on the brake.'

'Oh!' exclaimed Marion testily. 'Don't talk to me about motorcars. Sports cars, racing cars, cars of all sorts have ruined my life.'

'It's practically impossible to get anything out of a man if one doesn't accept a lift in his car,' said Daisy. 'A man from my dance club took me out to dinner the other evening and afterwards insisted on driving out as far as the Crystal Palace. At 2 a.m. I found myself obliged to walk all the way back to town in an evening cloak and high-heeled shoes. It took so long that by the time I got to Balham the milkmen were already starting their first deliveries: "Good morning, Blondie!" they cried. "Have you been hitting the high spots all night?" At Brixton I looked at myself in the windows of the Bon Marché. I might have walked out of a pantomime. I arrived home by tramway with a workman's early morning ticket. But even that lesson won't teach me to say no another time. What else can a girl do if she wants to get dinner out of a man?'

'Dropping you off at the Crystal Palace was nothing,' said Marion. 'In my case he would have broken both my ribs before throwing me out.'

'Oh, come!' exclaimed Daisy. 'Men are not such brutes!' Matilda and Marion exchanged a swift glance. Daisy was full of hope, Marion was unable to overcome her bitterness. As for Matilda, she hesitated between desire and fear. Her hopes were centred on me.

Mr Darley arrived at the barber's shop anxious to read in my eyes the joys of possessing so magnificent a rug. His features, generally composed and serious, were bright with anticipation. 'What did you think of it?' he cried. 'Isn't it magnificent?'

I was longing to thank him for this beautiful gift, but life had not yet taught me how to hide the fact that neither my mother nor I possessed the necessary experience to appreciate it. To be exuberant would be to lie. The carpet had really given us no joy at all. Rolled up by Matilda and put back in its brown paper, it had remained in a corner of the room waiting for the Tall Louise to stack it on top of the cupboard. Nanny had examined the wrapping afresh but without great enthusiasm, and the gift stayed there as a rather unpleasant reminder that we had neither the money nor the courage to make a move. It was a proof of our utter incompetence, and every time I crossed the room I turned my eyes away from it.

'What animals are they?' I asked almost ironically, hating myself for doing the opposite to what I wanted to do, which was to give him pleasure.

'Jackals,' he said. 'I thought you might not know. They are fond of marauding by night in packs of over a hundred, sometimes twice as many. The shriek of a jackal is even more hideous and terrifying than that of a hyena. The Arabs call them howlers and they look like wolves with bushy tails. I shot the ones I have given you and had the skins made up into that superb carpet. I thought it would look wonderful in your new apartment. Have you made a decision yet?'

'Not yet. I don't somehow think we shall ever move.'

'Oh yes, you will one day. I feel sure that one day you will have the most sumptuous apartment and then I shall feel happy to know that my rug has an honoured place in it. I have so many lovely things and they give joy to nobody. It's sad to think of them all eating their hearts away in a cold and dusty depository. But my beautiful carpet of jackals will be trodden on every day by your pretty feet. Some day when you are a rich girl with a young and good-looking husband my carpet will make you think back on the days when you manicured my poor distorted nails.'

'Yes,' I agreed, my heart full of shame. 'It will help me remember you.'

I had brought *Lorna Doone* to read in my spare moments. The book was on my instrument table. Mr Darley saw it and asked:

'What's the book?'

'*Lorna Doone*. A very nice man who is something important at the National Gallery gave it to me. Have you read it?'

'Of course,' said Mr Darley. 'Lorna Doone . . . Lorna Doone. There was a Lorna I shall never forget. Lorna was the name of my dear, dear wife. I adored her. She hated me. Our marriage was what is known as a marriage of convenience. Our parents had arranged it because of respective financial interests, but though I considered her the most beautiful girl I had ever seen she would never allow me to touch her. Every time I sought to enter her room at night she threatened to commit suicide. By day we were able for a time to give the appearance of a loving couple. She was an admirable hostess and our house was full of friends. People envied our happiness. But every night the drama began all over again. Chekhov, if I remember rightly, wrote a short story about just such a situation. You may find it difficult to believe. It was not a question of age. I was only twenty-two years old at the time; she was nineteen.'

Curiously enough I did understand it. This man so full of

163

kindness could well, I thought, be repellent to a girl. But all the same my heart went out to him now that I knew the one love of his life had been unrequited, as indeed, to my shame, his gift to me had been received unfavourably.

'What happened?' I asked almost in a whisper.

'We were in India. I had gone up into the hills. She emptied the house of all that a woman can pack into several trunks and went off with another man. Nothing after her departure had any value in my eyes. The little I had was shipped back to England and put into storage. And now here I am back in the heart of the Empire with no safe anchorage. Perhaps my story will help you to realize what joy you give me in accepting my jackals!'

It was a Friday, and because we were already in December the spirit of Christmas was in the air. Shoppers crowded the streets and business became brisker. I had told my mother I would not come back for lunch if for no other reason than that it was a dark, rainy day and the journey to and from home at midday was sufficient to get one's shoes soaked and one's silk stockings caked with mud.

Wendy was singing quietly as she arranged her Christmas cartons. Her husband would be spending Christmas with her at home. As soon as I had a moment I went up to see her for our usual exchange of news. Our charwoman, whose name I had lately discovered was Nellie, had gone to hospital for an operation and had been temporarily replaced by a Mrs Brown. She had turned up one morning three weeks earlier under the protective wings of her friend Nellie, and was to take over all Nellie's jobs during her absence. But though Mrs Brown claimed to be her colleague's best friend she had exclaimed almost on the first morning: 'Anybody can see that Nellie wasn't herself these last weeks. It's time I was here to scrub the corners.' Mrs Brown wore a greyish-green plush coat with an incredible fur collar and never removed her black hat. She did not smoke but she whistled continually, and it was nearly always the same air: 'If I were the only girl in the world . . .' As soon as she ceased whistling she conversed with Wendy, who showed great tact in her dealings with the new char. Mrs Brown speculated about Nellie's immediate future after the operation. She doubted that her colleague would be strong enough to resume all her normal obligations and she prophesied for her a spell of charring at their local pub, or perhaps even in a public lavatory. The advantage, according to Mrs Brown, of work as a public lavatory attendant was that one could sit down. She herself had worked for a time as attendant at the public lavatory in Green Park, a job which had allowed her to arrive at work 'like a duchess' by bus at Green Park station—which during the war had gone by the name of Dover Street—and come up to the surface to take her lunch under the trees on a grassy mound.

Mrs Brown, amongst her friend's jobs, had inherited that of looking after the girl who took her stand after dark at the corner of Wardour Street and Leicester Square. She exclaimed to us indignantly: 'If you was to see her like I do in the morning she looks as honest as you and me.' This, for some reason, shocked Mrs Brown profoundly all the more so because the 'girl' in question was really a respectable married woman whose husband brought the children every week-end so that they could all go off to the country together.

I think Mrs Brown wanted to shock me even more than Wendy. I was in her eyes the young French girl capable of all vice, whereas Wendy had a truly honest air about her. At the beginning Mrs Brown showed the same suspicious aversion to Frenchy because of his foreign-looking beard and French accent, but Frenchy had a way with women—even women apparently as antagonistic as Mrs Brown. He said to her in his suave voice with diabolical cunning: 'One morning before Christmas, Mrs Brown, if you have finished your work in time I'll style your hair so that you will look like a real lady!' After that Mrs Brown never referred to Frenchy otherwise than 'that nice French gentleman'. She would even put down her shammy-leather and pail of soapy water and join us in a cup of strong tea.

The Christmas trade even brought a smile to Mr Y's grim features. What brought music to his ears was the sound of his assistants' voices crying out: 'Next, please!' That meant that they were working at full blast. The barbers had all adopted me by now and I was the spoilt child of the salon. They would whisper in the ears of their customers the advantages of calling for a manicurist, 'the little blonde girl in the corner' who would be sure to make them laugh. Daisy was quite right about her theory that an actress responds to the warmth of a full house. We all responded to the speed and effervescence of the approach of Christmas. Mr Y even decorated the mirrors with holly and sprigs of mistletoe. I no longer had a moment to read *Lorna Doone*. Also since my customer had told me the story of the other Lorna I felt less inclined to read about the fictional heroine.

7

I HAD NO SOONER put the key in the front door that evening than I heard voices in our room upstairs. As I had come back late I was annoyed to think that my mother had allowed some woman to stay gossiping for so long which would retard supper and my chance of going to bed early. I hurried upstairs ready to display my ill humour, but on entering the room I realized at a glance that the woman seated on the edge of my couch was no ordinary visitor.

She was stately and sat very erect.

Matilda said with ceremony: 'Mademoiselle Léona, this is my daughter Madeleine.'

My annoyance having quite vanished, I exclaimed with eagerness: 'You don't mean to say the Tall Louise's younger sister!'

Mlle Léona looked rather taken aback by my familiarity. The words had escaped me. In Berwick Market when speaking to her colleagues we referred to her as Mme Louise. But mother and I, when alone or with friends, never called her anything but the Tall Louise. My familiarity in front of her sister came from my affection, and though she was surprised Mlle Léona certainly perceived it.

Some days earlier I had followed the advice of my client from the National Gallery and spent an hour there in rapt admiration before the Flemish School. Here facing me at this instant in our more than modest room was a character straight out of a Brueghel the elder. The effect was so striking that I felt for her a veneration as if a miracle had brought her to us across four centuries, and this impression was made all the stronger by the fact of her intonation and language, that were incredibly guttural and colourful to the ears. I still see her as clearly as on that memorable Friday evening in 1926, a magnificent woman with her rich hair piled up into a chignon the colour of honey, her arms clad in black, her hands delicately poised on her knees. I imagined her plucking a fat bird against a farmhouse wall in the Flemish country side. My mother was visibly impressed, as she invariably was by extreme beauty of any kind. Her natural appreciation of the superb, from exquisite hand-made lace to the masterpieces of nature, made her realize that her unexpected guest was somebody to be treated with immense respect. Her conversation was like somebody feeling his way step by step with the help of a stick tapping the ground ahead. Even when she spoke to me it was in the knowledge that her words would but prove to Mlle Léona that we were honoured by her presence. Mlle Léona, she said, had arrived this morning by the Ostend mail packet. The train had arrived at Victoria station very early in the morning. She had waited on the platform for the best part of an hour expecting to see her sister, Mme Louise, but unfortunately Mme Louise had not received the letter that Mlle Léona had sent to her earlier in the week. This, alas, was explained by the fact that the said letter was still in Mme Louise's room, Matilda not having guessed the urgency of its contents. Her mail, when she had any, was of a nature that in normal circumstances could easily await her arrival at the week-end. It was true that Matilda had taken the telegram round to her mistress's apartment in George Street, but a telegram was by its very definition urgent. Well, at all events, after Mlle Léona had waited for an hour, or perhaps two, at Victoria station she made her way into the forecourt where she tried to give our address—which she had understood was her sister's—to the taxi-driver, but her explanation, partly in Flemish, partly in Walloon, was so confusing that he must have taken her half round London before depositing her outside our front door. There at last she had been able to make herself understood. Matilda added in her 'little girl' voice :

'There was seventeen shillings and sixpence on the clock!'

On all important occasions Matilda began by making fresh coffee. Still addressing me, Matilda said: 'I had to explain to Mademoiselle Léona that though Madame Louise occupies the room at the back of ours she only comes here at week-ends.'

Mlle Léona listened attentively, occasionally nodding compre-

168

hension in a grave way, but obviously still extremely puzzled. So were we for that matter. Our role to say the least of it was delicate. Whenever the Tall Louise had spoken to us about her little sister it was to stress her noble character and the still more noble family from which they both descended. On these occasions the Tall Louise would treat us almost with hauteur. Her personality was a split one. On the one side she was of noble though impoverished Flemish descent; on the other side she was the Tall Louise determined to do anything to send large money orders back to Belgium every week so that her sister could live as her rank demanded in a large and comfortable house. Here their mother had lived and died convinced to the end, as Mlle Léona still was, that Louise was governess in a titled English home.

Mlle Léona had enjoyed my mother's freshly made coffee, though this also had puzzled her at first. But what Mlle Léona showed most surprise about was the poverty of our single room. Why, she asked, were there no tall Flemish wardrobes? Where were the piles of linen sheets handed down to us by our ancestors? Did we have no oak furniture or lace cloths to throw over solidly made tables? Where had we stored the high-backed chairs and the solid silver ornaments? At home she had full drawers of Bruges and Malines lace.

What could she be expected to think about that clean but utterly bare back room with its hard bed and jug and wash-basin, supposed, if she had understood us rightly, to constitute her sister's London home?

'She is the baby of the family,' the Tall Louise had told us one night, speaking of her younger sister. 'She was an accident from the first, born by mistake at a time when our mother had imagined herself to be past the age when she could have another child.' Léona was born a baby, and had remained a baby ever since, at least in the eyes of the brothers and sisters. Certainly she had retained the innocence of youth, remaining at home to look after their mother till the end. Now she appeared to be lost rather than sad. She kept on repeating: 'The house! The house! What will become of the house?' Her whole ample person with her beautiful features and almost sixteenth-century black dress reflected a placid but proud nature. How could we possibly destroy in her the firm conviction that her elder sister was a sort of story-book governess in an English ancestral home? How else could she have sent back to Belgium those immense sums of money to keep up a noble establishment in some still medieval Flemish village?

As there was no hope of the Tall Louise making an appearance until the following day, which was Saturday—and even then not before midday, Matilda had prepared a simple but excellent dinner. Secretly my mother had been worrying over the fear that Gabrielle might suddenly turn up and drop into the conversation some allusion to the Tall Louise's veritable occupation, but fortunately Gabrielle had been going home early during the last few evenings to look after her daughter who was spending the Christmas holidays at home. My mother, in order to make the meal more convivial, sent me over to the public house just beyond Phoenix Street to buy some beer; but as, according to British custom, it was served at the temperature of the room, and not on ice as in Belgium, Mlle Léona, though clearly enjoying it, remarked:

'It has a strange taste and I would fear to drink too much of it.'

Actually she said: 'Je ne saurais pas en boire beaucoup,' which was a peculiarly Belgian way of putting it. However, she soon changed her mind and drank more than enough to bring a young flush to her healthy features.

Matilda winked at me. Supper was proceeding in a much more satisfactory manner than we might have feared. This beautiful creature, come down to us from another age, having drunk the best part of a quart bottle of stout, broke into robust laughter for the first time since her arrival. 'Here in England I can let myself go!' she confided in us. 'Nobody knows me.' In the midst of her gaiety she would remark on the curiousness of the fact that the Tall Louise had not come to meet her at the station and appeared not to occupy even at night the room in which she was supposed to live.

'As for your coffee,' she said to Matilda, 'I find it strangely bitter. How is it that you don't make it with chicory as we do?'

'In France,' said Matilda gently, 'the addition of chicory makes it a poor man's drink. What I have served you is an excellent blend which, if I am to believe Madame Sandret, is appreciated by some of the oldest families in the land.'

Mlle Léona pondered over this. 'Life is full of surprises,' she said.

The bells of St Giles struck ten and we put Mlle Léona to bed in the Tall Louise's room where she soon fell fast asleep. The poor thing had been up all the previous night, crossing the Channel in the Ostend packet.

Late as usual, I flew off to work the next morning before Matilda knocked at Mlle Léona's door. My mother had decided against going round to George Street, Hanover Square. It was a long walk for her and Saturday was a busy day. The Tall Louise followed a certain ritual on this particular morning of the week. The French girls' maids who did their week-end shopping in Berwick Market foregathered just after eleven at Bodega's near Piccadilly Circus where they drank port wine while discussing the whims and behaviour of the young mistresses. They generally carried two moleskin bags—one filled with the week-end provisions for their employers, the other with provisions for themselves. Thus towards midday the Tall Louise would arrive to deposit her own provisions in the back room, collect any letters that might have come for her during the week and fill the gas meter with pennies. A moment later she would knock on Matilda's door to leave the rent, which my mother would give, together with our own, to the rent collector who called every Monday afternoon.

Everything took place just as Matilda had foreseen. Just before midday the tall Louise's long elastic steps could be heard approaching our house. Oblivious of what awaited her, she put down her two laden bags and slipped the key in the lock. My mother listened to her climbing the stairs. The brown earthenware percolator was full of freshly made coffee. Léona was seated at our table clad in a long white cotton cambric nightdress, her beautiful hair hanging in a plait down her back. She had not brought a dressing-gown and looked rather strange and out of place, my mother said to me afterwards, in this modern setting. The Tall Louise gave a piercing cry of surprise. Emotion and the two glasses of port wine she had drunk at Bodega's with her colleagues brought a flood of tears to her eyes. Léona rose to her feet. The Tall Louise dropped her shopping bags. They threw themselves into each other's arms.

I fancy that Matilda was no less affected than the sisters. She had, after all, played the major role in their reunion and later often tried to describe to me her impressions of the scene. For instance, the Tall Louise, said my mother, seemed quite a different person in Léona's presence. Normally brash, noisy, familiar, the Tall Louise manifested an almost shy respect for her sister. There was not between them, said my mother, the same warmth (in spite of their many quarrels) as had always united Matilda to Marie-Thérèse. And if the Tall Louise showed this shy respect for Léona, the young sister for her part showed an awareness for the prerogatives of the Tall Louise in her capacity as the elder. It was as if Léona wished to prove to the Tall Louise that since the death of their mother the younger was to a great extent dependent on the goodwill of the elder. The Tall Louise, however, had no desire to fill the role of matriarch. The free and happy existence she led in London delighted her. Moreover she considered her life to be utterly beyond reproach. Her own opinions and morals were in no way affected by her young mistress's way of earning a living. In addition to this what the Tall Louise did was nothing whatsoever to do with the members of her family in Belgium. Her role was simply to provide enough money for Léona to live as her condition demanded in their house where Flemish furniture, handmade lace and silver ornaments gave them the right status amongst their neighbours. Léona must, now that their mother was dead, succeed as head of the Belgian household until at some future date the Tall Louise might consider the moment appropriate to retire. When that moment came the Tall Louise would return to Belgium and find a noble home awaiting her.

There were, of course, a number of immediate problems. Within a matter of a few hours the whole of Soho, not to mention George Street, Conduit Street and Bond Street, would be aware of the arrival of the Tall Louise's young sister. Though Léona did not know a soul, except the Tall Louise, in London, the whole of the Tall Louise's London world knew everything about Léona. The Tall Louise for months, if not years past, had described her family in detail over countless glasses of port wine at Bodega's, and just as soon as Mlle Léona in her black clothes and general appearance of having stepped out of a Brueghel was seen walking down Old Compton Street she would be recognized and her sister's colleagues would welcome her in guttural Flemish.

Sunday, of course, was bound to prove the great day. Fortunately I would again become a direct witness of this colourful drama. Our modest house was already a diminutive tower of Babel, what with the Italian cook's family in the basement and poor Mrs Mead from Tipperary on the floor above ours. She paid a rent of five shillings a week and made buttonholes for gentlemen's waist-coats. We used to cross from time to time on the landing where there was a cold-water tap. She would be filling her pail there and would literally flatten herself against the wall at the approach of a tenant, so modest was she. The very essence of humility. Her mouth seemed to be full of good mornings and sorry, her slim body a mass of rheumatics. One knew of her existence because one met her at the water tap. Otherwise, except for an occasional Irish air, moaned rather than sung, she lived like a shadow. Mr Darley used to say of our street: 'Most of your neighbours appear to come to London as we English go to the colonies, to make a fortune and then return home. Because that is what we British tend to do in India and Africa, is it not?' Of course he was only joking and there are no jackals to shoot in Soho. But certainly the Tall Louise did look on George Street as a wealthy hunting ground.

Mr Darley often found some excuse to look in at the barber's shop towards four o'clock, which was the tea break. He would take me across the street to Lyons and order tea for two and a vanilla ice. I no longer even noticed his poor turned-in fingers and I kept on telling myself that I ought one day to bring him home and introduce him to Matilda. It was no longer a sense of shame that restrained me but the fear that he would ask what had happened to his carpet of jackals which was rolled up and stored on top of our wardrobe.

But to return to the Sunday lunch. As some days earlier we had invited Daisy, my mother had decided to buy a leg of lamb. The Tall Louise and Léona had slept together in the Tall Louise's bed, and though ten o'clock had struck on the clock at the church of St Giles no sound came from the back room. We had heard them talking half in French, half in Flemish, till very late the previous night. Their voices made a soft droning sound that kept Nanny on the alert. Though she was curled up as usual on my pillow her ears pricked up from time to time as if she did not quite dare to allow herself to fall asleep. Yet she liked the Tall Louise and knew all about the back room in which my mother locked her up on occasion to keep the mice at bay.

By midday the leg of lamb was beginning to smell delicious. My mother, who appreciated English cooking, as indeed she appreciated everything in this land which she loved, was making mint sauce, a delicacy frowned upon in foreign countries. But it was like Mme Sandret's coffee versus chicory. Her guests would have to learn to like it and at least Daisy was North Country. Here in fact came Daisy looking like a flower on a slender stalk, wearing a bottle-green pleated dress in *crêpe de Chine*, and a beige coat which she had bought from a girl friend who worked at her dance club. Matilda was just bringing the leg of lamb out of the oven when in walked the Tall Louise, bearing in her left hand a huge Belgian apple tart which she had gone out to buy at the Belgian pastrycook's in Old Compton Street—the one opposite the Librairie Parisienne, the paper shop in which I had worked for a time as a girl, my first job in London. The Tall Louise had obviously taken it for granted that she and Léona would be invited to our table for lunch and she had slipped out of the back room so quietly to do her shopping that we had never heard her go. 'And this is not all!' she cried, running back into the passage. 'I've brought the wine.'

Matilda made a sign to me to bring up chairs and lay two extra places. As she had more or less taken it for granted that the Tall Louise and her sister would arrive at the last moment she was not surprised. Early that morning we had put as many pennies in the gas meter as it would take, so that nothing should go wrong with the preparation of the meal. The meters in our street were all geared to receive not shillings or sixpences but pennies on the assumption, I suppose, that they would be less worth tampering with. One Sunday morning, expecting to find our roast waiting for us after a joyous expedition to Petticoat Lane, we found the gas out and the meat still raw. We had forgotten the pennies!

Léona now made an appearance rather like Brunhilda in the *Nibelungenlied* with her fair hair still in a plait hanging down her back and in that long white nightgown whose tight puckered sleeves and high neckline were more modest than any dress. She brought with her the elegant simplicity of another age and her presence dominated the company. An ordinary kitchen chair assumed the proportions as soon as she sat on it of a throne. She had majesty. Daisy fell in love with her at first sight. What impressed her was Mlle Léona's almost theatrical stateliness. One expected to hear at any moment the sounds of Wagnerian music. Daisy embarked on the beauties of Brussels, its flower market, its ancient buildings, its restaurants, its tramways. One would never have supposed that her most recent venture there had met with so little success; but above all Daisy was a charmer and those dark eyes of hers entirely won the Flemish woman over.

Meanwhile the Tall Louise was delighted to bask in her sister's reflected glory. Leaning over she whispered in Matilda's ear loud enough for us all to hear: 'What would you say if I were to tell you that this very evening "Mine" has invited Mademoiselle Léona to dinner in her maisonette in George Street, Hanover Square?'

My mother's brow darkened. How could the Tall Louise have dared to do such a thing? How far could she carry cynicism?

The Tall Louise, noticing that her young sister was entirely absorbed by Daisy's lyrical descriptions of her journey to Brussels, added in a much lower voice: 'I have warned my sister Léona that "Mine's" husband will not be present. He has gone on a business trip to Australia.'

'That her "husband" has gone to Australia!' repeated Matilda, quite stupefied by our friend's effrontery. 'But why Australia?'

'Because,' answered the Tall Louise, 'one apparently needs forty days to go there and forty days to come back.'

By this time Daisy and Mlle Léona, enjoying themselves hugely, had emptied the best part of a bottle of wine by themselves, and Nanny, our cat, seated on the table beside my mother, was daintily eating choice morsels of lamb which Matilda, in spite of reproving glances from the Tall Louise, had arranged on

the side of her plate. The Tall Louise who saw nothing repre-
hensible in having invented a husband for her 'Mine', began telling
us about a society wedding that had taken place the previous day
at the church of St George's, Hanover Square. Mine had sent her
out to exercise her little dog Lolotte and she came upon the crowd
gathered in front of the awning under which the bride and bride-
groom would pass after the ceremony. She was shocked because
when the happy couple eventually emerged, to pass under the
drawn swords of the groom's fellow officers in the Brigade of
Guards, she saw that the bride in her beautiful white satin dress
with a train wore gardenias instead of orange blossom.

'It struck me,' said the Tall Louise, addressing all of us at table,
'that I would never think of myself as well and truly married if I
didn't have a headpiece of real orange blossom! The one our
mother wore at her wedding, for instance, has always stood under
a glass bowl above the fireplace—unless, of course, my sister
Léona has removed it.'

'Indeed not,' said Léona, shocked at the mere suggestion.

'What a curious idea to attach such exaggerated importance to
orange blossom!' said Daisy.

'Oh!' cried the Tall Louise. 'How can you say such a thing.
Orange blossom has a significance. In our dear mother's case, for
instance, it showed that she came into marriage a virgin—pure as
driven snow!'

My mother and I looked at the Tall Louise, wondering if she
was serious, or if the wine had gone to her head. But on reflection,
and looking back on the years, I think she was serious. She was
this incredible being, an innocent in the midst of vice. But then,
strange as it may seem, so were we all.

My mother served fresh coffee and liqueurs and Daisy opened
a box of rose-tipped Turkish cigarettes which she had bought in
Bond Street specially for the occasion, though of course she did
not know at that time that we would have other guests. Turkish
tobacco was still very much appreciated in spite of the growing
number of people who thought it affected. However, these were
Abdullas, that young Guardees offered their girl friends, and they
gave Daisy an opportunity to turn the conversation to her
mother's adventures in Cairo. As for me, wine, the liqueurs, the

aroma of Turkish tobacco and a heavy Sunday lunch made me once again feel rather sick and I longed to find some excuse to go out into the fresh air, although I no longer dared tell anybody about these moments of malaise. I had learnt my lesson.

Léona had lost some of her shy embarrassment. She said rather severely to her sister: 'Your absence was much noticed at the funeral.'

The Tall Louise was a trifle ashamed of having made no effort to cross the Channel. She answered with great dignity, 'You know very well that it was impossible for me to go. With the master having just left for Australia it would not have been right for me to have left madame alone. Supposing I had lost my job, who would pay the expenses of our home in Belgium? Have you thought about that? All the responsibility rests on my shoulders.' The Tall Louise felt sure of herself now. The tables had been turned. Her young sister was again subdued. The Tall Louise added as a last thrust: 'I have no doubt that you blame me for not appearing today in a black dress, but we don't wear mourning any longer in England. It's not the custom.' She turned to Daisy, the only one to own a British passport. 'Tell them that it's not the custom.'

'Oh!' I cried. 'There's the muffin man!'

The afternoon was half over, and out in the street the muffin man with his tray balanced on his head and his bell in hand was slowly advancing as he cried:

'Muffins for tea! Muffins for tea!'

What a splendid excuse to run out into the lovely cool air of the street.

'Let me go out and buy some muffins and crumpets,' I said to Matilda. 'They would amuse Mademoiselle Léona.'

Matilda pointed to her purse on the sideboard.

'Go!' she said.

I think she had guessed the reason for my insistence.

8

I WOKE LATE ON MONDAY morning; the wine, the liqueurs and the Turkish cigarettes that Daisy had persuaded me to smoke had given me a disturbed night. The postman brought Matilda another letter from Marie-Thérèse, but I left for work before she had time to read it. I had wrapped up some of the remains of our copious lunch to give to the birds in St Giles churchyard. The plane trees had grown immense, and the tall, naked boughs were alive with sparrows that darted down at my approach to perch on the gravestones of men and women who had lived and died when this part of London was a village set amongst green fields. Daisy also had taken a liking to the area, claiming that it had everything to make a person happy—a church, the pubs, a bookmaker, a fried fish shop in St Giles High Street and most of the London theatres within walking distance. Yet I had often been ashamed to tell people where I lived. My Rumanian, for instance, having invited me to dinner, was anxious to know where I lived, and that was exactly what I did not want to tell him. It had struck me that he would never want to see me again if ever he were to discover the extreme modesty of our lodging. The nearest I had been willing to go was to inform him that our window practically overlooked the front of the Palace Theatre. Even that had been too precise. One evening he drove very slowly round Cambridge Circus in his huge Isotta-Fraschini, then the most brash and shiny of all expensive cars, and, having noticed that Stacey Street could be seen exactly facing him on the other side of Cambridge Circus by anybody standing with his back to the foyer of the Palace Theatre, down he cruised peering up at every window to the immense excitement of all our inquisitive neighbours. What had impressed me about my Rumanian was the beautiful felt of his beige Homburg. Was I a snob?

Matilda had always accused her sister Marie-Thérèse of being a snob because she lived in the ultra-smart district of Paris near the Trocadero, whereas we inhabited the banks of the muddy, but oh so lovely, suburban reaches of the Seine at Clichy. No, I think it was merely that I was twenty and was instinctively reaching out towards all the wonders that I felt convinced awaited me in the not too distant future.

While reflecting upon all these grave matters I found myself passing that small restaurant called the *Quo Vadis*, presumably named after the novel by Henryk Sienkiewicz, the Pole who received the Nobel Prize for literature a year before I was born. Matilda and I had immersed ourselves with passionate interest in the society that surrounded Nero, but I never quite understood what had made the owner of this small restaurant identify himself with the Christians and the lions.

My client from the National Gallery kept on plying me with questions about *Lorna Doone* with which I was making scant progress. Chiefly I fancy it was the fault of Mlle Léona, who had arrived at such an inopportune moment for our reading; and yet I felt occasionally aghast at the number of books, both English and French, that since the days of Mme Maurer in Clichy I had devoured with an indiscriminate appetite. It was, I fear, a family fault which Matilda and Marie-Thérèse shared to a high degree. In principle we all read anything we could lay our hands on, shedding copious tears for the misfortunes of wronged heroines. My client from the National Gallery who, though he was only thirty, took a fatherly interest in me, was in despair.

'Without literature you will never step out into the world you dream about!' he said. 'When will you spend another lunch hour at the National Gallery? Books and pictures go together.' Then as an afterthought: 'You could bring your mother.'

'Actually,' I answered, 'we have had a genuine Brueghel at home.'

'Oh!' he said, humouring me. 'So we are interested in the Flemish School?'

'For the moment,' I said, 'but I expect it is only a passing phase.'

'Try to be serious,' he said. 'Did you have time to look at the French Impressionists?'

'Yes,' I said, 'but I lived with them most of my girlhood. Mother and I are rather glad to have escaped out of them into the English School. Personally we prefer it.'

Wendy had a terrible cold. She had wanted to wash down the window frames of her suburban home, but, unwilling to be seen doing so by the neighbours, had the mad idea of accomplishing this task after dark—in fact in the middle of the night. 'I must have caught a chill,' she complained. 'Aunt never lifted a finger to help me. She was propped up in bed reading *Blood and Sand*. When on earth shall I have the place to myself?'

In the barber's shop, before the arrival of the first customers, George was in the Hungarian's chair having his hair cut by his colleague. Mr Y was filling more bottles with lotion that he hoped would be bought by his customers during the festive season. I was hoping to make a record week in tips. The previous week I had made £5, for us an unheard-of sum, but when the Tall Louise heard me telling Matilda, she had laughed so cruelly at my naïve pleasure that my mother, pitying my sudden unhappiness, said:

'Don't worry, Madeleine, if you could bring £5 home every week we would live like millionaires!'

But of course this good fortune would not last. It was due to the general air of Christmas, the streets crowded, the shops garlanded with holly, mistletoe and brightly coloured ribbons. Frenchy had left his door ajar. He had set his client's hair and was now giving her those final touches that were so pretty to watch, almost dancing round her, very light of foot, comb in hand, like a harlequin in a pantomime. She was a beautiful girl and Frenchy's flicks with the comb had something amorous about them, and every time he bent over her one had the impression that he was lightly brushing his lips against her curls. His client was obviously happy under this tribute to her youth and pretty features. She was smiling. Occasionally she would say something, but I could not catch her words.

Now she had risen from the chair and Frenchy was helping her on with her beautiful grey squirrel coat. A moment later, standing in front of the mirror, she carefully put on her claret-coloured felt cloche, not unlike the one that Marion had worn that day when she first came half-way home with me. I stood back a little from the door. I did not want to be caught eavesdropping, though Frenchy never minded us admiring his peculiarly French skill with his younger and more attractive clients. This was when she opened her handbag and with her sweetest smile pressed a note into his hand, whispering: 'For you, Monsieur Alfred. After all, it's Christmas or nearly, isn't it?' Then coming out into the shop she smiled at me, though she had never seen me before, bought a box of fifty expensive cork-tipped cigarettes from Wendy and with a very graceful movement threw them at Frenchy who caught them with both hands like a child afraid to miss an indiarubber ball.

'These also are for your Christmas,' she said. Then turning to Wendy and me: 'Goodbye, girls. Happy Christmas!'

When she had disappeared into the crowd surging along Coventry Street, Frenchy said to us both reflectively: 'She has something, don't you think?'

'Everything!' I said with a touch of jealousy, thinking of her rather sweet, babyish features, her lovely hair, her grey squirrel coat and cloche hat. 'Everything,' I repeated almost bitterly, 'to succeed in life.'

Frenchy said: 'That's where you are wrong!'

Frenchy collected details about the lives of his clients as other men collected silver or postage stamps. He had a gift while dressing women's hair of encouraging them to lay bare their souls. They must have sensed that he loved them, irrespective of their age or looks, and that they could trust him. This was true. He was never happy outside his dark, airless, unhygienic salon in which it was very rare for him to have more than one customer at a time. The place was really too small.

'She was a manicurist at quite a famous establishment,' he said, 'and should have been an enormous success. She had every-thing for it—youth, beauty, gaiety and the necessary skill, but customers complained that they were embarrassed by the odour of her perspiration. She consulted famous specialists, experi-mented with modern pharmaceutical products, was scrupulous in her personal hygiene, but nothing could overcome the action of her glands at moments of stress or emotion. This young woman who had been given everything desirable by the gods at her birth had this one flaw, and that nullified the rest. As in Greek mythology there must have been one angry goddess who succeeded in undoing all the rich presents that the friendly ones had bestowed upon her.

'I already knew her in those days. She used to cry like a child at the repeated humiliations she suffered. Defiantly she threw herself into gallantry and before long her wealth gave her the assurance that she had lacked as an employee. She now owns a small Georgian house behind Bruton Street and the cynical part of this story is that since the days of her physical disgrace new products have reached us from America that have to a great extent obviated the reasons for her early misery. This is a tale without a moral, for with due respect to those present it is doubtful if without that evil wish of the angry goddess she would today own a house of her own behind Bruton Street, and be in a position to give me a £5 note and a box of fifty cigarettes for my Christmas present.'

'You corrupt the young,' said Wendy, who must already have known the story. The tale displeased her and she accused Frenchy of preferring his work to his home life. But Frenchy had two sons who despised him for being a modest women's hairdresser, and in their presence he felt humiliated. So the wheel turned. His broken home life had given him the humility to sympathize with other people's humiliations.

'What are you going to do with this box of fifty cork-tipped cigarettes?' asked Wendy, who was already repenting of her show of pique. 'If you smoke them you will harm your health. Would it not be better for you to give them back to me so that I in return can put the money to your credit?'

Frenchy hesitated. He had been looking forward to smoking them over Christmas.

On the other hand fifty were perhaps too many and Wendy was right. They were bad for his health.

'Very well,' he agreed. 'Buy them back from me.'

He turned to me and said:

'You see that I am right to listen to women. One woman gives me fifty cigarettes. Another persuades me for the sake of my health not to smoke them. Thus I am loved, spoilt and given affectionate advice.'

'Mademoiselle Léona is beginning to lose her virginity!' exclaimed Matilda that evening on my return home. 'No wonder we didn't hear her come back with the Tall Louise after their famous dinner with "Mine" in George Street, Hanover Square. Do you know why? Can you guess?'

'No, I can't,' I answered.

'The dinner was so successful that "Mine" invited Mademoiselle Léona to spend the night with her sister in the flat. This morning the Tall Louise introduced her to Nana, a Flemish colleague who, like the Tall Louise, works for a young French girl. So if Mademoiselle Léona has not guessed anything by now she must be dumber than I take her for. But tonight, I think that Mademoiselle Léona will have to come back here. Meanwhile she and Nana must have had a good old gossip in Flemish. I can just hear them!'

'Did Mr Jones call for the rent this afternoon?'

'Yes. You remember the woman who lives on the first floor of No. 4, and who earns her living, like the Irishwoman above us, by sewing buttonholes. Mr Jones told me that she is in arrears. Business has been less good lately.'

Matilda translated all the misfortunes of our neighbours into evil omens for ourselves. She was constantly worrying. A turn down in business could well affect us even worse than it would the rich.

The woman Mr Jones had told her about was the one who during short winter days used to place her chair on a table beside the window so that she could catch the very last rays of light. The Frenchwoman who lived in Holborn had also told Matilda that one of her gentleman friends had expressed fear of a coming recession. In the Town as a whole, however, there appeared no sign of it. Christmas trade was said to be as brisk as ever. After supper I asked Matilda:

'What did Marie-Thérèse tell you in her letter?'

'The aunt from Buenos Aires and her mother have apparently taken a small house in Viroflay,' said Matilda. 'The old lady is over eighty and is a little deranged in the head. She has been going round all the famous dealers in period furniture on the Left Bank of the Seine ordering valuable pieces to be delivered to her daughter at their new home. The Fabulous Aunt, who is no longer a millionaire, is obliged to send them all back and pay the expenses. She will end by driving her daughter as crazy as she drove her good husband. Your Uncle Louis is furious.'

'What about Marie-Thérèse?' I asked.

My mother looked guilty.

'I hope you will not mind,' she said. 'I sent her the £5 you brought home in tips last week. With the exchange as it is the money represents a small fortune for her. I did not tell you but she is on the point of having another operation, and though she and I have so often quarrelled I love her dearly. She is my favourite sister. It was she who more or less brought me up when I was little, who cared for me, who dressed me. One never forgets that sort of thing. With our mother continually muttering to herself as she washed those mountains of linen in the Loire, Marie-Thérèse was the only person who really mothered me. She taught me to say my prayers, to read, and we were never seen otherwise than together, hand in hand, in the streets of Blois. So it is only right, isn't it, that it should be my turn to help her when she is in trouble? And that in spite of the fact that she was always telling me that I was the one who would never do anything worth while in life, that you and I were bound to come to a bad end. Oh! The things she used to tell me. I had made a miserable marriage. I had red hair. My daughter was stupid, worse still, downright ugly! Shall I tell you how she ends her letter?'

Matilda fumbled amongst her sewing and brought it out. She read:

'I must tell you, my dear Matilda, that I who had such exaggerated admiration for money and those who possessed it have changed so much that you would no longer recognize me. True wealth, my dear Matilda, is this—just the fact of not being continually ill. It is, for instance, to wake up in the morning after a good night's sleep and to fill one's lungs with all the wonders of a new day. Health is freedom. Money has no importance whatsoever. At the moment of writing to you I have lost my health

184

and my daughter Rolande has lost hers. She is to go back into that sanatorium at Groslay. Is it all my fault? Am I entirely to blame? All I know is that I am utterly miserable and that it is too late for me to do anything about it.'

The wheel turns. Marie Thérèse and Rolande whom we had envied were treading the road of despair, while I who had done nothing to deserve it was possessed with this growing desire to face the future. Was I as utterly selfish as Marie-Thérèse was utterly miserable? 'We go round with our destinies strung round our silly necks!' Daisy had said during that lunch with Mlle Léona. Daisy appeared never to take anything seriously. I, on the other hand, was made of the same stuff as my mother. We were impressionable, proud, sensitive, easily affrighted. Matilda was in tears and, at the memory of all that lovely tulle that Marie-Thérèse had stuffed into my arms on that hot morning in August 1914, I also began to cry with pity for her. Out in the street somebody was singing a Christmas carol. My aunt's letter fluttered down from Matilda's limp hand onto the floor where Nanny, the cat, sleepily laid a paw upon it. It was getting late.

I felt rather vulnerable and unimportant as I slid into bed that evening. Was I becoming submerged by my surroundings? There were too many women, not enough men. Matilda and her women friends put into the characters of the men they talked about exactly what they wanted to see, just as a painter can endow a sitter with whatever quality or defect he wishes to show uppermost. Matilda accused Uncle Louis of being unfaithful to Marie-Thérèse, but had he not proved an ideal husband? My father, Milou, was not very capable when it came to earning money, but fortune had certainly not been kind to him in an age when men who were laid off in winter-time starved. Most of the men who came to our barber's shop were much better served in this respect. They had lighter loads to carry on their shoulders. Nor did I think that Marie-Thérèse had found any lasting solution with her theory that money had no importance whatsoever. An organ-grinder who came regularly down our street every Saturday night, when the pubs were at their fullest and rowdiest, played a tune, the words of which ran something like this:

I want some money
Gimme some money, Do,
Oh! Ain't it funny
The difference that money makes to you!

Marion had been unlucky with the men in her life and Daisy's happy spell with her husband was brief. The Tall Louise exhibited a warm but questionable admiration for her 'Mine' who believed in picking up men by the spadeful; but the fact remained that at the age of twenty I had not found a single one. And yet I was more than a girl. I was a woman with all that a woman needs to acquire a man.

In front of the house footsteps could be heard. A key was put into the door. The door opened and closed with a resounding bang. It was ten o'clock. The cook who worked at Claridge's was back home and his heavy tired steps could be heard descending into the basement. His back was bent and his poor legs heavy with varicose veins. Yet his was a good trade and he made steady money. In short he was a husband, like any other husband. The thought was not exactly what I needed to give me exciting dreams.

There were mornings when on my way to work our street smelt of coal dust as in a railway station. With Christmas only a fortnight away the coalman had finished making his rounds and nearly everybody had a fire. Wisps of smoke curled up from narrow red chimneys into a leaden sky. The cold weather had set in.

But how bright the shop windows had become! The public houses, doors wide open to let in the fresh morning air while the char kneeling on her straw mat scrubbed the floor, allowed one glimpses of whisky and gin bottles garlanded with tinsel and holly. In Old Compton Street the Italian grocers displayed huge Italian cheeses as round and as large as cartwheels, mountains of spaghetti, garlic sausages and boxes of sugar plums and almonds. The poulterer plucked birds behind a barbarous curtain of hanging turkeys, the smallest of which would have been much too large to go into our oven. The Tall Louise had decided to spend Christmas Day and Boxing Day with her sister Léona in Belgium. They would be leaving separately—the little sister with her sparse belongings tonight by the night packet via Ostend, the Tall Louise on Christmas Eve. When they were together the details of the succession could be discussed.

Mrs Brown, our new charwoman, was still finishing off the brass when I turned into the shop. Wendy's sailor husband was back home at last with a curious assortment of Christmas gifts for the wife who had waited so patiently for him, and here she was dusting her cigarette packs and cigar boxes while Mrs Brown whistled her repertoire from *Tea for Two* and *Chu Chin Chow*.

'He talks about renting a little house in Surrey against the time when we retire,' said Wendy. 'He wants a garden and an apple tree. I want whatever he wants—except a child. I don't want to be tied at home while he suddenly decides to go off round the world again.'

'Nelly won't be coming back!' said Mrs Brown triumphantly as she momentarily ceased whistling. 'It's 'er operation.'

'What? Another one?' asked Wendy.

'Yes, miss, just as you say. Another one.'

'I'll send her some cigarettes for Christmas,' said Wendy. 'You will have to tell me where to address them.'

'So will I,' said Frenchy who had emerged from his salon and now stood with one arm raised against the door, listening. His beady, friendly little eyes were fixed on Mrs Brown's tin of metal polish. Mrs Brown reminded him that he had promised to shampoo and set her hair for Christmas. What day could she come, because she had a nephew who was getting married to a girl who worked in a baker's shop near Covent Garden tube station, and the one hair styling could do for both the wedding and for her Christmas party at home.

Frenchy, turning to Wendy, said: 'When are you going to allow me to bob your hair? The chignon is no longer in fashion.' Wendy hesitated. He had been on at her for some time, but the sacrifice of her long hair was something that filled her with foreboding. She believed, probably rightly, that it might rob her of personality. Her calm, honest dignity did much to enhance her status behind the cash desk of the little shop. Men tarried to pass the time of day. They liked her gentle appearance.

I jumped to her defence. 'Leave Wendy as she is!' I cried. 'To alter her looks would be like removing the bright lights from Piccadilly Circus. London would no longer be the same.'

While we were still talking Mr Appenrodt arrived and we all sprang to our various occupations. If I did not hurry down to the barber's shop, Mr Y would think that I had arrived late and this would be unpardonable at the present time. Mr Appendrodt was already seated in George's chair, and George, whose features lately had turned to the colour of wax, was throwing a towel over him. I was beginning to worry about George. He had no longer the voracious appetite of the lovely summer days when he took such joy in sharing with me the German cake his dear wife packed for him with his sandwiches in a napkin of fine linen smelling of soap and lavender. November fogs had robbed him of his rosy cheeks. He was tired and getting old.

As these last days before Christmas slid past, the tempo of my life quickened but remained little changed. I was occasionally invited out in the evening to sup and to dance. My mother's friends continued to sit on the edge of my couch and recount their strange adventures. I am not sure that I always gave them the attention they deserved. I imagined they would be with me for ever. There was Nana, for instance, who lived with an Italian family in Camden Town. She was Flemish, just another friend of the Tall Louise, and engaged in the same sort of work but more forthright and violent, so that sitting beside her was like trying to make friends with a volcano in eruption. Though she was far from resembling the Nana of Emile Zola she doubtless had in her youth many of the same adventures, though perhaps in a less luxurious setting. At all events she had more than enough colour to intrigue the young girl that I was. The word LOVE assumed between her lips the rumble of thunder. It evoked something obscene, wicked, superb! She would declare in a tone that left no doubt about her meaning that she could not live without it. Matilda, whose nature on the whole was on the frigid side, almost religiously austere, while in no way judging her, treated Nana's outbursts with amused generosity. Nana was not liked in the circle of the Tall Louise's friends who frequented Bodega's on Saturday morning to recount their week's exploits over glasses of port wine. She took too great a pleasure in breaking into a sudden silence with mocking words. She liked to explode their harmless little bombasts and watch the result. All this of course in Flemish, which added piquancy to the scene. They were without defence, for in truth she knew all about their families in Belgium and those who liked to pretend that they came of distinguished stock heard from Nana the truth of their sordid beginnings. She knew all their families like the lines on her hands. She was still a very fine woman with hair only just beginning to turn grey at the temples but a skin so fresh and appetizing that she never used powder. Her cheeks were like two rosy English apples. Somewhat on the stout side, which in her time had been no disadvantage, her ample arms were healthy and firm. She and the Tall Louise quarrelled incessantly without being able to separate for long.

It was one day when she had come to call on the Tall Louise that she knocked on my mother's door and sat down for the first time on the edge of my couch. After that there was no stopping her. She arrived whenever she felt the need of a confidante, for it was thus that she treated Matilda, who was the world's best and most patient listener. She never referred to her friend the Tall Louise otherwise than as that 'poor imbecile of a Louise with her château in Belgium and her crazy family!' 'You ought to see them for what they are, a grasping, greedy lot who will end by killing her, the goose that lays the golden eggs!' She had, of course, our Nana—we used to call her the Fat Nana—her kind, sentimental side. She knew all the strange characters of Soho, was the keeper of their secrets and would visit them in hospital and often take them unobtrusively what they needed. It was this side of her that Matilda liked and appreciated. On the occasion of which I write she sat down on the edge of my couch and said:

'Today I went to visit the unfortunate Zulma in hospital!'

This name made me jump. When, as a very young girl, I worked in that newsagent's shop in Old Compton Street where we sold French, Italian and Spanish newspapers as well as foreign magazines and books, it was part of my duty to reserve the newspapers ordered in advance by regular customers. These great bundles arrived by van from Victoria station every evening from the continental boat train. As soon as they arrived we cut the rope that kept them together and folded the papers twice over and then once across as was the custom abroad. It was an arduous task that covered our hands with printer's ink, but as the shop, like Wendy's tobacconist shop in Coventry Street, had no door but only an opening that could be closed with a steel blind at night, we virtually worked in the open air, which was excellent for our health. Nobody ever had a cold even in the winter months. Every evening therefore, as soon as the foreign newspapers were folded, I would deal with those we reserved for regular customers, writing their names on the top right-hand corner and putting them away in a special place. Thus during the whole time I was there I never failed to put *Le Petit Parisien* and *Le Journal* aside for a certain Mme Zulma. How many scores of times did I write down her name in pencil! And every evening at about seven o'clock there walked into the shop a frail little woman dressed in black with a cloche hat pulled well over her rather sweet features. 'Good evening, Madame Zulma!' I would say. And Mme Zulma would take her two newspapers, smile and walk into Old Compton Street. I never conversed with her. She never once spoke to me except to thank me for my trouble. I used to wonder why she read two newspapers, but I was told that she took one for the news and the other for the serial. Lots of people in those days bought a newspaper merely to follow the serials. It was a form of keeping abreast with the literature of the day, for many of the great writers of the period were serialized in the mass-circulation papers. What else did I remember about Mme Zulma? That she nearly always arrived carrying two heavy bags full of provisions, and that in spite of her rather sweet expression she used to give me the uncomfortable feeling that her life had drained out of those sallow cheeks and expressionless eyes. There are people like that who look dead before their time.

'Who is she? What was she—this Madame Zulma?' I asked. 'I never even discovered her nationality.'

'In Edwardian days,' said Nana, 'Madame Zulma was one of the most famous beauties in Europe. She began, in extreme youth, by being a circus rider, dressed in tights and tinsel and careering round the ring as she stood upright on the wide back of her white circus horse. Before long she had all Paris at her feet, owned a mansion in Passy and drove her own four-in-hand in the Bois de Boulogne every morning.'

'I would never have guessed,' I murmured.

'No, you would not,' said Nana. 'You who have done nothing yet with your pretty face and twenty summers; the thought may never have struck you that others have made better use of their capital. She was rich and much admired at your age. She was already launched on a fabulous career.'

'Perhaps she travelled too far and too fast,' said Matilda gently. 'One cannot judge a person until youth is past.'

Nana's sarcasm had evoked in Matilda a desire to find excuses for her daughter, but Nana did not look very wicked sitting placidly on the edge of my couch with the cat purring on her lap.

'But if Madame Zulma was so successful,' I asked, 'why has she become so lonely and poor?'

'The sort of life she led costs a fortune,' said Nana. 'She squandered many fortunes. As soon as one was dissipated, another was offered to her on a gold platter. The problem in those cases is to know precisely at what point there will not be another. False timing is apt to leave one penniless.'

'I would have put money aside,' I said.

'Had you done that you would never have been offered it,' said Nana. 'Little people remain little all their lives.'

'One can't help feeling sorry for her,' said Matilda.

'She would be embarrassed by your sympathy,' said Nana. 'She appears not to have a single regret. The gods give. The gods take away. Madame Zulma is a fatalist.'

I wondered about her name. Had she sprung from the plains of central Europe? My Rumanian had once told me how gipsies in the village in which he was born taught bears to dance by making them stand on metal strips heated by a wood fire underneath. Was Zulma of Rumanian origin? How bitterly I now regretted not having taken better advantage of those evenings when she came so regularly so collect her newspapers. I hated myself for missing such golden opportunities.

Already my mind was on the clock. A customer of Wendy's who was staying at the Engineers' Club had invited me to dinner at the Piccadilly Hotel which was then famous for de Groot and his orchestra. Owing to Nana's presence I had not found a moment since my arrival to tell Matilda that I had accepted this date and I was suddenly acutely nervous of what she would say. I was not even sure of the man's name. I had implored him not to come personally to fetch me and we had reached a compromise whereby he would send a taxi to call for me at eight o'clock precisely. I hated having to put on a dance frock in front of Nana. I hated having to tell my mother in the presence of a stranger what I intended to do, and I feared most of all that when I was all dressed and made up for the occasion the taxi would not come after all. The thought of such humiliation was as much as I could bear.

'I am going out to dinner,' I said to Matilda.

'Oh?'

'With a man from the Engineers' Club.'

Matilda to my relief had remained dignified. Nana looked me up and down with impertinent interest. I changed into a supper dress, put on fine silk stockings and my silver shoes and, having done my hair, dabbed Quelques Fleurs behind my ears. I looked rather nice. The mirror told me so. I would wear my midnight blue velvet cloak with the lynx collar. The room was heavy with critical silence.

I found myself praying eagerly that the taxi might now arrive.

I emptied the contents of my handbag and put what I would need in an evening bag made of silver brocade. The house key was always a problem. It was far too big and heavy to fit comfortably into such a pretty thing.

'If you come in late,' said Matilda, 'try to prevent the taxi from coming all the way down the street. As it is a cul-de-sac he will need to reverse and the noise will wake all the neighbours up. They become furious and it is most vexatious for me in the morning.'

I made no answer. Though I loathed Nana sitting there silently on the edge of my couch, I was grateful for her presence which prevented Matilda from uttering the flood of directives that lay unsaid on the tip of her tongue. It was not that she had any desire to curb my pleasure. Far from it. What preoccupied her was my health, more than my health, my life. Would I catch my death of cold? Would I be murdered? Would I be run over?

A taxi rattled to a stop. The front door bell rang stridently. I was saved. The taxi drawn up at our door became Cinderella's coach about to take me to the ball. I kissed my mother, waved to Nana and was gone.

It was 2 a.m. when the man from the Engineers' Club put me off, at my request, at the top of the street. I waited till his cab had driven round Cambridge Circus and then hurried home, the high heels of my silver shoes echoing against the sleeping façades of the low houses on either side of the street lit only by a couple of gas-lit street-lamps. I turned the key gently in the lock, stole quietly up the stairs and opened the door. I undressed silently by the light of the lamp in the street, but, in spite of all these pre-cautions, Matilda was awake, watching me. I dared not look at her, but I sensed this. I could tell when her eyes were fixed on me. I should have gone over to her and kissed her but I had not the courage. I never quite dared do the things I should have done. Nanny, the cat, had jumped up on my pillow and was purring her heart out. It was as if she also had been to the ball. My head was in a turmoil with all the colours of the spectrum going round and round, fox-trotting, waltzing, breaking into jazz. The famous restaurant had been a riot of noise and colour, but what had enthused me most was the floor show and de Groot's orchestra, watching this man whose name was on everybody's lips softly playing the violin. I had not been very nice to my partner. He was a bad dancer and had merely invited me as a one-night girl to amuse him before leaving for Penang. He did not care a bit about me and it had vexed me to spend an entire evening with a man who did nothing else but talk to me about his Scottish fiancée. I had no idea where Penang might be and it had never struck me before that rubber was a product of trees. Obviously Penang was a long way away and I gathered that the weather was hot. After we had danced a couple of times he brought a photo-graph of his fiancée out of his wallet and explained that she came from Aberdeen. He had known her since childhood.

'I'm surer of her that way,' he said.

193

Surer of what? I did not consider it worth while to inquire.

The restaurant of the Piccadilly Hotel was gaily festooned for Christmas with bells and holly and tinsel and little Christmas trees on every table.

'We were at Aberdeen University together,' he said.

Clearly I was no nearer getting married myself. This charming evening was a waste of time. I wondered if the girl from Pembroke Square was engaged by now to some wealthy subaltern in Delhi.

'My fiancée will be very happy in Penang,' he said. 'She will have a comfortable house with a great many servants. If we have a son we shall have to send him back to school in England.'

I may not have been very nice to him but I think he enjoyed his evening—as indeed I enjoyed mine. He was so very confident. What could possibly destroy his future happiness in that lovely house with all those servants in far-off Penang?

The morning was dark and cold. I envied Matilda who could stay quietly at home without realizing that it was she who should be pitied, having to remain forlornly alone thinking back on lacklustre years and lost opportunities, while I rushed down into the street plunging into the adventures of a new day.

'It looks like snow,' she said. 'Drink your coffee while it's hot and wrap yourself up. You came in very late this morning. You have scarcely had five hours' sleep.'

Matilda had been right. It looked and felt like snow. Perhaps we would have a white Christmas. At the corner of Phoenix Street an ambulance was drawn up outside the house in which two hunchbacks lived. I dared not stop to question anybody in the little crowd assembled on the kerb. Matilda would doubtless tell me this evening which of them had been taken away, but already the sight of the ambulance had robbed me of all my joy. Supposing one evening on my return home I should see it drawn up outside our house for Matilda! The mere thought filled me with terror. It never struck me that I could be ill. What frightened me was the thought that my mother might be taken away from me, that I should be left alone in the world.

I found Wendy down in the barber's shop boiling water in the kettle to make early cups of tea, and telling George that she had made a Christmas pudding in honour of the returned sailor. Mr Y was going to run across to the post office, having just discovered that he had run out of insurance stamps for our employment cards.

He had no sooner disappeared than we all became very gay. Wendy was furious with her firm's inspector who had asked her why she had not pushed a line of long imitation-tortoiseshell cigarette-holders that looked as if they might well remain unsold on their hands. He had hoped she would dispose of at least fifty as suitable Christmas presents. Wendy had told him that her customers were all men and she could not imagine members of the Engineers' Club offering vamp-like cigarette-holders to one another. The inspector had chosen the wrong branch on which to foist them and it merely proved how little he knew about her clientèle. The inspector had answered that even engineers have wives and that cigarette-holders were an article that passed quickly out of fashion. He had been obliged to foist them on somebody. 'He'd better take care,' said Wendy, 'or I shall hand in my notice!'

This was the first time we had seen her otherwise than calm and self-possessed. What would Frenchy do if Wendy were no longer there to advise and comfort him? The break-up of our little band was something we had never thought about, and yet was I not secretly hoping to leave for the Savoy early in the New Year?

'Meanwhile,' said Wendy, 'there is the problem of Christmas festivities to think about.' There would be her husband, her aunt and doubtless a number of her husband's relations. She would be forced to buy a turkey.

'My dear wife will cook a goose,' said George.

As for me, there would be neither goose nor turkey. Matilda eschewed the month of December, the month in which her birthday fell and in which she lost my baby brother, a tragedy that was still so clear in her mind that she dreamt of it at night. I had learnt by long experience to exhibit two different faces at the approach of Christmas, one gay and full of anticipation in the lighted streets, the other at home, mournful and indifferent so as not to hurt Matilda's feelings. Quite apart from her personal sorrow she had a pinched attitude towards religious festivals, seeing in them only degrading manifestations of drunkenness and brawls. Also she had never possessed enough money to give to those she loved the things she would have liked them to have. In such circumstances it was small wonder that she felt bitter.

Once again I was to have a busy day.

The young man who had invited me to the Kit-Kat was back in London after being sent by his parents to spend a month with a firm of silk merchants in Lyons. His father was determined to put him into the family business to replace the elder brother who, having quarrelled with the father, had gone off to work with a rival firm in the Midlands. Almost imperceptibly my young friend was being drawn back into parental domination. Once a week his parents organized little dinner parties to which the young unmarried daughters of wealthy cotton spinners or silk merchants were invited. My young friend's healthy pink cheeks were toning down under the exhausting process of being rendered conformist and grown up. After telling me these things he instinctively put out a hand to feel the texture of the dress I was wearing. 'Nice quality marocain silk,' he said. 'How much did you pay for it the yard?'

After the lunch hour Mr Darley arrived. I was almost surprised to find myself greeting him like an old friend. I had come to look upon him with daughterly affection. I wished him a happy Christmas and asked him where he thought of spending it.

'I am going up north,' he said, 'to stay with an elder sister. We quarrelled at the time of my marriage and I have seen very little of her since. It's time we buried past grievances. She was against my marriage, which she predicted at the time would prove unhappy. Convinced that I knew best I told her to mind her own business. Alas, she was right and I was wrong, but is there not an old saying that a third person must never seek to interfere between the bark and the tree? Supposing you were to tell me what you propose to do over Christmas?'

Mr Darley was almost the only person to whom I could tell my little secrets. So I confided in him Matilda's views on the month of December.

'When she was little nobody ever gave her presents or wished her a happy Christmas,' I said. 'It's not that she loves me any less, but she has never learnt to be demonstrative. In some ways she may have rendered me a service. At twenty instead of being *blasée* I come to everything with stars in my eyes. It's much more fun.'

'I sympathize with your mother,' said Mr Darley. 'The more you tell me about her the more I am inclined to think that she and I have much in common. We have both in our different ways been buffeted by ill winds and life has become something of a bleak, stormy place. On the other hand she has you and I have nobody. So in a way I ought to envy her.'

'She would probably envy your comfortable life,' I said.

'Doubtless, and in a way she would be right. There are moments when I find myself forgetting my past unhappiness. Everything is effaced if one waits long enough—or if one is allowed to wait long enough. It's a matter of survival.'

He became bantering again. 'Tell me more about yourself. What have you been doing?' I told him about my evening at the Piccadilly Hotel and I described my dress and how impressed I had been by the floor show with the searchlights converging in an ever-moving circle upon the dancers.

His eyes had become bright with interest. He was sharing my own wonderment and pleasure and exclaimed: 'Yes, it must have been a wonderful sight. Did you have a marvellous time?'

'No,' I answered, 'not particularly, but I fancy that my dress and my silver shoes must have been happy to be at the ball. As for me, I was obliged to spend most of the time enthusing over the photograph of my host's fiancée. He was going to pick her up in Aberdeen and take her out to Penang to live on a rubber plantation. She will have a fine house and lots of servants, and presumably they will live happily ever after.'

'It depends,' said Mr Darley. 'It depends if they are left in peace to enjoy the spoils. I know that part of the world very well.'

'He said it was very hot,' I commented.

Mr Darley looked down at me as I continued to file his nails.

'All that is very pretty,' he said, 'but did you think of me?'

'No, not once!' I exclaimed truthfully, and we both laughed. 'Why should I have thought of you?'

'For an excellent reason,' he said. 'Because I have thought a great deal about you. To begin with it will soon be Christmas, which is the time of year when one tries to give pleasure to others. I went to my bank the other day where I keep a few things in a safe, the medals I won in the war, some personal documents and so on. And then I remembered you telling me that first time we met how you had bought a piece of boiling bacon for your mother at the Haymarket Stores. Do you recall that conversation?'

'Yes,' I answered, puzzled, 'It was the day that Mr Y sent me out to buy a quarter of a pound of tea and that George asked me to buy him a cheese sandwich because he had forgotten to lunch.'

'Exactly,' he answered, 'and so you hurried across Piccadilly Circus to the top of the Haymarket, where, before reaching the Haymarket Stores, something attracted your attention. Do you remember now?'

'Yes, a lump of gold and some rather pretty Victorian rings with diamonds in a jeweller's shop.'

'Correct!' said Mr Darley. 'That is what came to my mind while I was going through my safe in the bank.'

He gently pulled his left hand from my grasp (I was busy polishing his nails) and fumbling in a waistcoat pocket brought out a small square leather case which he opened to reveal a gold ring with a small but extremely pretty diamond solitaire. 'It struck me,' said Mr Darley, 'that this Victorian ring was sitting in the bank giving pleasure to nobody and that it would be much happier on one of your pretty fingers. Would you like to see if it fits you?' I slipped it on the fourth finger of my right hand, the ring finger, and looked at it ecstatically. The diamond shone brightly in the artificial light of the barber's salon.

'It's my first ring!' I exclaimed. 'My first diamond!' I found myself explaining to Mr Darley that the only other ring I had ever worn was of elephant hair bought for a shilling at Wembley during the British Empire Exhibition two years earlier when I was eighteen. 'But that wasn't really a ring at all,' I added. 'The Indian who sold it us claimed that it was a charm and would bring me luck.'

'Keep it on your finger,' said Mr Darley 'and don't take it off even when you wash your hands. A diamond is for ever.' He laughed. 'I hope it will bring you even more luck than the elephant hairs.'

'I have never been happier in all my life!' I cried. This tall man I had first seen dressed in black, whose sad features and maimed fingers did nothing to make him physically attractive to a girl, had given me my first beautiful shoes, my first real carpet, my first diamond ring. What a pity that he was not thirty instead of forty. Or better still twenty! I was already busy speculating on the effect that my ring would have at home. I could imagine Marion's sarcastic commentary, the expression on the Tall Louise's features as she gravely nodded her wise old head, my mother's disbelief when I tried to explain to her that it was merely because it had been sitting in the bank giving pleasure to nobody. I had a passion for rings and I would bear with all the scandalous talk my ring would be sure to evoke. Matilda had once owned a ring set with small pearls, but the pearls had disappeared in the soapy water on successive wash days. Nothing was left of it but the gold frame with unsightly holes in which the pearls had been retained between claws. She hoped to have it reset with turquoises for which she had a fondness. She had bought it herself when a young married woman, but was so afraid of what Milou, my father, would say that she never dared show it him, wearing it only by day, slipping it deftly into a drawer as soon as she heard him coming home. But when I was a little girl, and we were alone and I used to play at being grown up, wearing her fur and tottering about in her high-heeled shoes, she would slip the ring on my finger so that I could pretend that I was married.

By nightfall a damp fog had fallen over the London streets and it was drizzling, and yet what a wonderful day it had been for me! On my way home I kept on stopping in front of brilliantly lit shop windows to inspect my diamond ring on my right hand. I could have sworn that it shot little beams of fire into the night. To be wearing a ring had quite changed my outlook on life. I was not at all the same girl who had passed this way eight hours earlier. I was a mature young woman. I walked with assurance and a new sense of responsibility. But at the corner of Phoenix Street I suddenly remembered the ambulance I had seen drawn up outside the house in which the two hunchbacks lived. They were not, of course, the only tenants, these two curious hunchback women who used to lean out of their front window and insult all the young women who passed along the street as if in revenge for their own infirmities. There was also Mme Alba, who lived on the second floor. For whom had the ambulance been waiting this morning?

I ran up to Matilda, meaning to enthuse her with the sight of my diamond ring, but I saw that her eyes were running. She had a bad cold and looked rather miserable. I held my news back for a moment. I did not want to burst my happiness upon her now that I felt so sorry for her poor red eyes. Anxious as always to impart the latest news, she said to me:

'Did you notice an ambulance in the street this morning?'

'Yes,' I said. 'I meant to ask you.'

'They came to take Madame Alba away,' said Matilda. In truth neither Matilda nor I knew much about Mme Alba except that we occasionally saw her furtively sidling up to the bookies at the bottom of the street to give them some money wrapped up in a piece of paper on which she had written in pencil the name of the horse on which she wished to place her bet. Once or twice also we had watched her from our window collecting her winnings. 'Today,' said Matilda reflectively, blowing her nose, 'was not her lucky day!'

'No,' I answered, unable to contain my own great news any longer, 'but it was *my* lucky day. Look!' I held my right hand up to the gas jet so that the diamond should catch the warm yellow light.

'The woman who lives in the basement flat came up to complain that you left the front door open this morning,' said Matilda, 'and that a stray dog messed up her newly scrubbed stairs.'

'Oh!' I cried. 'How dare she say such a thing!' I was furious not only at this manifestly unfair accusation but also because Matilda had thought fit to pass on the woman's remark at the very moment when I had been hoping for a show of enthusiasm about my ring. And in any case I disliked the woman in question, for was it not she who always beat me to our occasional letters every time I ran down at the postman's knock?

Matilda, anxious to appease me, said: 'Her visit was not entirely unfriendly. It was she who told me about Madame Alba being taken away to Middlesex Hospital. Her remark about the front door being left open was merely a poisoned arrow as she was about to leave.'

'But I am twenty!' I exclaimed. 'You should have told her that!'

'Oh, I expect you are right,' said Matilda, 'but you must admit that if one bangs the front door too hard it is apt to spring open again. I expect you did not even notice.'

Was I passing through a difficult phase? I was at that troublesome age—twenty. Perhaps also I was over-sensitive, but something else happened the next day when I was at the barber's shop. Mr Appenrodt had just been shaved as usual by his compatriot, George, who brushed him down with his usual air of affectionate possession, when Mr Appenrodt took a wallet out of his vest pocket and started very solemnly to distribute Christmas largesse in the form of brand new ten-shilling notes. First Mr Y, then George, then the Hungarian barber, who all reciprocated his best wishes for a happy Christmas, making little bows of polite gratitude. The distribution had stopped short at me. Surprise and a touch of disappointment sent the blood rushing to my cheeks. Though it was true that I had never done his hands, yet neither had the Hungarian barber, or still less Mr Y, served Mr Appenrodt personally. We thought of him as belonging to us all. I sprang to the conclusion that if I had been left out it must surely be that I was by birth a French girl, and that there could only be a distant echo of the Franco-Prussian war in this studied mark of neglect. Hurt pride sent tears streaming down my cheeks as I turned aside so that nobody should notice my confusion.

But one person had noticed it—George. 'You mustn't take a little thing like that to heart,' he said gently during a lull in the morning's work. 'Mr Appenrodt did not intend to slight you.'

'I am less sure than you are,' I answered. 'I have the feeling that it was because he is a German and I a French girl. And yet, Mr George, the curious thing is that I should have become so fond of you—and you such a typical German! It shows that I have no animosity for your compatriots.'

'Neither have I for yours,' said George, 'and as we all love England, and London in particular, with the same fervour, be assured that Mr Appenrodt did not mean it. He is such a dear, good man!'

Wendy came to tell me that the girl who worked as a manicurist at the Savoy Hotel was having her hair tinted by Frenchy. 'She is not very talkative this morning,' said Wendy. 'It appears that her mother is ill, but I thought you would like to know.' She gave my arm a little squeeze to show me that I must not let slip so favourable an opportunity to pass as if by accident in front of Frenchy's door. She added: 'She's having her roots dabbed with henna. Frenchy pretends that he is merely putting scalp lotion on!'

'Hallo!' said the girl, looking up. 'How's life in the barber's shop?'

'Busy,' I said, trying to look casual.

'There's a problem at our place,' she said. 'One of the girls is leaving to have a baby. We can't figure out if Mr Adolphe, our manager, is going to replace her or whether he will decide to wait until the spring. Of course if we could abolish one manicurist altogether there would be more tips for the rest of us.'

'You hair is looking very nice,' said Frenchy. 'I intended to use a touch of henna. I don't even know if it's necessary.'

'Things will be pretty quiet with us after Christmas,' said the girl.

'It appears that with us it's not at all the same thing,' I said. 'Mr Y claims that January is a very busy time.'

'Not with hotels,' said the girl. 'Our best clients are American millionaires who start crossing the Atlantic in the spring.'

I felt crushed. What did I know about American millionaires? What chance did I have now of replacing the girl who was going to have a baby?

9

As MR Y HAD GIVEN ME the afternoon off I had been invited to tea in her small hotel in Bayswater by a certain Mme D who occupied the exalted position of *première* in a great Paris fashion house, the name of which would make any girl dream. Matilda was intrigued and even a trifle jealous, but as she had promised to call on the lady from Holborn, I said I would walk with her as far as Holborn tube station where I could jump on a bus to Lancaster Gate.

Matilda told me that Gabrielle had called on her during the morning. She had found herself a new job to replace her rather clandestine activities in Paddington. As she had allowed her husband and mother-in-law to believe that she had always worked in a Belgian pastrycook's shop in Baker Street, she had decided to turn her harmless little invention into fact. Now she really did serve in a Belgian pastrycook's shop, and though it was a good deal less remunerative than washing linen sheets in a Paddington hotel, yet it allowed her to come home earlier in the evening and spend the Christmas season with her husband, her mother-in-law and her little girl back from convent school.

'She did not possess a suitable dress to wear at her new job,' Matilda said, 'and so I gave her your black satin. I hope you don't mind. As she is only twenty-nine and very slim I had no trouble in adapting it to fit her, and in return for our gift she is going to bring me all the girls who work with her in the shop so that I shall have lots of new clients during the otherwise slack post-Christmas period.'

Mme Dussère was waiting for me in the lounge of her hotel. As soon as I introduced myself to her she exclaimed:

'Oh dear, how young and pretty you are! No wonder!'

I did not immediately understand the significance of her words. Puzzled, I sat beside her in front of a little table under a tall potted palm, but no sooner had I done so than she said to me:

'Let us go up to my room. The windows face the park and I will order tea. Our mutual friend in Paris has written asking that I should try to instil a little patience into you because you have not yet been engaged by the Savoy Hotel. I understand that you are not altogether happy in your present job.'

I followed her to the lift.

I now had time to look closely at my companion. A very fine woman with large grey eyes, she wore her hair short but styled cunningly by some fashionable hairdresser, probably in Paris. A long pearl necklace hung over a severely cut black dress of *crêpe marocain* whose extreme simplicity evoked the elegance of her famous house. I followed her out of the little gilt lift into the corridor to her room whose bay windows, as she had told me, overlooked Bayswater Road and the fountains beyond Marlborough Gate.

'So he followed you in the street,' she said, 'bought you a new handbag and showed you the hotel he is building near the Etoile?'

'I had just passed an examination in hairdressing and manicuring,' I said. 'The loss of my handbag was terrible. I think I must have been crying.'

The woman looked at me fixedly:

'Our mutual friend is forty and relies on his greying temples to produce their maximum effect. At that age a man is apt to fall for younger and younger women.'

She sat down, motioned me to be seated and went on:

'I once loved him very much. I know all his tricks. I am glad to say that I have got over it now.'

I was blushing deeply. The conversation—or to be more exact the monologue—had taken such an unexpected turn.

'It was something very deep and important for me,' she continued. 'My brother is a very famous lawyer and it was through him that we first met.'

She reached for a bell.

'I'll order tea. Indian or China?'

When the waiter had come and gone, she said:

'I surprise you, do I not? Forgive me. Why should we not talk frankly? It is partly due to him, our mutual friend, that I came to London. Maybe I needed the consolation that this beautiful town affords to those who learn to love it. I have the most wonderful job in the world. When I was a little girl and I first told my family, the menfolk of which are all leading lights in the legal profession, that I wanted to become a little *cousette*, a humble seamstress in a Paris dressmaking house, they were all bitterly shocked. They felt I was dragging them down, but I was born with a needle and thread between my fingers. Today I am what is known as a *première*, the most important person in a couture house. Meanwhile my friend married a much younger woman, an heiress, thanks to whom he is able to build this beautiful hotel in the centre of Paris. What is strange in my story is the fact that my name is Madeleine, her name is Madeleine and so is yours.'

She laughed, but her laughter was tinged with bitterness. As for me I sat very rigid, extremely embarrassed, on the edge of my chair.

'How is it,' she asked, 'that though born in Paris you have become so much a London girl?'

In order to divert my thoughts from the uncomfortable side of this meeting, I began plunging into my life story. I must have gone on and on. She listened to me in a kind of stupor and ended by saying:

'How curious. I hoped to draw on my experience to teach you something of use, and instead of that it is you who fill me with wonder and surprise. How charming for me to discover that you are the daughter of a home dressmaker. Consider that never since the days of Worth have the great Paris dressmaking houses enjoyed such international fame as they do today. Where do you suppose your dismal job in a Coventry Street barber's shop will lead you? Give up that menial task while you are still young enough to learn a worth-while profession. With your skill with the needle and your striking appearance and lovely blonde hair you are the sort of girl who could make a meteoric career in the Grande Couture. Let me use my influence to get you started right away in the rue de la Paix!'

'I would not want to leave London,' I said.

'When a girl has a real profession she automatically becomes a superior being. She does not need to depend on anybody—least of all on men. Come and call on me one day and I will imbue you with the feel and the love of work supremely well done. You will blush to have stooped so low as to have accepted tips from balding men.'

I looked from the small diamond on my finger to the six-carat solitaire so blindingly blue-white on that of my elegant hostess and I felt terrible. 'I think that Mother will be waiting for me at home,' I said lamely. 'Thank you so much for the tea.'

Night had fallen and I ran in between the traffic across Bayswater Road and into the park. I needed to take great breaths of air in order to recover from the disagreeableness of my interview. But I soon began to shiver in my little coat under the damp gaunt winter trees. How ashamed I felt that I had been forced to allow that woman's grey eyes to dissect this poor little coat that my mother had made out of a remnant—this woman who dressed queens and princesses, film stars and stage actresses, society women in the entourage of the Prince of Wales—this *première* of the most famous dressmaking house in the world. What a fool she must have thought me.

Chilled to the bones, I hurried out of the park, crossed the street again and jumped on a bus bound for Tottenham Court Road. I wondered if Gabrielle would already be at work at the Belgian pastrycook's shop in Baker Street. I tried to picture her wearing my black satin. I blushed at the thought that under the trees in Hyde Park I had momentarily been so ashamed of my mother.

My bus had been empty, or almost, when I boarded it, but by the time we reached Oxford Circus the traffic was dense and here we were stopped in front of the scintillating windows of the Louvre—that London replica of the great Paris store. One large window was filled with model figures wearing simple little black dresses and gay cloche hats. Cambridge Circus. The clock of St Giles was striking eight. Matilda would be getting anxious. I felt suddenly happy to be back in my own little world.

Neverthless on reaching home I found Matilda, as I had rather imagined, with her stern look. 'You must be frozen,' she said. 'Why are you back so late?'

'I tried to walk for a while in Hyde Park,' I answered, 'but it was damp under the trees and I started to shiver.'

'I'll make you a hot chocolate,' she said.

She was eager to hear my story and I lost no time in recounting it in detail. When I had finished she said:

'Your fine lady of the Haute Couture is mad. What she told you is all very fine for her. She comes of a wealthy family, a long line of judges, learned counsel and so on, and is at the top of the most famous dress house in the world. But that you, at the age of twenty, should even consider starting in a new profession is crazy. Haven't you already worked in a newspaper shop in Old Compton Street, as a typist in the City, with Gaumont in Denman Street, as a salesgirl at the Galeries Lafayette and now as a manicurist in a barber's shop? And you have the effrontery to tell me that you are seriously thinking of becoming a seamstress in a dressmaking house? Have you any idea what sort of life a simple little seamstress enjoys in an overcrowded *atelier* from early morning till late at night? Straining her eyes as she bends over a seam or a *volant* bunched up with a whole lot of other girls? And never a man in sight? And so, if I gather right, she accused you of mendicity because you accept tips from the men whose hands you care for? Tell me, please, what name you would give to the humiliation of having to kneel at the foot of some woman, your mouth full of pins as she tries on a dress? At least in your present job you have the good fortune to meet a whole range of men who are kind to you and seek to widen your interests. One shoots tigers in India, another holds an important post at the National Gallery, yet another goes to Africa with Pearl White! Who knows that yet another might not one day ship you off to Hollywood and make a star out of you? At least I would have the satisfaction of knowing that my daughter was not going to have to stitch all day and half the night in a one-room apartment all her life. If you were to follow in my footsteps I would die of disappointment.'

'A great couture house would be different,' I suggested without much conviction.

'Oh, would it?' cried my mother. 'Think of your cousin Rolande who, younger than you are now, was already working in the *atelier* of a top Paris milliner, so gifted that she was herself designing hats for them, considered a child genius, and where is she now? In a sanatorium at Groslay dying of consumption.'

Her features were contorted with rage as she bent over a stuffed mannequin which we had called Rosalie and on the shoulders of which Nanny, the cat, liked to perch. Matilda was mounting gored flounces on a beautiful dress that the Tall Louise's 'Mine' was to wear at a Christmas dance. The flounces were bound with narrow strips of the same material cut on the cross. The bodices of evening dresses were comparatively simple because it was the fashion to wear long pearl necklaces that dangled over flattened bosoms. Now that we showed our legs so brazenly (these had become of great importance to a girl) the great idea was to complicate a dress from the hips downward with flounces or other devices. These would spin and whirl when one danced the Charleston so that our legs in flesh-coloured silk stockings looked as if they emerged from the petals of a flower.

'Aren't you going to bed soon?' I asked. I had drunk my chocolate and was beginning to feel sleepy after the emotions of the afternoon.

'Not yet,' she answered. 'I must get it tacked this evening so that I can sew it by daylight tomorrow morning.'

I could tell that she was quite worn out. The dress was in jade green *crêpe*, a very fashionable colour, and I was already mentally counting the snips and pieces that I guessed would be left over and which Matilda with her usual cunning might be prevailed upon to put together to make me a dress nearly as beautiful as the one she was assembling on the mannequin. Or at least if there was not enough material left over for a dress there might be sufficient for a blouse. The newly cut silk smelt good and the colour was truly bewitching.

'Who is the lucky client?' I asked.

Matilda's mouth was full of pins and she did not answer. Her right hand kept on flying from the pins in her mouth to the flounces on the mannequin, and I watched her pricking the material with angry little stabs. What was she thinking about? Her mind was not entirely on the jade dress, I decided. What she was really doing was sticking pins into the woman she called 'your fine lady of the Haute Couture'. I felt a bit guilty because to be honest I fancied that Mme D had merely wished to give me the most affectionate advice, but all the same Matilda knew better than anybody the servitude of her thankless profession.

The Tall Louise returned from her short holiday in Belgium on Boxing Day. She had crossed over from Ostend on the day packet and, having deposited her bags in the back room, came to tell us all the news. The house which since the mother's death she had thought of as being mostly her own with Mlle Léona as its guardian was now being fought over by obscure brothers and sisters and other relatives. As none of them had contributed to its upkeep she was bitter about these sudden claims that apparently had some substance in law. Léona also, during these short days since her visit to London, had become quite a different person. She who had been of such extreme propriety both in conduct and speech now had her head filled with thoughts about love. She talked about nothing else.

'You must admit,' said Matilda with a gay little laugh, 'that though she was a late starter she had an opportunity in London to learn a great deal in a very short time!'

'You don't understand,' objected the Tall Louise, annoyed by my mother's hilarity. 'It's not that at all. She wants to get married!' The Tall Louise snorted: 'At her age it's a positive disgrace. She's forty!'

'And I am forty also,' said Matilda. 'What's so strange about that?'

'Yes, but you are the mother of a girl of twenty!' said the Tall Louise. 'That alters everything.'

My mother winced. She did not particularly like being thought of as a woman who was now permanently on the shelf. In fact she looked so young that we were still occasionally taken for sisters. But there was no stopping the Tall Louise.

'That big fat goose of a Léona!' she went on. 'Can you picture her in a wedding dress with a wreath of orange blossom on her head? It's too comical for words. Well, believe it or not, that's all she thinks about.'

'Would there be a gentleman in her mind?' asked Matilda.

'Yes, indeed, but it's she who makes advances. She finds an

excuse to cross the road every morning to wave to him when he sets off for his office. The poor man is thoroughly embarrassed. Her visit to London has changed her completely. She has become a personality. If she marries him, are all my savings to pass into the hands of a total stranger? I could not stand the atmosphere a moment longer. I came back a day early.'

Though everybody was back at work the next morning, a slight malaise appeared to hang over the town as if the holiday had exhausted even those who had so feverishly looked forward to its coming. Wendy had a cold. Gloomily she felt that it might be more serious than an ordinary cold—influenza perhaps, which so often made its first appearance at this time of year. This morning Matilda also had not been gay. At breakfast she complained that the clients who had ordered pretty dresses for Christmas dances would try to make do with them on New Year's Eve. Her only order was from a dry cleaner at the bottom of the street—a new lining for a coat and some buttons to sew on.

Mr Y was engrossed in end-of-year accounts. The Hungarian barber had momentarily ceased to talk about racing form, either because he felt we were tired of listening to his predictions or because there was no racing. Mr Appenrodt, however, made his usual courteous matutinal appearance. Upon seeing Wendy he removed his hat and made her a little bow. She bade him good morning. So did I. Moved by the benign expression on his kindly face I inquired whether he had enjoyed himself over the holiday. He looked at me searchingly, perhaps even wondering where he had seen me before. Then suddenly, as if remembering a half-forgotten incident, he dived into a pocket and handed me a ten-shilling note, saying:

'This is for you, mademoiselle!'

The swift wiping out of his unintentional pre-Christmas slight moved me so deeply that I caught myself beginning to cry.

'Thank you! Oh, thank you, Mr Appenrodt!' I exclaimed. My emotion had nothing to do with the gift as such. It sprang from the idea that he might after all have a certain affection for me, that he had not secretly hated me, perhaps because I was a French girl or because of some other unknown reason. His action now seemed to me immensely important, so important that after all these years I recall it with fresh tears welling up in my eyes. I was not after all a subject of dislike. It would be terrible to be disliked when one is only twenty!

I waited a while before going down to the salon. By the time I had regained my composure George was brushing Mr Appenrodt's coat and handing him his hat. As soon as his compatriot had gone I exclaimed:

'Look what Mr Appenrodt gave me, George. It shows that his slight was unintentional. You can't imagine how happy he has made me.'

George looked at me very seriously and said: 'How could you have supposed for a single moment that a man of Mr Appenrodt's calibre could hold a snippet of a girl like you responsible for the 1914–18 war! Poor stupid little mademoiselle!'

'Poor Mademoiselle from Armentières,' echoed the Hungarian barber half mockingly. The barber's shop had suddenly become gay. Everybody was as pleased as I was. Even Mr Y was laughing as he looked up from his accounts. The post-holiday gloom was dissipated. And all because of a ten-shilling note given to the least important member of the staff and a general feeling that Mr Appenrodt's gentle features and spontaneous act represented the true spirit of an old-world Christmas.

A moment later steps could be heard descending into the basement. Lights were switched on. We sprang to our posts. 'Never give a customer the feeling that you are idle,' Mr Y would say. 'Make him feel how fortunate he is to find an unoccupied chair.'

On my return home that night I found Daisy sitting on the edge of my couch. She was radiant. She had spent a wonderful Christmas with her two boys. Matilda was transformed. The lady from Holborn had called to order a spring-like ensemble to wear at Nice where she was planning to spend ten days with a friend in one of the most expensive hotels. The friend, of course, was an admirer. He had booked a suite overlooking the Promenade des Ar glais and he had told her that she could look forward to a veritable orgy of spending. She would buy enough pairs of gloves to last the whole year, a new handbag and lots of gay hats. She had said to Matilda: 'This sort of experience is very agreeable to a woman like me who has never been officially married. Consider what fun it will be for me to have a man standing interestedly at my side while I do my shopping—just like a husband!'

Matilda had helped her choose the ensemble from amongst the models illustrated in a current copy of *Chiffons*, a Paris fashion magazine that showed the styles from the great couture houses in full colour. This operation required considerable skill on my mother's part, because while choosing something really becoming it was yet necessary to influence the customer in favour of an ensemble that would not be beyond Matilda's professional capabilities. The dress with wide pleats that would open and sway as the wearer walked was both gracious and relatively simple to cut. The *crêpe de Chine* in *bois-de-rose* to make it had already been bought. So had the gaberdine of the same delicate shade for the coat. 'The coat,' my mother explained, pointing it out in the magazine, 'is straight but lined entirely in the identical *crêpe de Chine* of the dress so that the effect, as you see, is truly lovely and ideal for the Riviera.'

'Don't you think she's old to wear *bois-de-rose*?' I asked with a touch of jealousy. 'It's a lingerie colour for a young girl.'

'I don't agree,' said Matilda. 'Of course it's young and I shall do my best to make you something in the same silk, but delicate shades are equally becoming for older women on the Mediterranean. The sun and the blue water call for gay colours.'

'I agree,' said Daisy, 'and when she comes back to Town it will be spring and she can wear her bright ensemble right through an English summer.'

Marion had come in while Daisy was speaking and asked:

'Who is to wear a bright ensemble right through spring and summer?'

Matilda told her about the woman from Holborn and showed her the fashion plate in the copy of *Chiffons*. Marion listened carefully. Daisy said:

'I admire her. She has organized her life wonderfully. I only wish some man would pay my rent for the next twenty years.'

Marion said:

'You all admire her because she has arranged things with

meticulous care. A departed lover to set up a sum in trust to pay her rent, gentlemen friends to provide the housekeeping money and a special lover to take her for a winter vacation in Nice and stock her up with clothes for the rest of the year. Well, all that's fine and it will probably continue to be so until she falls in love with a man younger than herself. Then how long will her money last? The cuckoo will be in the nest and the ladybird will find herself ruined.'

'She's such an unglamorous little mouse,' I exclaimed. 'I can't imagine her allowing herself to be ruined by a great love.'

'What do you know about love?' asked Marion, turning angrily upon me. 'A girl at twenty who has not yet had a single serious love affair! You know nothing about the subject we are discussing. First lesson: never judge by appearances. It's seldom the prettiest girls who have the most sensational adventures. Didn't somebody tell me that Mademoiselle Léona is on the verge of throwing her Flemish bonnet over the banks of the good River Scheldt?'

Hardly had our guests departed than Gabrielle arrived. 'I've brought you a present,' she said, depositing, on that part of the table not encumbered by the length of *bois-de-rose crêpe de Chine*, the gaberdine and my mother's copy of the magazine *Chiffons*, a carrier bag.

'May I look?' I asked, longing to peep inside.

'They are for you and your mother,' said Gabrielle, 'but mostly for Madame Gal because on several occasions she has confided in me that she has a sweet tooth.' It was true that Matilda was greedy, perhaps the only chink in her otherwise austere character. Gabrielle had brought her a Belgian cake with sugar icing and several pounds of delicious chocolates with exciting interiors. 'They are in part a belated Christmas gift,' explained Gabrielle, 'but also a celebration. This is my lucky day!'

We waited expectantly for Gabrielle to spill out her news.

'I have been appointed manageress!' she said.

'Already?' exclaimed my mother.

'Oh, and I am so happy in this job!' said Gabrielle. 'I am quite a different woman. Something extraordinary has come over me. I do really believe that I could have got married half a dozen times in the last week. I who had almost settled down into the inevitable dullness of being over thirty, now find myself behaving as if I were ten years younger.' She laughed, a wry little laugh. 'Not that I made the best of being twenty. That leaves a pretty sour taste in my mouth.'

'Perhaps,' suggested Matilda philosophically, 'one would need to efface the mistakes of one's twentieth year?'

She turned her eyes on me and I realized with something of a shock that I, yes I, was perhaps the mistake she was thinking about, for had she not made me when she was that age?

But Gabrielle had her own daughter in mind, the one in the rich convent, and she said to Matilda:

'I envy you, Madame Gal. You live here with your daughter, free as the air you breathe, able to do just what you want. If I could stay with my daughter and have her all to myself without husband or mother-in-law, what a paradise it would be! By the way, I was almost forgetting. Now that I am manageress I shall need a new black dress. Something particularly elegant because as I shall be wearing it without an apron the customers will notice all the details.' She added in her delightful Belgian accent, jumping from one idea to the other:

'What surprises me is that both in the kitchens and in the shop everybody appears to like me. Yet I am strict, very strict. I've already made a great many changes. The staff take them very well. This is what I do. Before giving an order, I recall the words of that wonderful surgeon who saved my poor deformed leg. He used to massage it, pulling it this way and that. "My dear little Gabrielle," he would say, "what I am going to tell you may sound very difficult, but your leg has got to be made to obey you." He was such a good man, so full of patience that I did my utmost to do as he wanted. So when I need to give an order to my personnel, to one of the waitresses, for instance, whom I find gossiping in a corner while her customers are waiting for their tea and pastries, I try to explain things as my surgeon explained them to me.' She laughed. 'The owner said to me this morning: "You are a funny person, Madame Gabrielle. You arrived after all my other employees and here you are the first amongst them, the most important after me!" He's leaving for Dijon for a whole month during which time I shall be in charge of everything.'

Gabrielle looked at my mother and said: 'You are the only person to whom I would dare say all this, Madame Gal, for if I were to recount my happiness to the Tall Louise, do you know what she would say? She would say: "But of course you have jumped ahead of all the other girls, Madame Gabrielle. The reason is obvious. You sleep with your boss!" But it isn't true, Madame Gal, and that is the solemn truth as you alone will have the good sense to realize. So with everybody else I shall remain silent. I shall hide my good news as wise people hide their joy when they suddenly come into money. Least of all shall I inform the members of my family. My mother-in-law would scent a rise in salary and start spending money right and left whilst my husband would go straight to his tailor's and order a new suit.'

She opened her handbag and rather mysteriously took out of it an envelope which she handed to Matilda, saying: 'This is a little something for my daughter's birthday, but I am so terrified of my mother-in-law or my husband melting my heart when they implore me for money tonight that I would like you to keep it in a safe place—if you would be so kind, one of you.'

'You are quite right,' said Matilda, 'it is unwise to shout one's good fortune from the housetop, but I concede that it is not easy. For if it is nice to have people feel sorry for one when things go wrong, one should be ready to give them the pleasure of sharing one's joys. But we are all the same. I caught myself telling my charming lady who lived in Pembroke Square that I envied her having so beautiful a daughter, whereas had I told her the truth I would have said that I was the fortunate one because my daughter was even prettier than hers. But had I told her that she would have dispensed with my services right away. A lady's dressmaker remains her dressmaker, and if she has a daughter she should become a seamstress or a lady's maid. Yet my lady from Pembroke Square was utterly charming and treated me with infinite kindness. She plied me with rich gifts, and not one amongst all the beautiful dresses and skirts she gave me was soiled or out of fashion. Those I adapted for Madeleine look as smart on her as they must have looked on the right owner, the rich girl for whom they were bought. You see, they are sisters under the skin, but there is a subtle difference.'

I had become suddenly attentive at the part of Matilda's discourse concerning myself. So she thought me prettier than the rich girl who had sailed with her mother to India! This was something she would never have admitted to me personally. From somebody as mean with her compliments as Matilda this was surprising indeed. I took the envelope containing the money that Gabrielle was going to give her daughter on her birthday and promised to make myself responsible for it. I would lock it up in the drawer where we kept our savings. I had a Post Office savings book, but it gave me no satisfaction. I wanted to watch my hoard growing in size physically. Wendy had promised to give me the next golden sovereign that came her way, but she had received none since that of the South African customer. The costers in Seven Dials threaded golden sovereigns on their massive watch chains suspended from their waistcoat pockets. They had obviously become rare and precious coins.

We began sampling the chocolates that Gabrielle had brought us, cutting the Belgian cake.

After a while my mother turned to Gabrielle and asked: 'Have you bought the material yet?' Her question, supposedly inspired by the belief that it was probably time to start paying for the chocolate and cake, raised a delicate point in my mind. All summer and autumn the errand boys in the West End, not to mention the bus conductors and taxi-drivers, had been whistling the title tune from *Lady be Good*, the show at the Empire Theatre, Leicester Square, in which Fred and Adele Astaire were dancing and singing to the delight of Londoners. My feet were itching to be given greater scope to dance the Charleston than on those two lamentable occasions, one at the Kit-Kat, the other at the Piccadilly Hotel. I was pinning my hopes on New Year's Eve, and my mother, who was always secretly on my side, had started to make me a perfectly lovely dress out of what had been left over from that beautiful jade green *crêpe* dress with flounces that I had found her tacking the evening I came home tired and cold from a walk in Hyde Park following my interview with Mme D in her hotel in the Bayswater Road. She had made me something so wonderful that I caught myself dreaming about it at night. So complicated that I had already had three fittings. But would she have time to finish it with these new orders in hand, that of the woman from Holborn whose *bois-de-rose crêpe de Chine* lay on the table and the one she had just promised to make in black for Gabrielle?

'Yes,' said Gabrielle, 'I went to Selfridges this afternoon and bought several yards of exquisite *crêpe marocain*. Between ourselves more than I need, but the owner of the pastrycook's shop who, as I told you, is off to Dijon, told me to enter it on his charge account, so I let myself go. When you have taken what you need for the dress there might be enough left over to make me a skirt! I had a bit of a conscience, but, after all, I shall probably wear both at work.' She looked archly at my mother for approval.

'Let us see what we can find in *Chiffons*,' said Matilda, picking up the magazine and meditatively turning the pages. 'We might hem the skirt with a band of black satin which would be very effective on the lustreless *crêpe marocain*.'

'Oh!' I exclaimed, laughing. 'Do you remember?' Matilda smiled, but Gabrielle looked at me with an anxious, puzzled expression.

Black marocain was all the fashion that year. All the smartest women wanted at least one dress made of it. My mother had a very wealthy client, half French, half Spanish, who wore her dress of this material to attend a bullfight in Madrid. She was a small, dark woman with large expressive eyes and of rare beauty. As the crowd left the arena after the farewell performance of a famous toreador a thunderstorm broke over the city and rain fell in sheets, soaking the spectators hurrying away. The Señora's beautiful tight-fitting black marocain dress shrank by degrees so alarmingly that her husband and the other members in the party were obliged to keep on tugging at the hem to prevent her showing all that was most shocking to the Spaniards of that period in Madrid. Eventually she brought the dress back to Matilda, more in the way of a museum piece than anything else, just to show what in certain circumstances can happen to *crêpe marocain*. My mother, who never wasted anything, patiently unpicked the stitches and made what remained of the dress into a skirt for me. Even so there was not quite enough of the material in its shrunken state, so my mother had the idea of adding a strip of shiny black satin to the hem, and this contrast between the bright silk and the dull *crêpe marocain* had proved sufficiently effective to inspire Matilda to do likewise with Gabrielle's new dress.

These last days of the year were spiced with picturesque little happenings at home. Our street retained a faint echo of the effervescence of other times and there was always some triviality to be watched from our first-floor window. In our one-room abode also I often had the impression of watching a play as exciting as any in the West End theatres all around us. Besides the bookies in front of St Giles churchyard and Mr Jones, the rent collector, who came round every Monday morning, the coal-heaver with his cart and horse, and the muffin man with his bell and tray on Sundays, the hunchback sisters leaning out of their window hurling insults at the girls who passed by and a great many other performers in this medieval scene, there was what everybody called the Death Man. He must have had a real title, but I never heard it. He went round collecting subscriptions to give one a decent funeral. Matilda never subscribed to anything and we did not believe so much in our own deaths as in the ever-present danger of illness. The Italians didn't like the idea either on religious grounds, but the Irish may not have minded so much because Mr Mackenzie who was Irish in spite of his name had subscribed for a long time and on his death was paraded down the street with a mountain of arum lilies on his coffin. This Mr Mackenzie, who had always struck me as being incredibly old, was the odd-job man employed by the owners of these insanitary but cheap and picturesque houses all along the street. One used to see him hurrying along with a roll of wallpaper under an arm, and this was the sign that somebody had gone away and there was a room to let. Mr Mackenzie would then arrive and with great dexterity paste wallpaper all over the ceiling and the walls. He said it was quicker and faster than paint. But he also did other things. If the plumbing went wrong one hurried to Mr Mackenzie's basement room and told him about it, and an hour or so later Mr Mackenzie would arrive with the necessary tools. His death was an event. Dressed in his best suit he was taken off to a funeral parlour, but, as it was the custom to parade the coffin down the street of the dead man's abode before taking him off to the cemetery, everybody in

Stacey Street leaned out of the window to bid a last farewell to Mr Mackenzie under his mountain of arum lilies. Matilda could hardly believe her eyes. All those white arum lilies would have proved more appropriate, she claimed, for a virgin. I had intended to go to the pictures that evening, but Nana arrived and I had to abandon the project.

'I have been to see Madame Zulma in hospital again,' she said. 'I fear she is dying!'

At the close of a day, when we had watched the coffin of Mr Mackenzie going past, this news depressed me. As usual Nana was sitting on the edge of my couch. I see her as if it were yesterday. Her hair, the colour of salt and pepper, was shaggy like a carpet, her thick black eyebrows and square face made her look like a matron in Roman times, her blueish grey eyes were at one moment cold as steel, the next caressing and full of tenderness, her wide shoulders and strong arms gave her authority and the physical strength so necessary to bundle an obstreperous man out of a girl's flat if he showed signs of wanting to start a brawl. Most of the Flemish maids who worked for girls gave this effect of being carved like a statue out of granite. The Tall Louise was the same. It would not have done for a man to try any nonsense with them. Or with their mistresses. Nana was a case in point.

She did not work regularly for any one particular girl, but hired herself out as a temporary maid, replacing a colleague who had gone to Belgium for a short holiday, or another who was ill and so on. For this reason her over-all knowledge was perhaps greater than anybody else's. One morning the previous summer she had returned to the apartment of the girl for whom she was working, having bought the provisions for the day, when she found her young mistress naked on the bed with the blood still running from a multitude of deep knife wounds. She did not need to be told the name of the aggressor. The work bore the signature of the girl's ponce. She called the police and denounced him and he appeared before a magistrate who sentenced him to twenty strokes of the cat-o'-nine-tails. Few of her colleagues would have dared do as much, and much of her bravado may have hidden a fear of revenge. Nevertheless Nana carried her head high. When, after filling a temporary job, she needed another, she would show herself on a Saturday morning at a certain spot in Berwick Street and she would be quickly hired—much as servant girls in Brittany used to stand in the market-place at the approach of autumn so as to get themselves hired for a year by some local farmer.

I was sometimes puzzled by Nana's refusal to take a steady job. I even put the question to her. She answered in a mixture of Flemish and French that she was devoured by the constant need to make love, and that by taking temporary jobs she could have frequent periods of amorous orgy. She used to tell my mother and any other stray guest who happened to be in our apartment at the time that this need of hers was so strong and so constant that even the swaying of a London bus when she was seated over the wheels made so devastating an effect on her that she would look at the nearest male passenger and have a spasm. Nobody was shocked by these confidences. Our world was full of picturesque characters, right down to the woman who, armed with an immense carving knife and trolley, came down the street to sell cat's meat and who with her incredible hat and vast bosom could quite easily have stepped out of a Hogarth drawing.

'Yes, I fear she is dying,' said Nana.

Matilda was tidying her threads and this was something she took hours over. She arranged the reels of cotton by colours in a box and now and again Nanny the cat would fish one out and send it rolling on the floor. Matilda pretended not to see.

'Who is Madame Zulma?' asked Marion, who had just arrived.

I told her all about Mme Zulma, what she had been and how I had known her at the French newspaper shop in Old Compton Street.

'You can't have looked at her properly,' said Marion. 'Any woman who has been as beautiful as you claim Madame Zulma was retains something of her past magnificence. There must still have been fire in her eyes.'

'Her eyes were lifeless,' I persisted. 'They were tired and sad.'

'Be that as it may,' said Nana, 'she has come to die in a hospital in a foreign land. I am sad for her.'

Just now Nana was working for Mme Zulma's pretty young employer.

'Do I know her?' asked Matilda.

'I doubt it,' said Nana. 'She has just arrived from Venezuela, a tigress, a vampire, an eater of men!' Nana looked us up and down and added: 'And all that work for a single man. And what sort of a man? A ponce like any other ponce. An obscenity of a man!'

One felt that Nana would not have any hesitation in sending him also up to a magistrate for several well-deserved lashes of the cat-o'-nine-tails. Matilda looked at her with eyes that said: 'Beware, Madame Nana. Beware!'

There was a pause.

'Coffee?' asked Matilda.

My mother made a sign to me to fetch the cups and saucers. I laid them out on a tray and served the coffee like the dutiful daughter that I was. Twenty years old and a virgin, severely brought up by a mother with principles. My nerves were on edge. How would Matilda ever get my lovely new jade green dress finished with all these gossiping females around? Yet I was vastly intrigued and would not have missed a word of what was said.

'I found Madame Zulma's Post Office savings book,' said Nana, sipping her coffee, and eating one of Gabrielle's chocolates. 'There'll be just enough for the funeral but no more. And not so long ago one of the wealthiest women in Paris.'

'We women are all alike,' said Marion, 'and yet different! We eternally surprise!'

Now my jade dress was nearly ready—but not quite. Matilda was seeking a way to eke out the beautiful material of which there was not quite enough. As I was confident she would succeed I remained in a state of delicious suspense, thinking of New Year's Eve when I would wear it.

The following evening I saw my mother diving under the table to bring out a cardboard box of the kind in which dry cleaners in those days delivered some delicate dress, which they invariably returned to one between layers of delicate tissue paper. I knew the box well. Matilda had brought it back one summer evening from the lady of Pembroke Square who, with rare sensitivity, had given her as a present one of her own dresses made of beige lace. When we had first unpacked it I was most intrigued. It was not at all what I had expected, but, as I longed to try it on, my mother, while I was undressing to go to bed, laid it out for me on the sofa. It proved so large that my feet disappeared under the folds of the skirt, and my hands were quite hidden in the sleeves that were made in the form of pointed wings so closely sewn together that they gave one the impression of some ethereal, fairylike mail.

I was on the point of laughing at this strange creation when Matilda informed me that her wealthy client had worn it for the Gold Cup at Ascot the summer following the Armistice. All the ladies in the Royal Enclosure had admired it. 'It may well appear strange to us today,' commented my mother, 'but though the beige lace is machine-made it is of rare beauty, and I intend to unpick it to use as trimming. I hope to make several beautiful models out of it.' She added that the lace somewhat reminded her of those real museum pieces that as a young woman shortly after my birth she bought from Mme Gaillard who in Paris exhibited her stock-in-trade under a large red umbrella with a cherry-wood handle rubbed to a shine. My mother, carried forward on the wings of creation, put together veritable lace blouses, Valencienne laces of exquisite beauty, which were immediately sold to wealthy South American customers. For these she had become famous.

'The first thing to do,' said my mother, 'is to remove the lace from the muslin lining that diminishes its airy lightness. You will be surprised at the result.'

We put the dress back in the box and I thought no more about it. Matilda's head was always full of ideas. Her pleasure in life was to overcome seemingly impossible difficulties and thereby create something wonderful in spite of a lack of material. She was less anxious to excite exclamations of surprise or praise than to win a victory over herself. 'One needs to sew with one's heart and one's head,' said she to me. 'A little of both. Always remember that. Otherwise anything one does with a needle will resolve itself merely into heartbreak. My lady from Pembroke Square had flair. She guessed that in making me this gift it would be appreciated.'

Well, this particular idea lay fallow until a few hours before New Year's Eve when of a sudden it was I who was to benefit from it. Matilda had sadly confessed to me that my green dress which she was making from the left-over snippets from that superb masterpiece she had created for the Tall Louise's young mistress—her 'Mine'—had in spite of her imagination and cunning, all for the want of a tiny piece more material, failed to come up to expectations.

'The skirt needs something to make it dance!' she exclaimed ruefully, looking at the dress on the lay figure. 'It needs to come to life when you pirouette. Weight is what it lacks.' Then, as her mind continued to turn the problem over, 'More fullness, to be precise.'

I felt like tears.

'Oh!' she exclaimed.

I looked up hopefully at her smiling features.

'The beige lace of the lady of Pembroke Square's Gold Cup dress! Don't you see?'

Her idea, executed on the spot, was to place a V-shaped apron in front of the skirt—a half-open fan of diaphanous beige lace, arms stretched outwards and upwards from the hem. The effect was enchanting.

I would go to the ball after all.

On New Year's Eve when I put on my dress I loved it—the jade green looked even lovelier for the billowing lace of its open fan.

I had been invited to the Italian Ball.

My friend Lucille and I had dreamt of it all the year through. One had to be invited by a club member, and as neither of us was Italian, we felt twice foreigners in a foreign land. In another sense it was like being invited to a foreign embassy. The Italian mothers, seated very solemnly with their backs to the wall, watched their children jealously, noting with extreme severity their every gesture.

Our young Italian host, having met us at the door, led us across the enchanted threshold and, crossing the room, introduced us to his Mamma. The 'Mamma' looked me up and down with a singular lack of tenderness. She was already suspicious. Her intention was to see that her son did not dance with me more often than propriety allowed. My partner, heedful of my pleasure, but terrified of his 'Mamma', would suddenly abandon me to long moments of miserable loneliness during which I did not dare accept the advances of any other young man for fear of hurting my host's Italian susceptibilities. 'Mamma' in voluble conversation with the 'Mammas' on either side of her never took her eyes off me. She also wanted to be sure that I danced with nobody but her son. Had I done so she would have taxed me with being a 'giddy young girl'. The evening was not quite what I had dreamt it would be. There was something foreboding about this etiquette to which I was not accustomed. Nevertheless when my host invited me to dance a tango my heart beat with happy anticipation. Of course he danced admirably, but so did all the young Italians in the room. What is more they sang as they danced, and this New Year's Eve it was *Gigoletta* and *Madre*. We all sang and danced together and it was wonderful. The tunes still echo in my ears.

When I walked home through the streets of Soho all the bells of London were ringing in the New Year. Matilda was waiting up for me. She had lowered the gas in the jet and she, who had passionately loved dancing when she was a girl, plied me with eager questions.

'Did you have a wonderful time?'

I told her about those Italian 'Mammas', lugubrious, like birds of prey, lined up against the wall—and about those long moments when I had remained all alone not daring to answer the smile in another man's eyes.

'I don't see myself marrying an Italian!' I said.

When I took off my beautiful green dress I already liked it rather less. Oh! It was not fair on the dress of course. But when I hung it up in the wardrobe I put it slightly at the back as if I were punishing it, poor innocent thing—and almost at the same time I gently patted the one with the narrow pleats in which I had received so many lovely compliments.

Matilda had fallen asleep. She was tired out and had kept awake only long enough to welcome me home. She slept the sleep of the utmost fatigue and worry—worry about the days to come.

I turned down the gas and slipped into bed. Nanny, our cat, who had left my mother's bed, came into mine. The lilting air of *Gigoletta* and Nanny's soft purring filled my ears So all of us together—my mother, myself and Nanny—drifted into the hopes and uncertainties of 1927.